PENG

AROU
IN SEVEI
OTHER WRITINGS

NELLIE BLY was born Elizabeth Jane Cochran on May 5, 1864, in Cochran's Mills (formerly Pitt's Mills), a small town about 40 miles northeast of Pittsburgh, Pennsylvania. As a child she was called "Pink" after the color in which her mother most often dressed her. Later she dropped the nickname. She added an "e" to her surname when she enrolled in the Indiana State Normal School to study teaching. After financial troubles forced her to drop out after less than a year, Cochrane sought work to bolster her family's income and grew frustrated by the scarcity of job opportunities for women. In 1885, when the *Pittsburg Dispatch* ran a column entitled "What Girls Are Good For" that mocked women who sought work outside the home, she wrote an anonymous response so scathing it gained notice from the paper's editor, who advertised for the author to reveal herself so he could hire her. She was encouraged to use a pseudonym—a common practice for women writers at the time—and she took "Nellie Bly," a misspelled reference to a song by Pittsburgh native Stephen Foster. Dissatisfied by the women's-page assignments she often received, she soon became a freelancer and traveled to Mexico with her mother to gain experience as a foreign correspondent. She moved to New York in 1887, where Joseph Pulitzer's *New York World* offered her a job after she agreed to commit herself to the Women's Lunatic Asylum on Blackwell's Island to write about the atrocious conditions there. The report aided attempts to reform mental health care, while also gaining Bly personal fame and inspiring imitators at rival newspapers. She went on to write about domestic servitude, political corruption, religious sects, baby-selling rings, swindlers, woman suffrage, anarchist and socialist movements, workers' strikes, and women in combat. Her unconventional approach to reporting combined personal opinion and investigatory journalism. In 1889, she became a national figure when she traveled around the world faster than the hero of Jules Verne's popular novel *Around the World in Eighty Days*.

After several years at the *World*, Bly took a hiatus from writing. She married and became deeply involved in her husband's lucrative manufacturing business. She marketed the first steel barrels in America and filed several patent applications for inventions, including a stacking garbage can. But hired managers mishandled the company's finances and it spiraled into bankruptcy. She returned to journalism in 1912, when she began writing for the *New York Evening Journal*. She sailed for Austria days after World War I began and filed firsthand reports from the Russian and Serbian fronts. Her calls for aid to Austrians would complicate her return to America after the war. Back in the States, she wrote an advice column and continued her activist work, assisting orphans and the poor, but as women became more accepted as journalists, public interest in Bly and her work diminished. In 1922, she died of pneumonia in New York City at age fifty-seven.

MAUREEN CORRIGAN is the book critic for NPR's *Fresh Air* and a critic-in-residence and lecturer at Georgetown University. She is an associate editor of and contributor to *Mystery and Suspense Writers* and the winner of the 1999 Edgar Award for Criticism. Corrigan's literary memoir, *Leave Me Alone, I'm Reading!* was published in 2005. Her new book, *So We Read On*, is about America's enduring fascination with *The Great Gatsby*. Corrigan is also a reviewer and columnist for *The Washington Post Book World*. In addition to serving on the jury for the 2012 Pulitzer Prize in Fiction and the advisory panel of *The American Heritage Dictionary*, she has chaired the Mystery and Suspense judges' panel of the *Los Angeles Times* Book Prize.

JEAN MARIE LUTES is an associate professor of English and director of academics for Gender and Women's Studies at Villanova University. Her first book, *Front-Page Girls: Women Journalists in American Literature and Culture*, was published by Cornell University Press in 2006.

NELLIE BLY

Around the World in Seventy-Two Days and Other Writings

Edited with an Introduction and Notes by
JEAN MARIE LUTES

Foreword by
MAUREEN CORRIGAN

PENGUIN BOOKS

PENGUIN BOOKS

Published by the Penguin Group
Penguin Group (USA) LLC
375 Hudson Street
New York, New York 10014

USA | Canada | UK | Ireland | Australia | New Zealand | India | South Africa | China
penguin.com
A Penguin Random House Company

Around the World in Seventy-Two Days first published in the United States of America
by The Pictorial Weeklies Company 1890
This edition with additional writings by Nellie Bly, an introduction by Jean Marie Lutes
and a foreword by Maureen Corrigan published in Penguin Books 2014

Introduction copyright © 2014 by Jean Marie Lutes
Foreword copyright © 2014 by Maureen Corrigan
ISBN 978-0-14-310740-8

Printed in the United States of America
5   7   9   10   8   6

Contents

AROUND THE WORLD IN SEVENTY-TWO DAYS AND OTHER WRITINGS

Foreword

Every fall semester, the requests pop up on my university e-mail. The writers range in age from middle school to high school and they come from all over the country, but without exception, they're always female. "Dear Ms. Corrigan," the letters usually begin, "I am working on a project for the National History Day competition and I've chosen to research Nellie Bly." Some of these students are writing papers or making poster boards; a few ambitious ones are making documentaries. They pepper me with questions they think I can answer because they've watched an *American Experience* documentary about Nellie Bly where I appeared as a talking head. One seventh grader tells me: "I became interested in her when I read a small story about her in my textbook." A high school junior from Florida begins by confessing: "She was once an aspiring female journalist, just like myself." The students say they want to know how Nellie Bly "affected the reform of asylum institutions," how she "impacted journalism," and how "she has influenced the women of today."

I suspect these young women want to know something else, too. I know I sure do. I want to know how a poor, skimpily educated teenager named Elizabeth Cochran found the guts to transform herself into a reporter named Nellie Bly who helped change the world by writing about it.

Where did Nellie Bly's strong sense of self come from? That, for me, is the central question at the heart of Bly's life story. You hear her self-assurance even early in her life, in the back talk young Bly gave to men in authority who tried to box her into polite categories. Her editor at the *Pittsburg Dispatch* insisted on burdening Bly with genteel assignments deemed appropriate for women (the flower show, ladies' lunches), despite the fact that she'd already made her mark on that newspaper's pages with exposés of the grim working conditions of local factory girls and the gender inequities of contemporary divorce laws. So Bly up and quit. Before she left, however, Bly left behind a note for her narrow-minded editor: "Dear Q.O., I'm off for New York. Look out for me. Bly."

The seedy boys' club that was the New York newspaper world of 1887 did not welcome the arrival of this exotic creature—a girl reporter—into its ranks. After four months of fruitlessly trying to find a job, Bly elbowed her way into the employ of Joseph Pulitzer's *New York World* by accepting a dangerous assignment: she agreed to pose as a madwoman and go under-cover at the infamous Women's Lunatic Asylum on Blackwell's Island. Her nightmarish account of her ten-day ordeal as a charity patient inside the walls of that institution reads like a chapter in a Gothic novel: Bly endured freezing baths in filthy water, rancid food, and the muted threat of physical and sex-ual abuse. Though Bly's body was weakened, her spirit was not. During her time at Blackwell's, she spoke up on behalf of more fragile inmates (some of them perfectly sane immigrant women who simply couldn't speak English), and she lectured the doctor in charge about fire safety.

If Bly gained renown by writing about imprisonment, she became even more famous by showing how fast a woman could race around the world, unfettered. As usual, Bly first had to fight for her right to do the globetrotting assignment. Even though the idea of besting the fictional travel record of Jules Verne's hero Phileas Fogg was Bly's own, her editor at the *New York World* wanted to give the story to a male reporter. It just wasn't done for a young lady to travel unescorted; moreover, she'd surely need to take along many steamer trunks for her wardrobe and other essentials. Ha! On two days' notice, Bly threw some un-derwear and a jar of cold cream into a gripsack; then, she hopped aboard a steamship bound for England and didn't stop moving until she reached the East Coast again seventy-two days later.

In fact, Bly never stopped moving. When she became a bride at the ripe old age of thirty, she took over the management of her husband's factory and created an on-site gymnasium, library, and recreation center for the workers. In her boundary-breaking career as a journalist and an industrialist, Nellie Bly could teach Sheryl Sandberg a thing or two about "leaning in."

I remember first learning about Nellie Bly the way a lot of girls still do: through an illustrated young adult biography. I must have been about ten when I read that book in my grammar school library and I was transported. In my imagination, Bly swirled together with Nancy Drew, Amelia Earhart, Jo March, and the few other autonomous female role models available to a girl growing up in the 1960s. I loved the way Bly looked in that famous photograph from her round-the-world trip: her ankle-length black checked coat and her cap were reminiscent of Sherlock Holmes and her travel bag looked like the one carried by Mary Poppins. She was young and pretty, but not so pretty that she was intimidating. And best of all she was a writer (like I wanted to be); yet she wasn't stuck at a desk. Long before Jack Kerouac made it a strictly macho thing to do, Nellie Bly went "on the road" to find her stories. She even picked up a pet monkey—shades of Pippi Longstocking!—in the East. What girl could resist?

Judging from my e-mail, lots of girls still can't resist the story of Nellie Bly, nor should they. I've noticed, though, that none of those middle and high school correspondents ever use the phrase "stunt journalist" in referring to Bly, although that's the kind of reporting that Bly is credited with pioneering. Maybe that term sounds too frivolous and self-promoting, especially for a National History Day project. It's true that many of Bly's assignments were often more than stunts, but it's also true that Bly reveled in the spotlight. Bly's fans these days seem to want to stress the social justice aspect of her escapades, as if to excuse all the publicity she generated about herself. In my letters back to Bly's admirers, I always emphasize that she was both a reformer and a performer, a crusader and a one-woman sensation. I want these young women to understand what a huge achievement it was for Bly to insist on her own byline, her picture in the newspaper, and her own self-worth. Had Nellie Bly modestly hid her light under a bushel, it would have stayed there. I want these students to be vaccinated by Bly's story against the career-crippling feminine desire to be liked; to be thought of as nice by their coworkers and bosses.

So where did it come from—Bly's famous moxie—a quality that girls even in our own post-feminist age struggle to attain and hold on to? The rocky circumstances of Bly's childhood and adolescence surely contributed to her independent attitude. The death of Bly's father when she was six coupled with her mother's disastrous remarriage to a drunken bully taught Bly not to rely on men for financial security. She also came of age during a time when the New Woman was pushing against traditional gender constraints in education, work, and even the domestic sphere. But beyond those explanations, there still lurks much mystery about the female force of nature known as Nellie Bly. She seems as self-generated as that fictional other Great American Enigma, Jay Gatsby. Like Gatsby, Bly came out of the nowhere of a small town to become the toast of New York City. Her ambitions—again, like Gatsby's—drove her farther and faster; for a time, she even became wealthy and powerful. Fortunately for Bly, her fall was much gentler than Gatsby's: she died at fifty-seven of pneumonia, bilked out of her factory's profits but still industriously filing newspaper stories.

F. Scott Fitzgerald directly inserted Nellie Bly into his greatest novel: she briefly appears as Ella Kaye, the tough newspaperwoman who consorts with Dan Cody, the young Jay Gatsby's mentor. It's not a flattering portrait, but to Fitzgerald and his Jazz Age contemporaries, Bly's stunts probably seemed as quaintly rough-and-tumble as Annie Oakley's. Despite that quick brush-off, however, Nellie Bly never entirely faded from twentieth-century cultural memory. She lived on in inspirational biographies for juvenile readers (like the one in which I first learned about her) and eventually also caught the serious attention of feminist scholars influenced by the second wave women's movement. The students who write to me these days may or may not consciously self-identify as feminists, but they're motivated by impulses I would certainly call feminist to seek out information about a woman whose life story might teach them something about the freedom to dream big, about the need to develop self-reliance, and about the courage to speak on behalf of those who can't speak up for themselves. Nellie Bly doesn't let these young fans down. In 1885 the teen-aged Bly published her very first piece: a response to a patronizing column in the *Pittsburg Dispatch* headlined, "What Girls Are Good For." (Birthing babies was the answer.) Bly talked back to that reductionist argument, loudly and passionately. She wrote about the lives of girls like herself, girls who worked to support themselves and often their families; girls who felt a weary pride in their self-sufficiency. For over a hundred years, Nellie Bly has remained hard at work rebutting sexist stereotypes and instilling—particularly in her female readers—a sense of adventure and possibility.

Introduction

Nellie Bly (1864–1922) made herself into the most famous newspaper reporter in the United States by embracing the idea that a woman writer was, by definition, a bit of a spectacle. In an era when reporters rarely got bylines, Bly's name appeared in the headline of almost every story she wrote. In lively prose, she produced her own brand of sensational news. Equal parts self-exhibition and self-deprecation, her stories featured a winning combination of ordinary common sense and extraordinary daring. At a time when newspaper editors hired women mostly to write about high society, fashion, recipes, and household hints, Bly traveled to Mexico to become a foreign correspondent. She got herself committed to New York City's most notorious insane asylum to write an exposé. She specialized in what came to be known as stunt reporting. She worked in a factory, spent the night at a homeless shelter for women, visited an opium den, and posed as a desperate job seeker at a corrupt employment agency. She also tried out ballet dancing, elephant training, and prizefighting. In her most famous stunt, she raced around the world on two days' notice. Although her undercover work often involved deception, the stories she delivered to her readers were always anchored in her own unique perceptions of people, places, and things. Turning the most demeaning assumptions about women upside down, Bly made a career out of being herself. She was often called plucky. I would rather call her brave.

Her life was as improbable as many of her journalistic escapades. Raised in near poverty with very little formal education, she rocketed to newspaper stardom in 1887, when she was still in her early twenties. In 1895, at the age of thirty, she married a millionaire industrialist nearly forty years her senior and lived abroad for several years. When her husband's interest in running his own businesses flagged, she became head of his large manufacturing company and embarked on a second career as a businesswoman. When World War I broke out in 1914, she traveled to Europe and filed rare firsthand reports from the front lines in Austria and Serbia. Toward the end of her life, when she had lost her fortune through a combination of family conflict, poor financial oversight, and thefts from embezzlers, she supported herself by writing an advice column. She also served as an unofficial social worker, making appeals and setting up adoptions on behalf of abused and abandoned children. She took some breaks from newspaper work—most notably a sixteen-year hiatus that began just after her marriage—but she always returned to it. Her last newspaper column was published less than three weeks before she died.[1]

Bly's personality has been celebrated much more often than her writing, and the outlines of her career have been kept alive in American popular consciousness largely by the many children's books that have been written about her.[2] Most of her work was published in newspapers that were discarded within a day, and the few books she published—three collections of her journalism and one undistinguished novel—were out of print long before she died. In the last three decades, Bly has inspired some renewed interest. A major biography of her came out in 1994.[3] New editions of *Around the World* began seeing print in the 1990s, about a hundred years after her circumnavigation of the world, and new editions of *Ten Days in a Mad-House* began to appear in 2008.[4] Some are even in foreign languages.[5] Bly's books and a substantial sampling of her journalism can now be found online, too, thanks to digital editions and fan websites.[6] But these sources, welcome as they are, give readers little or no help in understanding the historical events and people she mentions in her work or the circumstances in which she wrote. Because it is simply not possible to appreciate Bly's writing fully without the benefit of some context, Bly's work has remained, for the most part, inaccessible to modern readers.

While this volume includes only a fraction of her published work, it aims to give readers a sense of the breadth and depth of Bly's always lively reportage, along with just enough context to let the sparks in her prose fly once again. In addition to her two most famous stories, the asylum exposé and the trip around the world, both of which were published in Joseph Pulitzer's *New York World*, readers will find Bly's first published article, a defense of working women that appeared in the *Pittsburg Dispatch*; an article from her work as a correspondent in Mexico; two undercover investigations for the *World*; three articles about women's issues for the *World* ("Should Women Propose?" and two interviews with women's rights pioneers); four dispatches from the eastern front of World War I for the *New York Evening Journal*; and two advice columns, also published in the *Journal*, written in the final phase of Bly's career. Although the selected writings span the length of Bly's career, many come from the late 1880s, a period of relentless productivity for Bly in which she helped the *World*'s circulation numbers climb to an unprecedented high. In November 1888, a trade journal reprinted an item from the magazine *Puck*: "When a charming young lady comes into your office and smilingly announces she wants to ask you a few questions regarding the possibility of improving New York's moral tone, don't stop to parley. Just say, 'Excuse me, Nellie Bly,' and shin down the fire escape."[7]

Bly tends to be remembered as a headline, not an author. But the skills at self-promotion that made her career possible would have been useless if they had not been combined with an imaginative mind, a wry sensibility, an eye for telling details, a light touch with dialogue, and a finely honed sense of how to cast herself as a character in her own news stories. Many women imitated Bly's stunt reporting style, but no one succeeded quite the way she did. She wasn't just the first; she was the best. When the novelty waned and public tolerance for sensational journalism declined, Bly found new ways to make her reporting relevant to her readers. Throughout her career, she wrote intensely subjective news reports. Her focus on her feelings may have run counter to the rise of professional objectivity as a journalistic standard, but Bly's professionalism was of a different sort: as a journalist, she never pretended *not* to have feelings about her assignments. Even when she wasn't putting herself literally in the place of her subjects, she was always imaginatively doing so. Yes, Bly's stories were biased. In essence, she trotted out the limits of her judgment for all to see, taking her readers with her on her own journeys of self-discovery. If those journeys did not, as a general rule, end in transcendent truths, they offered something else instead—an irresistible invitation to a risk-free adventure, as well as a vivid sense of what it was like to be an ambitious woman in a world that was as likely to laugh at you as anything else.

Bly's early life was marked by some of the same abrupt changes in fortune that would characterize her adulthood. She was born Elizabeth Jane Cochran in a small western Pennsylvania town that had been renamed Cochran's Mills in honor of her father, Michael Cochran, a mill owner and real estate speculator who was known as "the Judge" in recognition of his five-year term as an elected county judge. Judge Cochran had ten children with his first wife; when she died he married again and started a second family. Bly, a member of that second family, was nicknamed "Pink" as an infant because of her mother Mary Jane's fondness for dressing her in attention-getting pink instead of more conventional dark colors. The family lived comfortably until Pink was six and her beloved father abruptly died without a will. By the time his estate was finally settled, Mary Jane's large house had been sold and she was left with only a meager income to support four young children and a four-month-old infant. She struggled on alone for two years; then, perhaps in desperation, married John Jackson Ford, who turned out to be a poor provider and a mean drunk. At least once, he threatened Mary Jane with a loaded gun in front of witnesses. Five years into the marriage, Mary Jane took the unusual (and scandalous for the time) step of filing for divorce. Pink, along with many others, testified in court against her stepfather. She was fourteen.

By the time her mother's divorce was granted, Pink had been well educated in the need for female self-reliance, if nothing else, and she was eager for a career. Teaching was an obvious choice. She headed off to boarding school in Indiana, Pennsylvania, where she stopped calling herself Pink.[8] But lack of funds forced her to leave before finishing a single term, and for the next few years, she watched as her brothers, with even less education, found better jobs than she could. In 1880 the family moved to Pittsburgh, where she became an enthusiastic reader of *The Pittsburg Dispatch*. In 1885, she wrote a letter to the editor about the status of women that caught the eye of managing editor George Madden, who invited her to write a column on the topic. She did, and shortly after was hired on a weekly salary. Madden gave her her pen name, accidentally misspelling his reference to the title character of the popular minstrel song "Nelly Bly," by Pittsburgh native Stephen Foster. The song, so the story goes, was inspired by Foster's chance encounter with a young, pretty African American servant, the daughter of a former slave, who stopped her work for a moment to listen to Foster play the piano. The song's lilting melody and lyrics, written in black dialect, appear to have had little concrete connection to white "Orphan Girl" Pink Cochrane, but the name did link her to blackface minstrelsy, one of the most enduring performance traditions in the United States. At the time, no one knew just how much—or how well—the newly minted newspaperwoman would perform. But they were about to find out. She would be known as Nellie Bly for the rest of her life.

Bly was thrilled to have the job but she soon grew frustrated with her *Dispatch* assignments, which were too often about gardens, fashion, and butterfly collections, rather than the plight of working women or other subjects she considered more worthy. She longed for a change. Inspired by the prospect of being a foreign correspondent and undaunted by her lack of travel experience or language skills, she left the relative security of Pittsburgh in 1886. With her mother as a chaperone, she traveled to Mexico and spent several months writing features as "Nellie in Mexico," about the customs, politics, and culture she encountered. Her return to the *Dispatch* was short-lived; in spring 1887 she moved to New York, intent on finding a newspaper job in the media capital of the nation.

It was a heady time to be a journalist, especially in New York, which was home to the world's first mass-circulation newspapers. More people, from more different walks of life, were reading newspapers than ever before. Between 1870 and 1900, the number of newspaper copies sold each day rose almost sixfold, outstripping even the rapid population growth of the cities that was fueling the rise. When the price of newsprint plummeted, the average newspaper expanded dramatically in size, too, and with more pages came bolder headlines, more illustrations, more advertising, and more experimentation with content. Joseph Pulitzer, publisher of the *New York World*, was one of the era's most influential innovators. Unlike more staid newspapers like the *New York Times*, journals like Pulitzer's did not shrink from manipulating events and sensationalizing the news. Pulitzer courted not just middle-class readers but also marginalized groups such as women, immigrants, the working poor, and even the barely literate. Under his leadership, the *World* specialized in self-promoting campaigns for social justice; headlines and editorials frequently called attention to the newspaper's powerful role in bringing about reforms.

Women played a special role in this sensational age, as both readers and writers of news. Because advertising had become such a crucial source of revenue for newspapers (rather than political parties, which had funded journals since colonial times), news organizations were working much harder to appeal to women, who purchased most household goods. Although newsrooms remained almost entirely dominated by men, editors slowly began to hire more women, as Bly's experience in Pittsburgh suggested, especially to write for women's pages. Bly, of course, was much more interested in writing for the front page than the women's page. But avoiding the garden show beat turned out to be the least of her problems when she got to New York. For months, she failed to get any newspaper job at all. She made a few dollars by sending stories back to the *Dispatch*, including a striking report that showcased her already impressive ability to turn her personal circumstances into news: She interviewed the most powerful newspaper editors in New York, asking them whether the city was the best place for aspiring female journalists to get started.[9] Her report on their responses, which were full of prejudice against women writers, was picked up by other newspapers around the country.

Still unemployed, she earned her big break by completing an assignment for the *New York World* that, her editor admitted, seemed nearly impossible. He suggested that she try to get herself committed to the city's insane asylum in order to investigate the notoriously poor conditions there. She jumped at the chance. The resulting exposé was such a success that the *World* offered her a staff position, and stunt reporting became her trademark. It also turned her into an author: the asylum story was later issued as a book titled *Ten Days in a Mad-House*. As the popularity of stunt reporting makes clear, the now familiar ideal of objective journalism—in which reporters produce neutral accounts of events and make every effort to represent multiple sides of issues in an impartial manner—was not yet firmly established as an industry standard. Today, when we generally assume the value and superiority of objective reporting, we often neglect to consider how convenient it was for newspaper publishers to "go neutral." By vowing to serve the public interest by representing all sides of an issue, newspapers gave themselves permission to avoid taking stands that might upset advertisers. Bly, however, never worried much about upsetting anyone. She specialized in a deeply personal form of newsgathering. Her own feelings about what she was doing and how people treated her were always a central element in her reports. More than a hundred years before reality television would transform American popular culture, Bly pioneered reality news. She got herself arrested, tried out the newfangled bicycle, and asked a voodoo practitioner to make her a love charm. Among her more outrageous stunts was her announcement, in 1896, that she would raise a regiment and go fight for Cuba's independence from Spain. Nothing ever came of those plans.

Not all of her stories were stunts, however. She turned out to be a highly successful interviewer, adept at establishing intimacy and soliciting candid remarks, and she interviewed a broad range of people, from down-and-out prisoners to high-flying celebrities. Her colleagues rolled their eyes at her practice of always reporting what interviewees said about *her*, but Bly's self-indulgence didn't seem to bother her subjects. She covered political conventions, too. She wrote a long feature about the Oneida Community, an experiment in communal living. She visited the midway at the Chicago World's Fair. She also tried her hand at fiction, without much success.[10]

Bly became a national icon in 1889, the year she embarked on her race around the world. The *World* promoted her trip as a real-life challenge to the fictional record set by Phileas Fogg in Jules Verne's bestselling novel *Around the World in Eighty Days*. Bly—who traveled alone, with a single bag so small that she had a hard time fitting her jar of cold cream into it—made it home in seventy-two days, setting a record and beating the rival newspaperwoman whom a competing journal had sent around the world in the opposite direction. Bly's venture became a national sensation, thanks in part to a contest the *World* sponsored, which promised a free trip to Europe to the entrant who came closest to guessing the length of Bly's trip down to the second. The spectacle of a single intrepid American girl speeding through distant lands and oceans proved irresistible to readers and advertisers alike. On the final leg of her trip—a railway journey from San Francisco to New Jersey—crowds cheered her at every stop. Bly's face and figure adorned not only front pages but also advertising trade cards and even a board game. On February 2, 1890, the *World* distributed a free photograph of her with every Sunday edition.[11] Her account of her trip was published to great fanfare in the *World* in four installments, and shortly after, it appeared in book form, as did a collection of her correspondence from Mexico, which had first appeared in the *Dispatch* four years earlier.

Bly's globe-circling success, thrilling as it was, brought challenges. Given her heightened visibility, the undercover investigations that had been the cornerstone of her career were no longer viable. Even worse, from Bly's perspective, was the way the *World* was taking her for granted. Her editors offered her no raise and no bonus, despite the high profile her globe-trotting adventure had helped to give the paper. Shortly after her "Around the World" series appeared, she quit, privately bitter about what she described as her poor treatment. A few months later, she signed a lucrative three-year contract to write fiction for Norman L. Munro's *New York Family Story Paper*. Bly wasn't cut out to be a novelist, however, and her fiction career fizzled. Although incomplete *Story Paper* archives make it impossible to know for certain, it seems likely that she did not fulfill the terms of her contract.[12]

Within three years, she had accepted a new offer of employment from the *World* and was back to reporting, starting off with a sympathetic front-page interview with anarchist Emma

Goldman, whom she visited in prison, where the fiery orator was facing charges of incitement to riot. In 1894, with the nation mired in a deep economic recession, Bly visited Chicago to report on the famous Pullman strike, called by railway workers to protest layoffs, wage cuts, and poor living conditions. With the strikers threatening to shut down the national rail system and riots erupting, federal troops had been called in to restore order. Bly arrived strongly inclined to favor management's position, but her attitude changed quickly and she wrote movingly from the viewpoint of the railway workers. She produced a steady stream of stories in these years, but grew tired of the editorial upheavals at the *World*. She left to work briefly for the *Chicago Times-Herald* in 1895. Then, she surprised just about everyone by getting married to longtime bachelor Robert Livingston Seaman, seventy, a rich New York businessman who dressed well and didn't quite look his age.

Bly's new husband made her a significant player in his business interests, particularly the still-growing Iron Clad Manufacturing Company. Seaman, who started out working as a clerk at a wholesale grocery, had made his fortune in two industries: groceries and manufacturing. By the time he met Bly, he had sold the grocery business and relied on hired managers to run the daily operations of Iron Clad, which produced, among other things, containers for rail transport, milk cans, dairy supplies, boilers, hot water heaters, air tanks, and enamelware. Bly immersed herself in the business, learning how to operate every machine, overseeing a reorganization of the plant, and building new facilities for the recreation and education of Iron Clad employees. Working with a hired manager, Bly started the first plant in the United States to manufacture steel barrels. She was delighted with her success, and she had business cards printed up with an elegant photograph of herself and text that read, "The Iron Clad factories are the Largest of their kind and are owned exclusively by NELLIE BLY, The only woman in the world personally managing Industries of such magnitude."[13] Her celebrity and experience certainly helped the company. But embezzlement and forgery, aided by Bly's inattention to the account books, drained the resources of Iron Clad. Shortly after Seaman died in February 1904, Bly discovered evidence that the company had been defrauded. Bly spent years in court over the problems at the company, testifying against former employees, battling creditors, fighting to save the original company, and arguing that her still-profitable steel barrel company was separate from the embattled Iron Clad.

Overwhelmed by legal wrangling, Bly did what she always did: returned to newspaper work. In the summer of 1912, she went to Chicago to cover the Republican National Convention for *The New York Evening Journal*. In March 1913, she wrote about riding, decked out in a brand-new riding outfit, on a horse in a suffragist parade in Washington, D.C. Meanwhile, the court cases began to resolve: the bankruptcy proceedings for Iron Clad finally came to an end and the creditors' claims were settled. But in July 1914, when Bly refused to obey a judge's order to produce the books for her steel barrel company—which she was still trying to protect as an independent entity—Bly came under a new indictment on the charge of obstructing justice. To gain some time and to prevail upon a rich friend in Vienna to help finance her steel barrel business, Bly sailed for Europe. It was four days after Emperor Franz Joseph of Austria-Hungary had declared war on Serbia. World War I had just begun.

As the fighting spread, Bly got an emergency passport at the U.S. Embassy in Paris and made her way to Vienna. Ensconced in the elegant Hotel Imperial, she devised a new goal: to be one of the first foreigners (and the first woman) to visit the front lines. Always good at making contacts, she reached out to anyone—other reporters, American officials, wealthy Austrian aristocrats—who might help her get press credentials for the war zone. It helped that she knew the U.S. ambassador to Austria, Frederic C. Penfield, personally. By late October, Bly was part of a small group making its way to Przemysl, a heavily fortified Austrian city on the Russian border. Very few American journalists had access to the eastern front, and Bly sent back idiosyncratic, compelling reports unlike anything else that was being published about the war. *The New York Evening Journal* published her dispatches in brief installments between December 1914 and February 1915. Bly's reports were short on big picture context and long on details about the conditions at field hospitals, the suffering of the wounded, and the inadequate food available at the front. In their emphasis on physical peril and suffering, they are reminiscent of the madhouse series that had launched her into stardom nearly three decades earlier.

When Bly left for Europe, she told her assistant that she would be back in three weeks. In fact, she would be gone for three and a half years. During that time, the news blackout in Austria prevented her from any access to Allied propaganda, and she remained a firm supporter of Austria, even after the United States, a latecomer to the Great War, had joined the Allies (which included France, the British Empire, and Russia) in their fight against the Central Powers (which included Austria-Hungary and Germany). She made repeated appeals in the American press for aid to help suffering Austrians. Given her outspoken defense of America's enemies, U.S. military intelligence officers took a long look at her application when she requested permission to return to the United States in early 1919. Eventually, despite her defiance, they decided she posed no serious threat to American interests. Once back in the United States, Bly appears to have learned not to discuss the war too much. When a reporter asked her about her wartime mission in enemy Austria, Bly said it was a secret.[14]

Bly's homecoming was not warm. She found her assets gone, her hostile brother Albert in charge of her steel barrel company, and her mother's home closed to her. In her long absence, her elderly but fully lucid mother had turned to Albert for help, and he had enlisted her as his ally in a bitter fight for control of the steel barrel company. More litigation ensued, as Bly and her siblings fought. Once again, Bly needed to work to pay her bills. *The New York Evening Journal* hired her back, this time as a columnist. She started at $100 a week, half what she had been making in her stunt reporting heyday. Readers wrote so many letters in response to her initial articles that Bly began to write her own advice column, modeled in part after the popular lovelorn columns developed in the 1890s by Beatrice Fairfax and Dorothy Dix. With typical energy, Bly went beyond simply advising her readers. She regularly published appeals addressed to specific anonymous correspondents such as "Nameless" or "Worried Mother," asking them to identify themselves so she could meet them in person and help them find jobs, adopt children, or keep their families together. Now well into middle age, the woman who started her journalism career as "Orphan Girl" returned to the old problem of getting women jobs and making sure that children were cared for. She was no national phenomenon but she attracted a substantial following. Her column featured a whole series of foundling stories, in which Bly played fairy godmother to abandoned babies, arranging adoptions herself with her characteristic confidence that she was always doing the right thing (not everyone agreed). She also voiced her support for birth control. She published her address in her column and often found needy visitors waiting in the lobby of the hotel where she lived. She still wrote an occasional news report, too. When she witnessed the electrocution of convicted murderer Gordon Fawcett Hamby at Sing Sing on January 29, 1920, her graphic report stressed the horror and injustice of capital punishment.

Bly continued to write and to operate as an informal social worker for the next two years, even as her health declined. On January 9, 1922, at the age of fifty-seven, Bly checked into St. Mark's Hospital with a severe case of pneumonia complicated by heart disease. She died eighteen days later. Bly's longtime friend and supporter, distinguished newspaper editor Arthur Brisbane, called her "the best reporter in America" in a column published the day after her death. "Her life was useful and she takes with her from this earth all that she cared for, an honorable name, the respect and affection of her fellow workers, the memory of good fights well fought and of many good deeds never to be forgotten by those that had no friend but Nellie Bly. Happy the man or woman that can leave as good a record."[15]

Acknowledgments

My first thanks go to Henry Freedland, who sent me an e-mail out of the blue and gave me the opportunity to create this edition. I also thank Lydia Browning, my research assistant, whose meticulous, thoughtful, and resourceful labor allowed me to come close to making my deadline for this project; the staff at Villanova's Falvey Library, especially Laura Bang, Luisa Cywinski, Jesse Flavin, Trisha Kemp, and Jutta Siebert; and my friends and colleagues who offered instructive feedback on preliminary drafts, particularly Ashley Cross, Alan Drew, Heather Hicks, Megan Quigley, and Erin Smith. I also thank the College of Arts and Sciences at Villanova University for granting me the research sabbatical during which I completed most of the work for this edition.

My greatest debt is to my family. I thank my mother, Mary O'Neil Lutes, for a lifetime of love and encouragement, and my sister, Beth Hillman, for her wisdom and courage. I thank my children, Will and Evelyn DiPatri, for showing me what really matters and for filling my life with joy. The framed "Around the World with Nellie Bly" board game that hangs in Evelyn's bedroom will, I hope, inspire her to embark on incredible journeys of her own choosing. I thank my in-laws, Joy and Nick DiPatri Sr., and my extended family, Kim, Anthony, and Gianna Hollywood, for helping to keep Will and Evelyn occupied and well loved when I needed extra weekends to work.

Finally, I thank Nick DiPatri, my husband, a man who can take anything apart and put it back together again, but whose greatest gift is his generosity of spirit, which has enriched my life beyond measure. His love and support made this edition possible.

JEAN MARIE LUTES

Suggestions for Further Reading

PRIMARY SOURCES

Traditional print editions

Bly, Nellie. *Nellie Bly's Book: Around the World in Seventy-Two Days*. Rockville, MD: Wildside Press, 2009.

Bly, Nelly [*sic*]. *Ten Days in a Mad-House*. Rockville, MD: Wildside Press, 2009.

Digital editions

Bly, Nellie. *Nellie Bly's Book: Around the World in Seventy-Two Days*. Open access web edition. Philadelphia, PA: University of Pennsylvania Digital Library, 1890.

Bly, Nellie. *Six Months in Mexico*. Amazon Digital Services Kindle edition, 2010.

Bly, Nellie. *Ten Days in a Mad-House*. Open access web edition. Philadelphia, PA: University of Pennsylvania Digital Library, n.d.

SECONDARY SOURCES

Beasley, Maurine H., and Sheila J. Gibbons, ed. *Taking Their Place: A Documentary History of Women and Journalism*. State College, PA: Strata, 2003.

Goodman, Matthew. *Eighty Days: Nellie Bly and Elizabeth Bisland's History-Making Race Around the World*. New York: Ballantine Books, 2013.

Kroeger, Brooke. *Nellie Bly: Daredevil, Reporter, Feminist.* New York: Random House, 1994.

Lutes, Jean Marie. *Front-Page Girls: Women Journalists in American Literature and Culture, 1880–1930.* Ithaca, NY: Cornell University Press, 2006.

Marks, Jason. *Around the Word in 72 Days.* Pittsburgh, PA: Sterlinghouse, 1999.

Roggenkamp, Karen. *Narrating the News: New Journalism and Literary Genre in Late Nineteenth-Century American Newspapers and Fiction.* Kent, OH: Kent State University Press, 2005.

Wong, Edlie L. "Around the World and Across the Board: Nellie Bly and the Geography of Games." In *American Literary Geographies: Spatial Practice and Cultural Production, 1500–1900.* Ed. Martin Bruckner and Hsuan L. Hsu. Newark, DE: University of Delaware Press, 2007, pp. 296–324.

A Note on the Texts

The texts used in this collection are, with one exception, taken from Bly's original articles, published in the *Pittsburg Dispatch*, the *New York World*, and *The New York Evening Journal*. To represent Bly's trip around the world as fully as possible, I drew from her book based on the trip, published in 1890 by the Pictorial Weeklies Company, rather than the originally published articles. I also included excerpts from the newspaper updates about her that appeared while she was racing around the world.

Throughout the manuscript, I have regularized hyphenations and silently corrected misspellings and obvious errors. I have also eliminated nineteenth-century typographical features such as the use of periods after titles. In texts that have been abridged, omitted passages are marked by ellipses.

ALL RECORDS BROKEN

The New York World published both of these illustrations, the guessing match coupon on December 8, 1889, and the board game on January 26, 1890.

THE GUESSING MATCH COUPON

The guessing contest, which asked readers to estimate, down to the second, how long it would take Bly to race around the world, attracted more than 900,000 entries from across the nation. F. W. Stevens—the lucky New Yorker who came closest to guessing Bly's actual time of 72 days, 6 hours, 11 minutes, and 14 seconds—won a free trip to Europe. The image of Bly girdling the globe was probably drawn by *World* staff cartoonist Walt McDougall, who often illustrated Bly's stories.

THE COUPON.

THE NELLIE BLY

GUESSING MATCH.

Cut out this coupon. Make your guess up:n it, with date of guess. Give your name and address. Send the coupon, filled out, to European Trip Editor, THE WORLD, New York. All guesses must be made on this coupon. Only one guess allowed to a single coupon. But by securing extra copies you CAN

GUESS EARLY AND OFTEN.

To the European Trip Editor:

MY GUESS AS TO THE EXACT TIME OF NELLIE BLY'S TOUR OF THE WORLD IS AS FOLLOWS:

DAYS.	HOURS.	MINUTES.	SECONDS.

NAME OF GUESSER—

....

RESIDENCE OF GUESSER

....

DATE OF GUESS—

....

GUESS EARLY AND OFTEN!

THE BOARD GAME

The instructions on the board game, "Round the World with Nellie Bly," told readers to cut it out and place it on a table or paste it on cardboard. The spiral of seventy-two squares was a facsimile of the more durable, brightly colored board game issued in 1890 by the McLoughlin Brothers to celebrate and capitalize on Bly's trip.

Directions for players: Any number of Persons can play. Use checkers, pennies or any kind of counters to represent the voyagers. Use either a "teetotum" or dice.* A play of "one" puts voyagers at first day, a play of "two" at second day and so on. Follow directions on any given day or space that player may happen to reach, i.e., "go back a day;" "lose one throw," etc. If no directions are given, remain on space. The directions, however, are to be followed only when player reaches a space by the throw of dice or turn of the "teetotum." For instance, having gone back a day or more as directed, players are to disregard the directions found at second resting place. The object of the "game" is to complete the circuit of the world and reach New York first.

---

*Teetotum: Small four-sided disk or die with an inscription on each side and a spindle by which it could be twirled like a small top.

ROUND THE WORLD WITH NELLIE BLY

CUT OUT THIS GAME, PLACE IT ON A TABLE OR PASTE IT ON CARDBOARD AND PLAY ACCORDING TO SIMPLE DIRECTIONS BELOW.

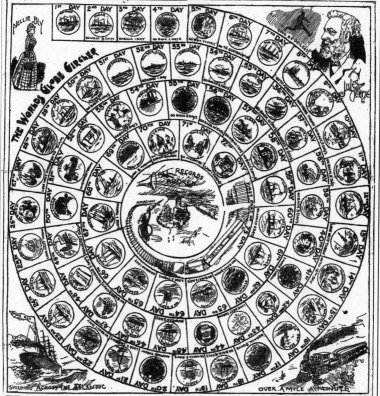

SPEEDING ACROSS THE ATLANTIC

OVER A MILE A MINUTE

I.

GATHER UP THE REAL SMART GIRLS

THE GIRL PUZZLE

Bly's journalism career began with a brisk letter of protest that got the attention of a newspaper editor. An "Anxious Father" had written to popular *Pittsburg Dispatch* columnist Erasmus Wilson, asking for advice about what to do with his five unmarried daughters, aged eighteen to twenty-six. In his published reply, Wilson did not answer the question. Instead, he insisted that homemaking was the only proper occupation for women, criticized a society in which parents did not have time to raise their children properly, and suggested, in jest, that the United States might eventually have to follow China's example and kill their girl babies.[1] Twenty-year-old Elizabeth Jane Cochrane—who had not yet adopted her famous pen name—was one of the many women who wrote to the *Dispatch* to protest Wilson's remarks. Managing editor George Madden was struck by her letter, signed "Lonely Orphan Girl," and printed a notice asking the author to identify herself. When she showed up, visibly nervous, at the *Dispatch* office the next day, Madden asked her to write a column about "the woman's sphere." In "The Girl Puzzle," her first published article, Bly took seriously the anxious father's question about what to do with girls and women.

THE GIRL PUZZLE

Some Suggestions on What to Do With
the Daughters of Mother Eve

THE OLD FIELDS OF LABOR OVERCROWDED

How the Average Employer Discriminates Against
Petticoated Workers

THE ROAD AS SAFE AS THE FACTORY

What shall we do with our girls?

Not our Madame Neilsons;[2] nor our Mary Andersons;[3] not our Bessie Brambles[4] nor Maggie Mitchells;[5] not our beauty or our heiress; not any of these, but those without talent, without beauty, without money.

What shall we do with them?

The anxious father still wants to know what to do with his five daughters. Well indeed may he inquire and wonder. Girls, since the existence of Eve, have been a source of worriment, to themselves as well as to their parents, as to what shall be done with them. They cannot, or will not, as the case may be, all marry. Few, very few, possess the mighty pen of the late Jane Grey Swisshelm,[6] and even writers, lecturers, doctors, preachers and editors must have money as well as ability to fit them to be such. What is to be done with the poor ones?

The schools are overrun with teachers, the stores with clerks, the factories with employees. There are more cooks, chambermaids and washerwomen than can find employment. In fact, all places that are filled by women are overrun, and still there are idle girls, some that have aged parents depending on them. We cannot let them starve. Can they that have full and plenty of this world's goods realize what it is to be a poor working woman, abiding in one or two bare rooms, without fire enough to keep warm, while her threadbare clothes refuse to protect her from the wind and cold, and denying herself necessary food that her little ones may not go hungry; fearing the land-lord's frown and threat to cast her out and sell what little she has, begging for employment of any kind that she may earn enough to pay for the bare rooms she calls home, no one to speak kindly to or encourage her, nothing to make life worth the living? If sin in the form of man comes forward with a wily smile and says "fear no more, your debts shall be paid," she cannot let her children freeze or starve, and so falls. Well, who shall blame her? Will it be you that have a comfortable home, a loving husband, sturdy, healthy children, fond friends—shall you cast the first stone? It must be so; assuredly it would not be cast by one similarly situated. Not only the widow, but the poor maiden needs employment. Perhaps father is dead and mother helpless, or just the reverse; or may be both are depending on her exertions, or an orphan entirely, as the case may be.

GIRLS POORLY PAID

What is she to do? Perhaps she had not the advantage of a good education, consequently cannot teach; or, providing she is capable, the girl that needs it not half as much, but has the influential friends, gets the preference. Let her get a position as clerk. The salary given would not pay for food, without counting rent and clothing. Let her go to the factory; the pay may in some instances be better, but from 7 a.m. until 6 p.m., except for 30 minutes at noon, she is shut up in a noisy, unwholesome place. When duties are over for the day, with tired limbs and aching head, she hastens sadly to a cheerless home. How eagerly she looks forward to pay day, for that little mite means so much at home. Thus day after day, week after week, sick or well, she labors on that she may live. What think you of this, butterflies of fashions, ladies of leisure? This poor girl does not win fame by running off with a coachman; she does not hug and kiss a pug dog nor judge people by their clothes and grammar; and some of them are ladies, perfect ladies, more so than many who have had every advantage.

Some say: "Well, such people are used to such things and do

not mind it." Ah, yes, Heaven pity them. They are in most cases used to it. Poor little ones put in factories while yet not in their teens so they can assist a widowed mother, or perhaps father is a drunkard or has run away; well they are used to it, but they mind it. They will very quickly see you draw your dress away that they may not touch it; they will very quickly hear your light remarks and sarcastic laugh about their exquisite taste in dress, and they mind it as much as you would, perhaps more. They soon learn of the vast difference between you and them. They often think of your life and compare it with theirs. They read of what your last pug dog cost and think of what that vast sum would have done for them—paid father's doctor bill, bought mother a new dress, shoes for the little ones, and imagine how nice it would be could baby have the beef tea that is made for your favorite pug, or the care and kindness that is bestowed upon it.

But what is to be done with the girls? Mr. Quiet Observations says: "In China they kill girl babies. Who knows but that this country may have to resort to this sometime."[7] Would it not be well, as in some cases it would save a life of misery and sin and many a lost soul?

IF GIRLS WERE BOYS

If girls were boys quickly would it be said: start them where they will, they can, if ambitious, win a name and fortune. How many wealthy and great men could be pointed out who started in the depths; but where are the many women? Let a youth start as errand boy and he will work his way up until he is one of the firm. Girls are just as smart, a great deal quicker to learn; why, then, can they not do the same? As all occupations for women are filled why not start some new ones. Instead of putting the little girls in factories let them be employed in the capacity of messenger boys or office boys. It would be healthier. They would have a chance to learn; their ideas would become broader and they would make as good, if not better, women in the end. It is asserted by storekeepers that women make the best clerks. Why not send them out as merchant travelers? They can talk as well as men—at least men claim that it is a noted fact that they talk a great deal more and faster. If their ability at home for selling exceeds a man's why would it not abroad? Their lives would be brighter, their health better, their pocketbooks fuller, unless their employers would do as now—give them half wages because they are women.

We have in mind an incident that happened in your city. A girl was engaged to fill a position that had always been occupied by men, who, for the same, received $2.00 a day. Her employer stated that he never had anyone in the same position that was as accurate, speedy and gave the same satisfaction; however, as she was "just a girl" he gave her $5.00 a week. Some call this equality.

The position of conductor on the Pullman Palace car is an easy, clean and good paying business.[8] Why not put girls at that? They do many things that are more difficult and more laborious.[9]

GIVE THE GIRLS A CHANCE

They can do the work as well, and, as a gentleman remarked, "It would have a purifying effect on the conversation." Some people claim it would not do to put woman where she will not be protected. In being a merchant traveler or filling similar positions a true woman will protect herself anywhere—as easily on the road as behind the counter, as easily as a Pullman conductor as in an office or factory. In such positions, receiving men's wages, she would feel independent; she could support herself. No more pinching and starving, no more hard work for little pay; in short, she would be a woman and would not be half as liable to forget the duty she owed to her own true womanhood as one pinched by poverty and without means of support. Here would be a good field for believers in women's rights. Let them forego their lecturing and writing and go to work; more work and less talk. Take some girls that have the ability, procure for them situations, start them on their way, and by so doing accomplish more than by years of talking.

Instead of gathering up the "real smart young men" gather up the real smart girls, pull them out of the mire, give them a shove up the ladder of life, and be amply repaid both by their success and unforgetfulness of those that held out the helping hand.

However visionary this may sound, those who are interested in humankind and wonder what to do with the girls might try it. George M. Pullman has tried and succeeded in bettering this poorer class.[10] Some of our purse-filled citizens might try it by way of variety, for, as some one says: "Variety is the spice of life." We all like the "spice of life": we long for it, except when it comes in the form of hash on our boarding-house table. We shall talk of amusements for our girls after we find them employment.

ORPHAN GIRL
The Pittsburg Dispatch, JAN. 25, 1885

NELLIE IN MEXICO

In 1886, after only nine months as a paid journalist, the twenty-one-year-old Bly grew impatient with her women's page assignments on fashion, gardening, and hair care. Although she spoke no Spanish and had never traveled abroad, she persuaded her very reluctant editor at the *Pittsburg Dispatch* to allow her to serve as the paper's correspondent to Mexico, got her mother to agree to accompany her, and embarked on the long train ride south. Within a month, the *Dispatch* published the first of more than thirty features that appeared under the headline "Nellie in Mexico." They included descriptions of working people, socialites, native Indians, tourist attractions, and ordinary life in both cities and rural areas, as well as details about the government's strict censorship of the press. Two years later, when her New York madhouse series had earned Bly even more name recognition, the reports were collected in a book titled *Six Months in Mexico*.[1] Bly actually spent only five months in Mexico; she planned to spend six, but she cut her visit short when she was threatened with jail for writing an article about the arrest of a local newspaper editor who had criticized the government.

NELLIE IN MEXICO

Random Notes Gathered from the Streets
of the Ancient City

PEEPS AT THE LIVES OF THE LOWLY

Meat Markets Established on the Backs
of Rickety Old Mules

AMUSING SCENES, AS WELL AS SAD

Special Correspondence of the *Dispatch*

CITY OF MEXICO, FEBRUARY 25.

In Mexico, as in all other countries, the average tourist rushes
to the cathedrals and places of historic note, wholly unmind-
ful of the most intensely interesting feature the country contains: the people.

Street scenes in the City of Mexico form a brilliant and
entertaining panorama, for which no charge is made. Even
photographers slight this wonderful picture. If you ask for
Mexican scenes they show you cathedrals, saints, cities and
mountains, but never the wonderful things that are right under
their eyes daily. Likewise, journalists describe this cathedral,
tell you the age of that one, paint you the beauties of another,
but the people, the living, moving masses that go so far toward
making the population of Mexico, are passed by with scarce a
mention.

It is not a clean, inviting crowd, with blue eyes and sunny
hair I would take you among, but a short, heavy-set people,
with almost black skins, topped off with the blackest eyes and
masses of raven hair. Their lives are as dark as their skins and
hair, and are invaded by no hope that through effort their lives
may amount to something.

Nine women out of ten in Mexico have babies. When at a very tender age, so young as five days, the babies are completely hidden in the folds of the *rebozo*[2] and strung to the mother's back, in close proximity to the mammoth baskets of vegetables on her head and suspended on either side of the human freight. When the babies get older their heads and feet appear, and soon they give their place to another or share their quarters, as it is no unusual sight to see a woman carry three babies at one time in her *rebozo*. They are always good. Their little coal-black eyes gaze out on what is to be their world, in solemn wonder. No baby smiles or babyish tears are ever seen on their faces. At the earliest date they are old, and appear to view life just as it is to them in all its blackness. They know no home, they have no school, and before they are able to talk they are taught to carry bundles on their heads or backs, or pack a younger member of the family while the mother carries merchandise, by which she gains her living. Their living is scarcely worth such a high title. They merely exist. Thousands of them are born and raised on the streets. They have no home and were never in a bed. Going along the streets of the city late at night, you will find dark groups huddled in the shadows, which, on investigation, will turn out to be whole families gone to bed. They never lie down, but sit with their heads on their knees, and so pass the night.

LIVING WITHOUT SHELTER

When they get hungry they seek the warm side of the street and there, hunkering down, devour what they scraped up during the day, consisting of refused meats and offal boiled over a handful of charcoal. A fresh tortilla is the sweetest of sweetbreads. The men appear very kind and are frequently to be seen with the little ones tied up in their serape.[3]

Groups of these at dinner would furnish rare studies for Rogers.[4] Several men and women will be walking along, when suddenly they will sit down in some sunny spot on the street. The women will bring fish or a lot of stuff out of a basket or poke, which is to constitute their coming meal. Meanwhile the men, who also sit flat on the street, will be looking on and accepting their portion like hungry, but well-bred, dogs.

This type of life, be it understood, is the lowest in Mexico, and connects in no way with the upper classes. The Mexicans are certainly misrepresented, most wrongfully so. They are not lazy, but just the opposite. From early dawn until late at night they can be seen filling their different occupations. The women sell papers and lottery tickets.

"See here, child," said a gray-haired lottery woman in Spanish. "Buy a ticket. A sure chance to get $10,000 for 25 cents." Being told that we had no faith in lotteries, she replied: "Buy one; the Blessed Virgin will bring you the money."

The laundry women, who, by the way, wash clothes whiter and iron them smoother even than the Chinese, carry the clothes home unwrapped. That is, they carry their hands high above their head, from which stream white skirts, laces, &c., furnishing a most novel sight. . . .

A peep into doorways shows the people at all manner of occupations. Men always use the machines. Women and men put chairs together and weave bottoms in them. They also make shoes, the finest and most artistic shoe in the world, and the cobblers can make a good shoe out of one that is so badly worn as to be useless to our grandmothers as a rod of correction. The water-carrier, aguador, is one of the most common objects on the street. They suspend water jars from their heads, one in front, one back. Around their bodies are leather aprons to protect them from the water, which they get at big fountains and basins distributed throughout the city.

As a people they do not seem malicious, quarrelsome, unkind or evil disposed. Drunkenness does not seem to be frequent, and the men, in their uncouth way, are more thoughtful of the women than many who belong to a higher class. The women, like other women, sometimes cry, doubtless for very good cause, and then the men stop to console them, patting them on the head, smoothing back their hair, gently wrapping them tighter in their rebozo. Late one night, when the weather was so cold, a young fellow sat on the curbstone and kept his arm around a pretty young girl. He had taken off his ragged serape and folded it around her shoulders, and as the tears ran down her face and she complained of the cold, he tried to comfort her, and that without a complaint of his own condition, being clad only in muslin trousers and waist, which hung in shreds from his body.

Thus we leave the largest part of the population of Mexico. Their condition is most touching. Homeless, poor, uncared for, untaught, they live and they die. They are worse off by thousands of times than were the slaves of the United States. Their lives are hopeless, and they know it. That they are capable of learning is proven by their work, and by their intelligence in other matters. They have a desire to gain book knowledge, or at least so says a servant who was taken from the streets, and now spends every nickel and every leisure moment in trying to learn wisdom from books.

FROM "NELLIE IN MEXICO," *The Pittsburg Dispatch*,
MARCH 7, 1886

II.

INTO THE
MADHOUSE

Nearly four months after moving to New York City to find work as a journalist, Bly had no job offers and she was running out of money. She borrowed carfare from her landlady, rode down to Park Row, talked her way past the guards at the *New York World* building, and somehow got an interview with the managing editor. When she offered to travel to Europe and return steerage class to report firsthand on the experiences of immigrants who were coming to the United States in record numbers, the editor rejected the idea as too far-flung for a newcomer. Instead, he asked if she was willing to get herself committed to the insane asylum on Blackwell's Island, a forbidding sliver of land in the East River that was home to most of New York City's prisons, charity hospitals, and workhouses.[1] She was and she did. Pretending insanity, Bly gained entrance to one of the city's most dreaded asylums, a charity ward where conditions were notoriously poor and patients were apparently mistreated on a regular basis. Her account, published in two illustrated installments, chronicled Bly's journey from a Lower East Side boardinghouse where she behaved erratically enough to make the matron in charge call the police, to an Essex Market courtroom where a sympathetic judge observed that she must be "somebody's darling" and thought she had been drugged but saw no other choice but to have her committed, to the city's psychiatric facility at Bellevue Hospital, where she was examined and declared "positively demented," and finally to Blackwell's Island, where she was incarcerated for ten days. Bly's performance as an insane woman was so compelling that her case attracted coverage from competing newspapers, whose reporters were not in on the ruse. When Bly's exposé appeared, the *World* editors delightedly reprinted the news reports in which their rivals detailed the "sad case" and speculated about the mystery of the unknown insane girl, who was described as pretty, well-dressed, and possibly Cuban.[2] (As part of her masquerade, Bly used some of the Spanish she had picked up on her travels in Mexico.) Bly's feat earned her a place on the *World*'s permanent staff and attracted notice from newspapers all over North America; many noted how troubling it was to discover that a young woman with no special training could fool so many scientific experts with such ease. Bly's madhouse reports also provided a crucial boost to the efforts that were already under way to improve the overcrowded, inadequate facilities at Blackwell's Island. By the end of the year, a city board had voted to substantially increase funds for the care of the insane: the budget appropriation for the Department of Public Charities and Corrections was increased from $1.5 million to $2.34 million, and $50,000 was earmarked for the Blackwell's Island asylum.[3]

BEHIND ASYLUM BARS

The Mystery of the Unknown Insane Girl

REMARKABLE STORY OF THE SUCCESSFUL IMPERSONATION OF INSANITY

How Nellie Brown Deceived Judges, Reporters and Medical Experts

SHE TELLS HER STORY OF HOW SHE PASSED AT BELLEVUE HOSPITAL

Studying the Role of Insanity Before Her Mirror and Practising It at the Temporary Home for Women—Arrested and Brought Before Judge Duffy—He Declares She is Some Mother's Darling and Resembles His Sister—Committed to the Care of the Physicians for the Insane at Bellevue—

Experts Declare Her Demented—Harsh Treatment of the Insane at Bellevue—"Charity Patients Should Not Complain"—Vivid Pictures of Hospital Life—How Our Esteemed Contemporaries Have Followed a False Trail—Some Needed Light Afforded Them—Chapters of Absorbing Interest in the Experience of a Feminine "Amateur Casual."

A DELICATE MISSION

I.

On the 22d of September I was asked by THE WORLD if I could have myself committed to one of the Asylums for the Insane in New York, with a view to writing a plain and unvarnished narrative of the treatment of the patients therein and the methods of management, &c. Did I think I had the courage to go through such an ordeal as the mission would demand? Could I assume the characteristics of insanity to such a degree that I could pass the doctors, live for a week among the insane without the authorities there finding out that I was only a "chiel amang 'em takin' notes?" I said I believed I could. I had some faith in my own ability as an actress and thought I could assume insanity long enough to accomplish any mission entrusted to me. Could I pass a week in the insane ward at Blackwell's Island? I said I could and I would. And I did. My instructions were simply to go on with my work as soon as I felt that I was ready. I was to chronicle faithfully the experiences I underwent, and when once within the walls of the asylum to find out and describe its inside workings, which are always so effectually hidden by white-capped nurses, as well as by bolts and bars, from the knowledge of the public. "We do not ask you to go there for the purpose of making sensational revelations. Write up things as you find them, good or bad; give praise or blame as you think best, and the truth all the time. But I am afraid of that chronic smile of yours," said the editor. "I will smile no more," I said, and I went away to execute my delicate and, as I found out, difficult mission.

The Preliminaries

All the preliminary preparations for my ordeal were left to be planned by myself. Only one thing was decided upon, namely, that I should pass under the pseudonym of Nellie Brown, the initials of which would agree with my own name and my linen, so that there would be no difficulty in keeping track of my movements and assisting me out of any difficulties or dangers I might get into. There were ways of getting into the insane ward, but I did not know them. I might adopt one of two courses. Either I could feign insanity at the house of friends and get myself committed on the decision of two competent physicians, or I could go to my goal by way of the police courts. On reflection I thought it wiser not to inflict myself upon my friends or to get any good-natured doctors to assist me in my purpose. Besides, to get to Blackwell's Island my friends would have had to feign poverty, and, unfortunately for the end I had in view, my acquaintance with the struggling poor, except my own self, was only very superficial. So I determined upon the plan which led me to the successful accomplishment of my mission and to which the bulk of the following narrative will be devoted. I succeeded in getting committed to the insane ward at Blackwell's Island, where I spent ten days and nights and had an experience which I shall never forget. I took upon myself to enact the part of a poor, unfortunate crazy girl and felt it my duty not to shirk any of the disagreeable results that should follow. I became one of the city's insane wards for that length of time, experienced much, and saw and heard more of the treatment accorded to this helpless class of our population, and when I had seen and heard enough my release was promptly secured. I left the insane ward with pleasure and regret—pleasure that I was once more able to enjoy the free breath of heaven; regret that I could not have brought with me some of the unfortunate women who lived and suffered with me, and who I am convinced are just as sane as I was and am now myself. But here let me say one thing: From the moment I entered the insane ward on the island I made no attempt to keep up the assumed role of insanity. I talked and acted just as I do in ordinary life. Yet strange to say, the more sanely I talked and acted the crazier I was thought to be by all except one physician, whose kindness and gentle ways I shall not soon forget.

Preparing for the Ordeal

But to return to my work and my mission. After receiving my instructions I returned to my boardinghouse, and when evening came I began to practise the role in which I was to make my debut on the morrow. What a difficult task, I thought, to appear before a crowd of people and convince them that I was insane. I had never been near insane persons before in my life and had not the faintest idea of what their actions were like. And then to be examined by a number of learned physicians who make insanity a specialty and who daily come in contact with insane people! How could I hope to pass these doctors and convince them that I was crazy? I feared that they could not be deceived. I began to think my task a hopeless one. But it had to be done. So I flew to the mirror and examined my face. I remembered all I had read of the doings of crazy people, how first of all they must have staring eyes, and so I opened mine as wide as possible and stared unblinkingly at my own reflection. I assure you the sight was not reassuring, even to myself, especially in the dead of night. I tried to turn the gas up higher in hopes that it would raise my courage. I succeeded only partially, but I consoled myself with the thought that in a few nights more I would not be there, but locked up in a cell with a lot of lunatics. The weather was not cold, but nevertheless when I thought of what was to come wintry chills ran races up and down my back in very mockery of the perspiration which was slowly but surely taking the curl out of my bangs. Between times practicing before the mirror and picturing my future as a lunatic I read snatches of improbable and impossible ghost stories, so that when the dawn came to chase away the night I felt that I was in a fit mood for my mission, yet hungry enough to feel keenly that I wanted my breakfast. Slowly and sadly I took my morning bath and quietly bade farewell to a few of the most precious articles known to modern civilization. Tenderly I put my toothbrush aside, and, when taking a final rub of the soap, I murmured, "It may be for days and it may be—for longer." Then I donned the old clothing I had selected for the occasion. I was in the mood to look at everything through very serious glasses. It's just as well to take a last "fond look," I mused, for who could tell but that the strain of playing crazy and being shut up with a crowd of mad people might turn my own brain and I would never get back. But not once did I think of shirking my mission. Calmly, outwardly at least, I went out to my crazy business. I walked down Second avenue. It had been arranged that I should enter one of the many temporary homes or shelters for females, and that once in I should do the best I could to get forwarded on my journey to Blackwell's Island. The place selected was the Temporary Home for Females, 84 Second avenue.[4]

IN THE TEMPORARY HOME

II.

I was left to begin my career as Nellie Brown, the insane girl. As I walked down the avenue I assumed the look which maidens wear in pictures entitled "Dreaming." I passed through the little paved yard to the entrance of the Home. I pulled the bell, which sounded loud enough for a church chime, and nervously awaited the opening of the door to the home which I intended should ere long cast me forth and out upon the charity of the police. The door was thrown back with a vengeance and a short, yellow-haired girl of some thirteen summers stood before me.

"Is the matron in?" I asked faintly.

"Yes, she's in; she's busy. Go to the back parlor," answered the girl in a loud voice, without one change in her peculiarly matured face.

I followed these not overkind or polite instructions and found myself in a dark, uncomfortable back parlor. There I awaited the arrival of my hostess. I had been seated some twenty minutes at the least, when a slender woman, clad in a plain dark dress, entered and, stopping before me, ejaculated inquiringly, "Well?"

"Are you the matron?" I asked.

"No," she replied; "the matron is sick; I am her assistant. What do you want?"

"I want to stay here for a few days, if you can accommodate me."

"Well, I have no single rooms; we are so crowded, but if you will occupy a room with another girl, I shall do that much for you."

"I shall be glad of that," I answered. "How much do you charge?" I had brought only about 70 cents along with me, knowing full well that the sooner my funds were exhausted the sooner I should be put out, and to be put out was what I was working for.

"We charge 30 cents a night," was her reply to my question, and with that I paid her for one night's lodging, and she left me on the plea of having something else to look after. Left to amuse myself as best I could, I took a survey of my surroundings. By the time I had become familiar with my quarters a bell, which rivaled the doorbell in its loudness, began clanging in the basement and simultaneously women went trooping downstairs from all parts of the house. I imagined, from the obvious signs, that dinner was served, but as no one had said anything to me I made no effort to follow in the hungry train. Yet I did wish that some one would invite me down, and I was glad when the assistant matron came up and asked me if I did not want something to eat. I replied that I did, and then I asked her what her name was. Mrs. Stanard, she said, and I immediately wrote it down in a notebook I had taken with me for the purpose of making memoranda, and in which I had written several pages of utter nonsense for inquisitive scientists. Thus equipped I awaited developments. But my dinner—well, I followed Mrs. Stanard down the uncarpeted stairs into the basement, where a large number of women were eating. She found room for me at a table with three other women. The short-haired slavey who had opened the door now put in an appearance as waiter. Placing her arms akimbo and starting me out of countenance she said:

"Boiled mutton, boiled beef, beans, potatoes, coffee or tea?"

"Beef, potatoes, coffee and bread," I responded.

"Bread goes in," she explained, as she made her way to the

kitchen, which was in the rear. It was not very long before she returned with what I had ordered on a large, badly battered tray, which she banged down before me. I began my simple meal. It was not very enticing, so while making a feint of eating I watched the others. After dinner I went upstairs and resumed my former place in the back parlor. I was quite cold and uncomfortable and had fully made up my mind that I could not endure that sort of business long, so the sooner I assumed my insane points the sooner I would be released from enforced idleness. Ah, that was indeed the longest day I had ever lived. I listlessly watched the women in the front parlor, where all sat except myself. One did nothing but read and scratch her head and occasionally call out mildly, "Georgie," without lifting her eyes from her book. "Georgie" was her over-frisky boy, who had more noise in him than any child I ever saw before. He did everything that was rude and unmannerly, I thought, and the mother never said a word unless she heard some one else yell at him. Another woman always kept going to sleep and waking herself up with her own snoring. I really felt wickedly thankful it was only herself she awakened. The majority of the women sat there doing nothing, but there were a few who made lace and knitted unceasingly. The enormous doorbell seemed to be going all the time and so did the short-haired girl. The latter was, besides, one of those girls who sing all the time snatches of all the songs and hymns that have been composed for the last fifty years. There is such a thing as martyrdom in these days. The ringing of the bell brought more people who wanted shelter for the night. Excepting one woman who was from the country on a day's shopping expedition, they were working women, some of them with children. As it drew towards evening Mrs. Stanard came to me and said:

She Begins to Show Signs

"What is wrong with you? Have you some sorrow or trouble?"

"No," I said, almost stunned at the suggestion. "Why?"

"Oh, because," she said, womanlike, "I can see it in your face. It tells the story of a great trouble."

"Yes, everything is so sad," I said in a haphazard way, which I had intended to reflect my craziness.

"But you must not allow that to worry you. We all have our troubles, but we get over them in good time. What kind of work are you trying to get?"

"I do not know; it's all so sad," I replied.

"Would you like to be a nurse for children and wear a nice white cap and apron?" she asked.

I put my handkerchief up to my face to hide a smile and replied in a muffled tone, "I never worked; I don't know how."

"But you must learn," she urged; "all these women here work."

"Do they?" I said in a low, thrilling whisper. "Why, they look horrible to me; just like crazy women. I am so afraid of them."

"They don't look very nice," she answered, assentingly, "but they are good, honest working women. We do not keep crazy people here."

I again used my handkerchief to hide a smile, as I thought that before morning she would at least think she had one crazy person among her flock.

"They all look crazy," I asserted again, "and I am afraid of them. There are so many crazy people about, and one can never tell what they will do. Then there are so many murders committed, and the police never catch the murderers," and I finished with a sob that would have broken up an audience of blasé critics. She gave a sudden and convulsive start, and I knew my first stroke had gone home. It was amusing to see what a remarkable short time it took her to get up from her chair and to whisper hurriedly: "I'll come back to talk with you after a while." I knew she would not come back, and she did not. When the supper-bell rang I went along with the others to the basement and partook of the evening meal, which was similar to dinner, except that there was a smaller bill of fare and more people, the women who are employed outside during the day having returned. After the evening meal we all adjourned to the parlors, where all sat, or stood, as there were not chairs enough to go round. I watched two women, who seemed of all the crowd to be the most sociable, and I selected them as the ones to work out my salvation, or, more properly speaking, my condemnation and conviction. Excusing myself and saying that I felt lonely, I asked if I might join their company. They graciously consented, so with my hat and gloves on, which no one had asked me to lay aside, I sat down and listened to the rather wearisome conversation, in which I took no part, merely keeping up my sad look, saying "Yes," or "No," or "I can't say," to their observations. Several times I told them I thought everybody in the house looked crazy, but they were slow to catch on to my very original remark. One said her name was Mrs. King and that she was a Southern woman. Then she said that I had a Southern accent. She asked me bluntly if I did not really come from the South. I said "Yes." Then the other woman got to talking about the Boston boats and asked me if I knew at what time they left. For a moment I forgot my role of assumed insanity and told her the correct hour of departure. She then asked me what work I was going to do or if I had ever done any. I replied that I thought it very sad that there were so many working people in the world. She said in reply that she had been unfortunate and had come to New York, where she had worked at correcting proofs on a medical dictionary for some time, but that her health had given way under the task and that she was now going to Boston again. When the maid came to tell us to go to bed I remarked that I was afraid, and again ventured the assertion that all the women in the house seemed to be crazy. The nurse insisted on my going to bed. I asked if I could not sit on the stairs, but she said decisively: "No; for every one in the house would think you were crazy." Finally I allowed them to take me to a room.

A Kind Soul Discovered

Here I must introduce a new personage by name into my narrative. It is the woman who had been a proof-reader and was about to return to Boston. She was a Mrs. Caine, who was as courageous as she was good-hearted. She came into my room and sat and talked with me a long time, taking down my hair with gentle ways. She tried to persuade me to undress and go to bed, but I stubbornly refused to do so. During this time a number of the inmates of the house had gathered around us. They expressed themselves in various ways. "Poor loon!" they said. "Why, she's crazy enough!" "I am afraid to stay with such a crazy being in the house." "She will murder us all before morning." One woman was for sending for a policeman to take me away at once. They were all in a terrible and real state of fright. No one wanted to be responsible for me, and the woman who was to occupy the room with me declared that she would not stay with that "crazy woman" for all the money of the Vanderbilts. It was then that Mrs. Caine said she would stay with me. I told her I would like to have her do so. So she was left with me. She didn't undress, but lay down on the bed, watchful of my movements. She tried to induce me to lie down, but I was afraid to do this. I knew that if I once gave way I should fall asleep and dream as pleasantly and peacefully as a child. I should, to use a slang expression, be liable to give myself dead away. I had made up my mind to stay awake all night. So I insisted on sitting on the side of the bed and staring blankly at vacancy. My poor companion was put into a wretched state of unhappiness. Every few moments she would rise up to look at me. She told me that my eyes shone terribly brightly and then began to question me, asking me where I had lived, how long I had been in New York, what I had been doing, and many things besides. To all her questionings I had but one response—I told her that I had forgotten everything, that ever since my headache had come on I could not remember.

Poor soul! How cruelly I tortured her and what a kind heart she had! But how I tortured all of them! One of them dreamed of me—as a nightmare. After I had been in the room an hour or so I was myself startled by hearing a woman screaming in the next room. I began to imagine that I was really in an insane asylum. Mrs. Caine woke up, looked around, frightened, and listened. She then went out and into the next room, and I heard her asking another woman some questions. When she came back she told me that the woman had had a hideous nightmare. She had been dreaming of me. She had seen me, she said, rushing at her with a knife in my hand, with the intention of killing her. In trying to escape me she had fortunately been able to scream, and so to awaken herself and scare off her nightmare. Then Mrs. Caine got into bed again, considerably agitated, but very sleepy. I was weary, too, but I had braced myself up to the work, and was determined to keep awake all night so as to carry on my work of impersonation to a successful end in the morning. I heard midnight. I had yet six hours to wait for daylight. The time passed with excruciating slowness. Minutes appeared hours. The noises in the house and on the avenue ceased. I kept thinking about the past events of my life. I began at the beginning and, after living over again fifteen or twenty years of my existence, found I had only spanned over a space of five minutes. Failing to find anything more to think about of the past I turned my thoughts bravely to the future, wondering, first, what the next day would bring forth, then making plans for the carrying out of my project. I wondered if I should be able to pass over the river to the goal of my strange ambition to become eventually an inmate of the halls inhabited by my mentally wrecked sisters. And then, once in, what would be my experience? And after? How to get out. Bah! I said, they will get me out.

I looked out towards the window and hailed with joy the slight shimmer of dawn. The light grew strong and gray, but the silence strikingly still. My companion slept. I had still an hour or two to pass over. Fortunately I found some employment for my mental activity. Robert Bruce in his captivity had won confidence in the future and passed his time as pleasantly as possible under the circumstances by watching the celebrated spider building his web.[5] I had less noble vermin to interest me. Yet I believe I made some valuable discoveries in natural history. I was about dropping off to sleep in spite of myself, when I was suddenly startled to wakefulness. I thought I heard something crawl and fall down upon the counterpane with an almost inaudible thud. I had the opportunity of studying these interesting animals very thoroughly. They had evidently come for breakfast, and were not a little disappointed to find that their principle *plat* was not there. They scampered up and down the pillow, came together, seemed to hold interesting converse and acted in every way as if they were puzzled by the absence of an appetizing breakfast. After one consultation of some length they finally disappeared, seeking victims elsewhere, and leaving me to pass the long minutes by giving my attention to cockroaches, whose size and agility were something of a surprise to me.

Sympathy in Trouble

My room companion had been sound asleep for a long time, but she now woke up, and expressed surprise at seeing me still awake and apparently as lively as a cricket. She was as sympathetic as ever. She came to me and took my hands and tried her best to console me, and asked me if I did not want to go home. She kept me upstairs until nearly everybody was out of the house, and then took me down to the basement for coffee and a bun. After that, partaken in silence, I went back to my room, where I sat down, moping. Mrs. Caine grew more and more anxious. "What is to be done?" she kept exclaiming. "Where are your friends?" "No," I answered, "I have no friends, but I have some trunks. Where are they? I want them." The good woman tried to pacify me, saying that they would be found in good time. She believed that I was insane. Yet I forgive her. It is only after one is in trouble that one realizes how little sympathy and kindness there are in the world. The women in the Home who were not afraid of me had wanted to have some amusement at my expense, and so they had bothered me with questions and remarks that had I been insane would have been cruel and inhumane. Only this one woman among the crowd, pretty and delicate Mrs. Caine, displayed true womanly feeling. She compelled the others to cease teasing me and took the bed of the woman who refused to sleep near me. She protested against the suggestion to leave me alone and to have me locked up for the night so that I could harm no one. She insisted on remaining with me in order to administer aid should I need it. She smoothed my hair and bathed my brow and talked as soothingly to me as a mother would do to an ailing child. By every means she tried to have me go to bed and rest, and when it drew towards morning she got up and wrapped a blanket around me for fear I might get cold; then she kissed me on the brow and whispered, compassionately, "Poor child, poor child!" How much I admired that little woman's courage and kindness. How I longed to reassure her and whisper that I was not insane, and how I hoped that if any poor girl should ever be so unfortunate as to be what I was pretending to be, she might meet with one who possessed the same spirit of human kindness possessed by Mrs. Ruth Caine.

THE ADVENT OF THE POLICE

III.

But to return to my story. I kept up my role until the assistant matron, Mrs. Stanard, came in. She tried to persuade me to be calm. I began to see clearly that she wanted to get me out of the house at all hazards, quietly if possible. This I did not want. I refused to move, but kept up ever the refrain of my lost trunks. Finally some one suggested that an officer be sent for. After a while Mrs. Stanard put on her bonnet and went out. Then I knew that I was making an advance towards the home of the insane. Soon she returned, bringing with her two policemen— big, strong men—who entered the room rather unceremoniously, evidently expecting to meet with a person violently crazy. The name of one of them was Tom Bockert. When they entered I pretended not to see them. "I want you to take her quietly," said Mrs. Stanard. "If she don't come along quietly," responded one of the men, "I will drag her through the streets." I still took no notice of them, but certainly wished to avoid raising a scandal outside. Fortunately Mrs. Caine came to my rescue. She told the officers about my outcries for my lost trunks, and together they made up a plan to get me to go along with them quietly by telling me they would go with me to look for my lost effects. They asked me if I would go. I said I was afraid to go alone. Mrs. Stanard then said she would accompany me, and she arranged that the two policemen should follow us at a respectful distance. She tied on my veil for me, and we left the house by the basement and started across town, the two officers following at some distance behind. We walked along very quietly and finally came to the station-house, which the good woman assured me was the express office and that there we should certainly find my missing effects. I went inside with fear and trembling, for good reason.

Before Capt. McCullagh

I remembered the police station well because only ten days before I had been there and had seen Capt. McCullagh, from whom I had asked for information in a case which I had written as a reporter. If he were in, would he not recognize me? And then all would be lost so far as getting to the island was concerned. I pulled my sailor hat as low down over my face as I possibly could, and prepared for the ordeal. Sure enough there was sturdy Capt. McCullagh standing near the desk. "Are you Nellie Brown?" he asked. I said I supposed I was. "Where do you come from?" he asked. I told him I did not know, and then Mrs. Stanard gave him a lot of information about me—told him how strangely I had acted at her home; how I had not slept a wink all night, and that in her opinion I was a poor unfortunate who had been driven crazy by inhuman treatment. There was some discussion between Capt. McCullagh, Mrs. Stanard and the two officers, and Tom Bockert was told to take us down to the court in a car.

"Come along," Bockert said, "I will find your trunk for you." We all went together, Mrs. Stanard, Tom Bockert and his companion and myself. I said it was very kind of them to go with me and I should not soon forget them. As we walked along I kept up my refrain about my trunks, interjecting occasionally some remark about the dirty condition of the streets and the curious character of the people we met on the way. "I don't think I have ever seen such people before," I said. "Who are they?" I asked, and my companions looked upon me with expressions of pity, evidently believing I was a foreigner, an emigrant or something of the sort. They told me that the people around me were working people. I remarked once more that I thought there were too many working people in the world for the amount of work to be done, at which remark Policeman P. T. Bockert eyed me closely, evidently thinking that my mind was gone for good. We passed several other policemen, who generally asked my two sturdy guardians what was the matter with me. By this time quite a number of ragged children were following us too, and they passed remarks about me that were to me original as well as amusing.

"What's she up for?" "Say, kop, where did ye get her?" "Where did yer pull 'er?" "She's a daisy!"

Poor Mrs. Stanard was more frightened than I was. The whole situation grew interesting, but I still had fears for my fate before the Judge.

Searching for Lost Trunks

At last we came to a low building, and Tom Bockert kindly volunteered the information: "Here's the express office. We shall soon find those trunks of yours."

I said that a great many people seemed to have lost their trunks. "Yes," he said, "nearly all these people are looking for trunks."

I said, "They all seem to be foreigners, too." "Yes," said Tom, "they are all foreigners, just landed. They have all lost their trunks, and it takes most of our time to help find them for them."

We entered the courtroom. It was the Essex Market Police courtroom. At last the question of my sanity or insanity was to be decided. Judge Duffy[6] sat behind the high desk, wearing a look which seemed to indicate that he was dealing out the milk of human kindness by wholesale. I rather feared I would not get the fate I sought because of the kindness I saw on every line of his face, and it was with rather a sinking heart that I followed Mrs. Stanard as she answered the summons to go up to the desk where Tom Bockert had just given an account of the affair. "Come here," said an officer. "What is your name?"

"Nellie Brown," I replied, with a little accent, "I have lost my trunks and would like if you could find them." "When did you come to New York?" he asked. "I did not come to New York," I replied (while I added mentally, "because I have been here some time"). "But you are in New York now," said the man. "No," I said, looking as incredulous as I thought a crazy person could, "I did not come to New York." "That girl is from the West," he said, in a tone that made me tremble. "She has a Western accent." Some one else who had been listening to the brief dialogue here asserted that he had lived South and that my accent was pure Southern, while another officer was positive it was Eastern. I felt much relieved when the first spokesman turned to the Judge and said, "Judge, here is a peculiar case of a young woman who doesn't know who she is or where came from. You had better attend to it at once."

I commenced to shake with more than the cold, and I looked around at the strange crowd about me, composed of poorly dressed men and women with stories printed on their faces of hard lives, abuse and poverty. Some were consulting eagerly with friends, while others sat still with a look of utter hopelessness. Everywhere was a sprinkling of well-dressed, well-fed officers watching the scene passively and almost indifferently. It was only an old story with them. One more unfortunate added to a long list which had long since ceased to be of any interest or concern to them.

Before Judge Duffy

"Come here, girl, and lift your veil," called out Judge Duffy in tones which surprised me by a harshness which I did not think from the kindly face he possessed.

"Who are you speaking to?" I inquired, in my stateliest manner.

"Come here, my dear, and lift your veil. You know the Queen of England, if she were here, would have to lift her veil," he said very kindly.

"That is much better," I replied. "I am not the Queen of England, but I'll lift my veil."

As I did so the little Judge looked at me, and then, in a very kind and gentle tone, he said:

"My dear child, what is wrong?"

"Nothing is wrong except that I have lost my trunks, and this man," indicating Policeman Bockert, "promised to bring me where they could be found."

"What do you know about this child?" asked the Judge sternly of Mrs. Stanard, who stood, pale and trembling, by my side.

"I know nothing of her except that she came to the home yesterday and asked to remain over night."

"The home! What do you mean by the home?" asked Judge Duffy, quickly.

"It is a temporary home kept for working women at No. 84 Second avenue."

"What is your position there?"

"I am assistant matron."

"Well, tell us all you know of the case."

"When I was going into the home yesterday I noticed her coming down the avenue. She was all alone. I had just got into the house when the bell rang and she came in. When I talked with her she wanted to know if she could stay all night, and I said she could. After awhile she said all the people in the house looked crazy and that she was afraid of them. Then she would not go to bed, but sat up all the night."

"Had she any money?"

"Yes," I replied, answering for her, "I paid her for everything, and the eating was the worst I ever tried."

There was a general smile at this, and some murmurs of "She's not so crazy on the food question."

"Poor child," said Judge Duffy, "she is well dressed and a lady. Her English is perfect, and I would stake everything on her being a good girl. I am positive she is somebody's darling."

At this announcement everybody laughed, and I put my handkerchief over my face and endeavored to choke the laughter that threatened to spoil my plans, in despite of my resolutions.

"I mean she is some woman's darling," hastily amended the Judge. "I am sure some one is searching for her. Poor girl, I will be good to her, for she looks like my sister, who is dead."

There was a hush for a moment after this announcement, and the officers glanced at me more kindly, while I silently blessed the kind-hearted Judge, and hoped that any poor creatures who might be afflicted as I pretended to be should have as kindly a man to deal with as Judge Duffy.

"I wish the reporters were here," he said at last. "They would be able to find out something about her."

I got very much frightened at this, for if there is any one who can ferret out a mystery it is a reporter. I felt that I would rather face a mass of expert doctors, policemen and detectives than two bright specimens of my craft, so I said:

"I don't see why all this is needed to help me find my trunks. These men are impudent and I do not want to be stared at. I will go away. I don't want to stay here."

So saying I pulled down my veil and secretly hoped the reporters would be detained elsewhere until I was sent to the asylum.

"I don't know what to do with the poor child," said the worried Judge. "She must be taken care of."

"Send her to the Island," suggested one of the officers.

"Oh, don't!" said Mrs. Stanard in evident alarm. "Don't! She is a lady and it would kill her to be put on the Island."

For once I felt like shaking that good woman. To think the Island was just the place I wanted to reach and here she was trying to keep me from going there! It was very kind of her, but rather provoking under the circumstances.

"There has been some foul work here," said the Judge. "I believe this child has been drugged and brought to this city. Make out the papers and we will send her to Bellevue for examination. Probably in a few days the effect of the drug will pass off and she will be able to tell us a story that will be startling. If the reporters would only come!"

I dreaded them, so I said something about not wishing to stay there any longer to be gazed at. Judge Duffy then told Policeman Bockert to take me to the back office. After we were seated there Judge Duffy came in and asked me if my home was in Cuba.

"Yes," I replied with a smile. "How did you know?"

"Oh, I knew it, my dear. Now, tell me where was it. In what part of Cuba?"

"On the hacienda," I replied.

"Ah," said the Judge, "on a farm. Do you remember Havana?"

"Si, senor," I answered. "It is near home. How did you know?"

"Oh, I knew all about it. Now, won't you tell me the name of your home?" he asked persuasively.

"That's what I forget," I answered sadly. "I have a headache all the time, and it makes me forget things. I don't want them to trouble me. Everybody is asking me questions, and it makes my head worse," and in truth it did.

"Well, no one shall trouble you any more. Sit down here and rest awhile," and the genial Judge left me alone with Mrs. Stanard.

A Reporter Interviews Her

Just then an officer came in with a reporter. I was so frightened and thought I would be recognized as a journalist, so I turned my head away and said, "I don't want to see any reporters; I will not see any; the Judge said I was not to be troubled."

"Well, there is no insanity in that," said the man who had brought the reporter, and together they left the room. Once again I had a fit of fear. Had I gone too far in not wanting to see a reporter, and was my sanity detected? If I had given the impression that I was sane I was determined to undo it, so I jumped up and ran back and forward through the office, Mrs. Stanard clinging terrified to my arm.

"I won't stay here; I want my trunks! Why do they bother me with so many people?" and thus I kept on until the ambulance surgeon came in, accompanied by the Judge.

The Ambulance Appears

"Here is a poor girl who has been drugged," explained the Judge. "She looks like my sister, and any one can see that she is a good girl. I am interested in the child, and I would do as much for her as if she were my own. I want you to be kind to her," he said to the ambulance surgeon. Then turning to Mrs. Stanard, he asked her if she could not keep me for a few days until my case was inquired into. Fortunately, she said she could not, because all the women at the home were afraid of me, and would leave if I were kept there. I was very much afraid she would keep me if the pay was assured her, and so I said something about the bad cooking and that I did not intend to go back to the home. Then came the examination. The doctor looked clever and I had not one hope of deceiving him, but I determined to keep up the farce. "Put out your tongue," he ordered briskly. I gave an inward chuckle at the thought. "Put out your tongue when I tell you," he said. "I don't want to," I answered truthfully enough. "You must. You are sick, and I am a doctor." "I am not sick and never was. I only want my trunks." But I put out my tongue, which he looked at in a sagacious manner. Then he felt my pulse and listened to the beating of my heart. I had not the least idea how the heart of an insane person beat, so I held my breath all the while he listened, until when he quit I had to give a gasp to regain it. Then he tried the effect of the light on the pupils of my eyes. Holding his hand within a half inch of my face he told me to look at it, then jerking it hastily away he would examine my eyes. I was puzzled to know what insanity was like in the eye, so I thought the best thing under the circumstances was to stare. This I did. I held my eyes riveted unblinkingly upon his hand, and when he removed it I exerted all my strength to still keep my eyes from blinking. "What drugs have you been taking?" he then asked me. "Drugs?" I repeated wonderingly. "I do not know what drugs are." "The pupils of her eyes have been enlarged ever since she came to the home. They have not changed once," explained Mrs. Stanard. I wondered how she knew whether they had or not, but I kept quiet. "I believe she has been using belladonna," said the doctor, and for the first time I was thankful that I was a little near-sighted, which of course answers for the enlargement of the pupils. I thought I might as well be truthful when I could without injuring my case, so I told him I was near-sighted, that I was not in the least ill, had never been sick, and that no one had a right to detain me when I wanted to find my trunks. I wanted to go home. He wrote a lot of things in a long, slender book and then said he was going to take me home. The Judge told him to take me and to be kind to me, and to tell the people at the hospital to be kind to me and to do all they could for me. If we only had more such men as Judge Duffy the poor unfortunates would not find life all darkness.

In the Ambulance Wagon

I began to have more confidence in my own ability now, since one Judge, one doctor and a mass of people had pronounced me insane, and I put on my veil quite gladly when I was told that I was to be taken in a carriage and that afterwards I could go home. "I am so glad to go with you," I said, and I meant it. I was very glad indeed. Once more, guarded by Policeman Bockert, I walked through the little crowded courtroom. I felt quite proud of myself as I went out a side door into an alleyway, where the ambulance was waiting. Near the closed and barred gates was a small office occupied by several men and large books. We all went in there, and when they began to ask me questions the doctor interposed and said he had all the papers and that it was useless to ask me anything further, because I was unable to answer questions. This was a great relief to me, for my nerves were already feeling the strain. A rough-looking man wanted to put me into the ambulance, but I refused his aid so decidedly that the doctor and the policeman told him to desist, and they performed that gallant office themselves. I did not enter the ambulance without protest. I made the remark that I had never seen a carriage of that make before and that I did not want to ride in it, but after a while I let them persuade me, as I had right along intended to do. I shall never forget that ride. After I was put in flat on the yellow blanket the doctor got in and sat near the door. The large gates were swung open and the curious crowd which had collected swayed back to make way for the ambulance as it backed out. How they tried to get a glimpse at the supposed crazy girl! The doctor saw that I did not like the people gazing at me and considerately put down the curtains, after asking my wishes in regard to it. Still that did not keep the people away. The children raced after us, yelling all sorts of slang expressions and trying to get a peep under the curtains. It was an interesting drive, but I must say that it was an excruciatingly rough one. I held on, only there was not much to hold on to, and the driver drove as if he feared some one would catch up with us.

IN BELLEVUE HOSPITAL

IV.

At last Bellevue was reached, the third station on my way to the island. I had passed through successfully the ordeals at the home and at Essex Market Police Court, and now felt confident that I should not fail. The ambulance stopped with a sudden jerk and the doctor jumped out. "How many have you?" I heard some one inquire. "Only one, for the pavilion," was the reply. A rough-looking man came forward, and catching hold of me attempted to drag me out as if I had the strength of an elephant and would resist. The doctor, seeing my look of disgust, ordered him to leave me alone, saying that he would take charge of me himself. He then lifted me carefully out and I walked with the grace of a queen past the crowd that had gathered curious to see the new unfortunate. Together with the doctor I entered a small dark office, where there were several men. The one behind the desk opened a book and began on the long string of questions which had been asked me so often. I refused to answer, and the doctor told him it was not necessary to trouble me further, as he had all the papers made out, and I was too insane to be able to tell anything that would be of consequence. I felt relieved that it was so easy here, as, though still undaunted, I had begun to feel faint for want of food. The order was then given to take me to the insane pavilion, and a muscular man came forward and caught me so tightly by the arm that a pain ran clear through me. It made me angry, and for a moment I forgot my role as I turned to him and said: "How dare you touch me?" At this he loosened his hold somewhat, and I shook him off with more strength than I thought I possessed. "I will go with no one but this man," I said, pointing to the ambulance surgeon. "The Judge said that he was to take care of me, and I will go with no one else." At this the surgeon said that he would take me, and so we went arm in arm, following the man who had at first been so rough with me. We passed through the well-cared-for grounds and finally reached the insane ward. A white-capped nurse was there to receive me. "This young girl is to wait here for the boat," said the surgeon, and then he started to leave me. I begged him not to go or to take me with him, but he said he wanted to get his dinner first, and that I should wait there for him. When I insisted on accompanying him he claimed that he had to assist at an amputation, and it would not look well for me to be present. It was evident that he believed he was dealing with an insane person. Just then the most horrible insane cries came from a yard in the rear. With all my bravery I felt a chill at the prospect of being shut up with a fellow-creature who was really insane. The doctor evidently noticed my nervousness, for he said to the attendant: "What a noise the carpenters make." Turning to me he offered me explanation to the effect that new buildings were being erected, and that the noise came from some of the workmen engaged upon it. I told him I did not want to stay there without him, and to pacify me he promised soon to return. He left me and I found myself at last an occupant of an insane asylum.

Some Interior Arrangements

I stood at the door and contemplated the scene before me. The long, uncarpeted hall was scrubbed to that peculiar whiteness seen only in public institutions. In the rear of the hall were large iron doors fastened by a padlock. Several stiff-looking benches and a number of willow chairs were the only articles of furniture. On either side of the hall were doors leading into what I supposed and what proved to be bedrooms. Near the entrance door, on the right-hand side, was a small sitting room for the nurses, and opposite it was a room where dinner was dished out. A nurse in a black dress, white cap and apron and armed with a bunch of keys had charge of the hall. I soon learned her name, Miss Ball. An old Irishwoman was maid of all work. I heard her called Mary, and I am glad to know that there is such a good-hearted woman in that place. I experienced only kindness and the utmost consideration from her. There were only three patients, as they are called. I made the fourth. I thought I might as well begin work at once, for I still expected that the very first doctor might declare me sane and send me out again into the wide, wide world. So I went down to the rear of the room and introduced myself to one of the women and asked her all about herself. Her name, she said, was Miss Anne Neville, and she had been sick from overwork. She had been working as a chambermaid, and when her health gave way she was sent to some Sisters' Home to be treated. Her nephew, who was a waiter, was out of work, and being unable to pay her expenses at the Home, had had her transferred to Bellevue.

"Is there anything wrong with you mentally as well?" I asked her.

"No," she said. "The doctors have been asking me many

curious questions and confusing me as much as possible, but I have nothing wrong with my brain."

"Do you know that only insane people are sent to this pavilion?" I asked.

"Yes, I know; but I am unable to do anything. The doctors refuse to listen to me, and it is useless to say anything to the nurses."

Among the Insane Patients

Satisfied from various reasons that Miss Neville was as sane as I was myself, I transferred my attentions to one of the other patients. I found her in need of medical aid and quite silly mentally, although I have seen many women in the lower walks of life, whose sanity was never questioned, who were not any brighter.

The third patient, Mrs. Fox, would not say much. She was very quiet, and after telling me that her case was hopeless she refused to talk. I began now to feel surer of my position, and I determined that no doctor should convince me that I was sane as long as I had the hope of accomplishing my mission. A small, fair-complexioned nurse arrived and, after putting on her cap, told Miss Ball to go to dinner. The new nurse, Miss Scott by name, came to me and said, rudely:

"Take off your hat."

"I shall not take off my hat," I answered. "I am waiting for the boat and I shall not remove it."

"Well, you are not going on any boat. You might as well know it now as later. You are in an asylum for the insane."

Although fully aware of that fact yet her unvarnished words gave me a shock. "I did not want to come here, I am not sick or insane and I will not stay," I said.

"It will be a long time before you get out if you don't do as you are told," answered Miss Scott. "You might as well take off your hat or I shall use force, and if I am not able to do it I have but to touch a bell and I shall get assistance. Will you take it off?"

"No, I will not. I am cold and I want my hat on, and you can't make me take it off."

"I shall give you a few more minutes and if you don't take it off then I shall use force, and I warn you it will not be very gentle."

"If you take my hat off I shall take your cap off; so now."

Miss Scott was called to the door then, and as I feared that an exhibition of temper might show too much sanity I took off my hat and gloves and was sitting quietly looking into space when she returned. I was hungry, and was quite pleased to see Mary make preparations for dinner. The preparations were simple. She merely pulled a straight bench up along the side of a bare table and ordered the patients to gather 'round the feast. Then she brought out a small tin plate on which was a piece of boiled meat and a potato. It could not have been colder had it been cooked the week before, and it had no chance to make acquaintance with salt or pepper. I would not go up to the table, so Mary came to where I sat in a corner and while handing out the tin plate asked:

"Have ye any pennies about ye, dearie?"

"What?" I said in my surprise.

"Have ye any pennies, dearie, that ye could give me. They'll take them all from ye any way, dearie, so I might as well have them."

I understood it fully now, but I had no intention of feeing Mary so early in the game, fearing it would have an influence on her treatment of me, so I said that I had lost my purse, which was quite true. But though I did not give Mary any money, she was nonetheless kind to me. When I objected to the tin plate in which she had brought my food she fetched a china one for me, and when I found it impossible to eat the food she presented she gave me a glass of milk and a soda cracker.

Only a Charity Ward

All the windows in the hall were open and the cold air began to tell on my Southern blood. It grew so cold indeed as to be almost unbearable, and I complained of it to Miss Scott and Miss Ball. But they answered curtly that as I was in a charity place I could not expect much else. All the other women were suffering from the cold and the nurses themselves had to wear heavy garments to keep themselves warm. I asked if I could go to bed.

They said "No!" At last Miss Scott got an old gray shawl and shaking some of the moths out of it told me to put it on. "It's rather a bad looking shawl," I said. "Well, some people would get along better if they were not so proud," said Miss Scott. "People on charity should not expect anything and should not complain." So I put the moth-eaten shawl with all its musty smell around me, and sat down on a wicker chair, wondering what would come next, whether I should freeze to death or survive. My nose was very cold, so I covered up my head and was in half a doze when the shawl was suddenly jerked from my face and a strange man and Miss Scott stood before me. The man proved to be a doctor, and his first greetings were, "I've seen that face before." "Then you know me?" I asked with a great show of eagerness. "I think I do. Where did you come from?" "From home." "Where is home?" "Don't you know? Cuba." He then sat down beside me, felt my pulse and examined my tongue, and at last said: "Tell Miss Scott all about yourself." "No, I will not. I will not talk with women." "What do you do in New York?" "Nothing." "Can you work?" "No, Senor." "Tell me, are you a woman of the town?" "I do not understand you," I replied, heartily disgusted with him.

"I mean have you allowed the men to provide for you and keep you."

I felt like slapping him in the face, but I had to maintain my composure, so I simply said: "I do not know what you are talking about. I always lived at home."

Positively Demented

After many more questions fully as useless and senseless, he left me and began to talk with the nurse. "Positively demented," he said. "I consider it a hopeless case. She needs to be put where some one will take care of her."

And so I passed my second medical expert.

After this I began to have a smaller regard for the ability of doctors than I had ever had before. I felt sure now that no doctor could tell whether people were insane or not, so long as the case was not violent.

Later in the afternoon a boy and a woman came. The woman sat down on a bench while the boy went in and talked

with Miss Scott. In a short time he came out, and, just nodding good-bye to the woman, who was his mother, went away.
She did not look insane, but as she was German I could not
learn her story. Her name, however, was Mrs. Louise Schanz.
She seemed quite lost, but when the nurses put her at some
sewing she did her work well and quickly. At 3 in the afternoon all the patients were given a gruel broth and at 5 a cup of
tea and a piece of bread. I was favored, for when they saw that
it was impossible for me to eat the bread or drink the stuff
honored by the name of tea they gave me a cup of milk and a
cracker, the same as I had at noon. Just as the gas was being
lighted another patient was added. She was a young girl,
twenty-five years old. She told me that she had just gotten up
from a sick bed. Her appearance confirmed her story. She
looked like one who had had a severe attack of fever. "I am
now suffering from nervous debility," she said, "and my
friends have sent me here to be treated for it." I did not tell her
where she was and she seemed quite satisfied. At 6.15 Miss
Ball said that she wanted to go away and so we would all have
to go to bed. Then each of us—we now numbered six—were
assigned a room and told to undress. I did so and was given a
short cotton-flannel gown to wear during the night. Then she
took every particle of the clothing I had worn during the day
and making it up in a bundle labelled it "Brown" and took it
away. The iron-barred window was locked, and Miss Ball,
after giving me an extra blanket, which, she said, was a favor
rarely granted, went out and left me alone. The bed was not a
comfortable one. It was so hard, indeed, that I could not make
a dent in it, and the pillow was stuffed with straw. Under the
sheet was an oilcloth spread. As the night grew colder I tried
to warm that oilcloth. I kept on trying, but when morning
dawned and it was still as cold as when I went to bed, and had
reduced me, too, to the temperature of an iceberg, I gave it up
as an impossible task.

Another Reporter Turns Up

I had hoped to get some rest on this my first night in an insane
asylum. But I was doomed to disappointment. When the night
nurses came in they were curious to see me and to find out

what I was like. No sooner had they left than I heard some one at the door inquiring for Nellie Brown, and I began to tremble, fearing always that my sanity would be discovered. By listening to the conversation I found it was a reporter in search of me, and I heard him ask for my clothing so that he might examine it. I listened quite anxiously to the talk about me, and was relieved to learn that I was considered hopelessly insane. That was encouraging. After the reporter left I heard new arrivals, and I learned that a doctor was there and intended to see me. For what purpose I knew not, and I imagined all sorts of horrible things, such as examinations and the rest of it, and when they got to my room I was shaking with more than fear. "Nellie Brown, here is the doctor. He wishes to speak with you," said the nurse. If that's all he wanted I thought I could endure it. I removed the blanket which I had put over my head in my sudden fright and looked up. The sight was reassuring.

A Handsome Doctor

He was a handsome young man. He had the air and address of a gentleman. The air he wore was somewhat deceptive. He came forward, seated himself on the side of my bed, and put his arm soothingly around my shoulders. It was a terrible task to play insane before this young man, and only a girl can sympathize with me in my position.

"How do you feel to-night, Nellie?" he asked, easily.

"Oh, I feel all right."

"But you are sick, you know," he said.

"Oh, am I?" I replied, and I turned my head on the pillow and smiled.

"When did you leave Cuba, Nellie?"

"Oh, you know my home?" I asked.

"Yes, very well. Don't you remember me? I remember you."

"Do you?" and I mentally said I should not forget him. He was accompanied by a friend who never ventured a remark, but stood staring at me as I lay in bed. After a great many questions, to which I answered truthfully, he left me. Then came other troubles. All night long the nurses read one to the other aloud, and I know that the other patients, as well as myself, were unable to sleep. Every half-hour or hour they would walk heavily down the halls, their boot-heels resounding like the march of a private of dragoons,[7] and take a look at every patient. Of course this helped to keep us awake. Then, as it came towards morning, they began to beat eggs for breakfast, and the sound made me realize how horribly hungry I was. Occasional yells and cries came from the male department, and that did not aid in making the night pass more cheerfully. Then the ambulance-gong, as it brought in more unfortunates, sounded as a knell to life and liberty. Thus I passed my first night as an insane girl at Bellevue.

THE GOAL IN SIGHT

V.

At 6 o'clock on Sunday morning, Sept. 25, the nurses pulled the covering from my bed. "Come, it's time for you to get out of bed," they said, and opened the window and let in the cold breeze. My clothing was then returned to me. After dressing I was shown to a washstand, where all the other patients were trying to rid their faces of all traces of sleep. At 7 o'clock we were given some horrible mess, which Mary told us was chicken broth. The cold, from which we had suffered enough the day previous, was bitter, and when I complained to the nurse she said it was one of the rules of the institution not to turn the heat on until October, and so we would have to endure it, as the steam-pipes had not even been put in order. The night nurses then, arming themselves with scissors, began to play manicure on the patients. They cut my nails to the quick, as they did those of several of the other patients. Shortly after this a handsome young doctor made his appearance and I was conducted into the sitting-room. "Who are you?" he asked. "Nellie Moreno,"[8] I replied. "Then why did you give the name of Brown?" he asked. "What is wrong with you?" "Nothing. I did not want to come here, but they brought me. I want to go away. Won't you let me out?"

Who Is This Man?

"If I take you out will you stay with me? Won't you run away from me when you get on the street?"

"I can't promise that I will not," I answered, with a smile and a sigh, for he was handsome.

He asked me many other questions. Did I ever see faces on the wall? Did I ever hear voices around? I answered him to the best of my ability.

"Do you ever hear voices at night?" he asked.

"Yes, there is so much talking I cannot sleep."

"I thought so," he said to himself. Then turning to me, he asked: "What do these voices say?"

"Well, I do not listen to them always. But sometimes, very often, they talk about Nellie Brown and then on other subjects that do not interest me half so much," I answered truthfully. "That will do," he said to Miss Scott, who was just on the outside. "Can I go away?" I asked. "Yes," he said, with a satisfied laugh, "we'll soon send you away." "It is so very cold here, I want to go out," I said. "That's true," he said to Miss Scott. "The cold is almost unbearable in here, and you will have some cases of pneumonia if you are not careful."

Tests for Insanity

With this I was led away and another patient was taken in. I sat right outside the door and waited to hear how he would test the sanity of the other patients. With little variation the examination was exactly the same as mine. All the patients were asked if they saw faces on the wall, heard voices, and what they said. I might also add each patient denied any such peculiar freaks of sight and hearing. At 10 o'clock we were given a cup of unsalted beef tea; at noon a bit of cold meat and a potato, at 3 o'clock a cup of oatmeal gruel and at 5.30 a cup of tea and a slice of unbuttered bread. We were all cold and hungry. After the physician left we were given shawls and told to walk up and down the halls in order to get warm. During the day the pavilion was visited by a number of people who were curious to see the crazy girl from Cuba. I kept my head

covered, on the plea of being cold, for fear some of the reporters would recognize me. Some of the visitors were apparently
in search of a missing girl, for I was made to take down the
shawl repeatedly, and after they looked at me they would say,
"I don't know her," or "she is not the one," for which I was secretly thankful. Warden O'Rourke[9] visited me and tried his
arts on an examination. Then he brought some well-dressed
women and some gentlemen at different times to have a glance
at the mysterious Nellie Brown.

Praise of the Reporters

The reporters were the most troublesome. Such a number of
them! And they were all so bright and clever that I was terribly
frightened lest they should see that I was sane. They were very
kind and nice to me, and very gentle in all their questionings.
My late visitor the night previous came to the window while
some reporters were interviewing me in the sitting-room and
told the nurse to allow them to see me as they would be of assistance in finding some clue as to my identity.

In the afternoon Dr. Field[10] came and examined me. He
asked me only a few questions, and ones that had no bearing
on such a case. The chief question was of my home and friends,
and if I had any lovers or had ever been married. The other patients were asked the same questions. As the doctor was about
to leave the pavilion Miss Tillie Mayard discovered that she
was in an insane ward. She went to Dr. Field and asked him
why she had been sent there. "Have you just found out you are
in an insane asylum?" asked the doctor. "Yes, my friends said
they were sending me to a convalescent ward to be treated for
nervous debility, from which I am suffering since my illness. I
want to get out of this place immediately." "Well, you won't
get out in a hurry," he said, with a quick laugh. "If you know
anything at all," she responded, "you should be able to tell
that I am perfectly sane. Why don't you test me?" "We know
all we want to on that score," said the Doctor, and he left the
poor girl condemned to an insane asylum, probably for life,
without giving her one feeble chance to prove her sanity.

Sunday night was but a repetition of Saturday. All night
long we were kept awake by the talk of the nurses and their

heavy walking through the uncarpeted halls. On Monday morning we were told we should be taken away at 1.30. The nurses questioned me unceasingly about my home, and all seemed to have an idea that I had a lover who had cast me forth on the world and wrecked my brain. The morning brought many reporters. How untiring they are in their efforts to get something new. Miss Scott refused to allow me to be seen, however, and for this I was thankful. Had they been given free access to me, I should probably not have been a mystery long, for many of them knew me by sight. Warden O'Rourke came for a final visit and had a short conversation with me. He wrote his name in my notebook, saying to the nurse that I would forget all about it in an hour. I smiled and thought I wasn't sure of that. Other people called to see me, but none knew me or could give any information about me.

Leaving Bellevue

Noon came. I grew nervous as the time approached to leave for the Island. I dreaded every new arrival, fearful that my secret would be discovered at the last moment. Then I was given a shawl and my hat and gloves. I could hardly put them on, my nerves were so unstrung. At last the attendant arrived, and I bade good-bye to Mary as I slipped "a few pennies" into her hand. "God bless you," she said; "I shall pray for you. Cheer up, dearie. You are young and will get over this." I told her I hoped so, and then I said good-bye to Miss Scott in Spanish. The rough-looking attendant twisted his arms around mine, and half led, half dragged me to an ambulance. A crowd of the students had assembled and they watched us curiously. I put the shawl over my face and sank thankfully into the wagon. Miss Neville, Miss Mayard, Mrs. Fox, and Mrs. Schanz were all put in after me, one at a time. A man got in with us; the doors were locked and we were driven out of the gates in great style on towards the insane asylum and victory! The patients made no move to escape. The odor of the male attendant's breath was enough to make one's head swim.

When we reached the wharf such a mob of people crowded around the wagon that the police were called to put them away, so that we could reach the boat. I was the last of the procession. I was escorted down the plank, the fresh breeze blowing the attendant's whiskey breath into my face until I staggered. I was taken into a dirty cabin, where I found my companions seated on a narrow bench. The small windows were closed, and, with the smell of the filthy room, the air was stifling. At one end of the cabin was a small bunk in such a condition that I had to hold my nose when I went near it. A sick girl was put on it. An old woman, with an enormous bonnet and a dirty basket filled with chunks of bread and bits of scrap meat, completed our company. The door was guarded by two female attendants. One was clad in a dress made of bed-ticking and the other was dressed with some attempt at style. They were coarse, massive women, and expectorated tobacco juice about on the floor in a manner more skillful than charming. One of these fearful creatures seemed to have much faith in the power of the glance on insane people, for when any one of us would move or go to look out of the high window, she would say, "Sit down," and would lower her brows and glare in a way that was simply terrifying. While guarding the door they talked with some men on the outside. They discussed the number of patients and then their own affairs in a manner neither edifying nor refined.

The boat stopped and the old woman and the sick girl were taken off. The rest of us were told to sit still. At the next stop my companions were taken off, one at a time. I was last, and it seemed to require a man and a woman to lead me up the plank to reach the shore. An ambulance was standing there, and in it were the four other patients.

"What is this place?" I asked of the man, who had his fingers sunk into the flesh of my arm.

"Blackwell's Island, an insane place, where you'll never get out of."

With this I was shoved into the ambulance, the springboard was put up, an officer and a mail-carrier jumped on behind, and I was swiftly driven to the Insane Asylum on Blackwell's Island. Of my ten days' experience there I have yet to tell.

New York World,
OCTOBER 9, 1887

INSIDE THE MADHOUSE

Nellie Bly's Experience in the Blackwell's
Island Asylum

CONTINUATION OF THE STORY OF TEN DAYS WITH LUNATICS

How the City's Unfortunate Wards Are Fed and Treated

THE TERRORS OF COLD BATHS AND CRUEL, UNSYMPATHETIC NURSES

Attendants Who Harass and Abuse Patients and Laugh at Their Miseries

---

Doctors Who Flirt with Pretty Nurses—A Queer Medical
Examination that Did Not Examine—Inmates of Hall No.
6—At the Piano—Taking Away Her Clothes—A Long Wait
in the Cold for Supper—No Knives nor Forks—Food Un-
salted and Unfit—Half Drowned in an Icy Bath—Soap Only
Once a Week—Put to Bed in Damp Clothing—Noises at
Night—The Horror of Fire in a Locked and Barred Room—
Hair Combed with a Public Comb—Nurses Who Vex
and Annoy Patients—Holding Them Under Water Until
Half Drowned—Punishing Unfortunates Who Appeal for
Protection—Attendants Curse Nellie—Set Free at Last.

As the wagon was rapidly driven through the beautiful lawns
up to the asylum my feelings of satisfaction at having attained
the object of my work were greatly dampened by the look of
distress on the faces of my companions. Poor women, they had
no hopes of a speedy delivery! On the wagon sped, and I, as
well as my comrades, gave a despairing farewell glance at freedom as we came in sight of the long stone buildings. We passed
one low building, and the stench was so horrible that I was

compelled to hold my breath, and I mentally decided that it was the kitchen. I afterwards found I was correct in my surmise, and smiled at the signboard at the end of the walk: "Visitors are not allowed on this road." I don't think the sign would be necessary if they once tried the road, especially on a warm day.

The wagon stopped and the nurse and officer in charge told us to get out. The nurse added: "Thank God! They came quietly." We obeyed orders to go ahead up a flight of narrow stone steps, which had evidently been built for the accommodation of people who climb stairs three at a time. I wondered if my companions knew where we were, so I said to Miss Tillie Mayard: "Where are we?" "At the Blackwell's Island Lunatic Asylum," she answered sadly. "Are you crazy?" I asked. "No," she replied, "but as we have been sent here we will have to be quiet until we find some means of escape. They will be few, though, if all the doctors, as Dr. Field, refuse to listen to me or give me a chance to prove my sanity." We were ushered into a narrow vestibule and the door was locked behind us.

In spite of the knowledge of my sanity and the assurance that I would be released in a few days, my heart gave a sharp twinge. Pronounced insane by four expert doctors and shut up behind the unmerciful bolts and bars of a madhouse! Not to be confined alone, but to be a companion, day and night, of senseless, chattering lunatics; to sleep with them, to eat with them, to be considered one of them, was an uncomfortable position. Timidly we followed the nurse up the long uncarpeted hall to a room filled by so-called crazy women. We were told to sit down, and some of the patients kindly made room for us. They looked at us curiously and one came up to me and asked: "Who sent you here?" "The doctors," I answered. "What for?" she persisted. "Well, they say I am insane," I admitted. "Insane!" she repeated incredulously. "It cannot be seen in your face."

This woman was too clever, I concluded, and was glad to answer the roughly given orders to follow the nurse to see the doctor. This nurse, Miss Grupe, by the way, had a nice German face, and if I had not detected certain hard lines about the mouth I might have expected, as did my companions, to receive but kindness from her. She left us in a small waiting room at the end of the hall, and left us alone while she went into a small office opening into the sitting or receiving-room. "I like to go down in the wagon," she said to the invisible party on the inside. "It helps to break up the day." He answered her that the open air improved her looks, and she again appeared before us all smiles and simpers.

"Come here, Tillie Mayard," she said. Miss Mayard obeyed, and, though I could not see into the office, I could hear her gently but firmly pleading her case. All her remarks were as rational as any I ever heard, and I thought no good physician could help but be impressed with her story. She told of her recent illness, that she was suffering from nervous debility. She begged that they try all their tests for insanity, if they had any, and give her justice. Poor girl, how my heart ached for her! I determined then and there that I would try by every means to make my mission of benefit to my suffering sisters; that I would show how they are committed without ample trial. Without one word of sympathy or encouragement she was brought back to where we sat.

Mrs. Louise Schanz was taken next into the presence of Dr. Kinier, the medical man. "Your name?" he asked, loudly. She answered in German, saying she did not speak English nor could she understand it. However, when he said Mrs. Louise Schanz she said "Yah, yah." Then he tried other questions, and when he found she could not understand one word of English he said to Miss Grupe: "You are German: speak to her for me." Miss Grupe proved to be one of those people who are ashamed of their nationality and she refused, saying she could understand but a few words of her mother tongue. "You know you speak German. Ask this woman what her husband does," and they both laughed as if they were enjoying a joke. "I can't speak but a few words," she protested, but at last she managed to ascertain the occupation of Mr. Schanz. "Now, what was the use of lying to me?" asked the doctor, with a laugh which dispelled the rudeness. "I can't speak any more," she said, and she did not.

Thus was Mrs. Louise Schanz consigned to the asylum without a chance to make herself understood. Can such carelessness

be excused, I wondered, when it was so easy to get an inter-
preter? If the confinement was for but a few days one might
question the necessity. But here was a woman taken without
her own consent from a free world to an asylum and there
given no chance to prove her sanity. Confined most probably
for life behind asylum bars, without even being told in her language the why and wherefore. Compare this with a criminal,
who is given every chance to prove his innocence. Who would
not rather be a murderer and take the chance for life than be
declared insane, without hope of escape? Mrs. Schanz begged
in German to know where she was and pleaded for liberty. Her
voice broken by sobs, she was led unheard out to us.

Mrs. Fox was then put through this weak, trifling examination and brought from the office, convicted. Miss Annie Neville took her turn and I was again left to the last. I had by this
time determined to act as I do when free, except that I would
refuse to tell who I was or where my home was.

THEY EXAMINE HER AGAIN

But the Doctor Paid More Attention to
the Nurse Than to His Patient

"Nellie Brown, the doctor wants you," said Miss Grupe. I
went in and was told to sit down opposite Dr. Kinier at the
desk. "What is your name?" he asked, without looking up.
"Nellie Brown," I replied easily. "Where is your home?" writing what I had said down in a large book. "In Cuba." "Oh!"
he ejaculated, with sudden understanding—then, addressing
the nurse: "Did you see anything in the papers about her?"
"Yes," she replied, "I saw a long account of this girl in the *Sun*
on Sunday." Then the doctor said: "Keep her here until I go to
the office and see the notice again." He left us and I was relieved of my hat and shawl. On his return he said he had been
unable to find the paper, but he related the story of my debut,
as he had read it, to the nurse. "What's the color of her eyes?"
Miss Grupe looked and answered "gray," although everybody
had always said my eyes were brown or hazel. "What's your

age," he asked, and as I answered, "Nineteen last May,"[1] he turned to the nurse and said, "When do you get your next pass?" This I ascertained was a leave of absence or "a day off." "Next Saturday," she said with a laugh. "You will go to town?" and they both laughed as she answered in the affirmative, and he said:

"Measure her." I was stood under a measure, and it was brought down tightly on my head. "What is it?" asked the doctor. "Now you know I can't tell," she said. "Yes, you can; go ahead. What height?" "I don't know; there are some figures there, but I can't tell." "Yes, you can. Now look and tell me." "I can't; do it yourself," and they laughed again as the doctor left his place at the desk and came forward to see for himself. "Five feet five inches; don't you see?" he said, taking her hand and touching the figures. By her voice I knew she did not understand yet, but that was no concern of mine, as the doctor seemed to find a pleasure in aiding her. Then I was put on the scales, and she worked around until she got them to balance. "How much?" asked the doctor, having resumed his position at the desk. "I don't know. You will have to see for yourself," she replied, calling him by his Christian name, which I have forgotten. He turned and also addressing her by her baptismal name, he said, "You are getting too fresh!" and they both laughed. I then told the weight—112 pounds—to the nurse, and she in turn told the doctor. "What time are you going to supper?" he asked, and she told him. He gave the nurse more attention than he did me, and asked her six questions to every one of me. Then he wrote my fate in the book before him. I said, "I am not sick and I do not want to stay here. No one has a right to shut me up in this manner." He took no notice of my remarks, and having completed his writings, as well as his talk with the nurse for a moment he said that would do, and with my companions, I went back to the sitting-room.

"You play the piano," they asked. "Oh, yes; ever since I was a child," I replied. Then they insisted that I should play, and they seated me on a wooden chair before an old-fashioned square. I struck a few notes, and the untuned response sent a grinding chill through me. "How horrible," I exclaimed, turning to a nurse, Miss McCarten, who stood at my side. "I never touched a piano as much out of tune." "It's a pity of you," she said spitefully, "we'll have to get one made to order for you." I began to play the variations of "Home, Sweet Home." The talking ceased and every patient sat silent, while my cold fingers moved slowly and stiffly over the keyboard. I finished in an aimless fashion and refused all requests to play more. Not seeing an available place to sit, I still occupied the chair in the front of the piano while I "sized up" my surroundings.

It was a long, bare room, with bare yellow benches encircling it. These benches, which were perfectly straight, and just as uncomfortable, would hold five people, although in almost every instance six were crowded on them. Barred windows, built about five feet from the floor, faced the two double doors which led into the hall. The bare white walls were somewhat relieved by three lithographs, one of Fritz Emmet[2] and the others of Negro minstrels. In the centre of the room was a large table covered with a white bedspread and around it sat the nurses. Everything was spotlessly clean and I thought what good workers the nurses must be to keep such order. In a few days after how I laughed at my own stupidity to think the nurses would work. When they found I would not play any more, Miss McCarten came up to me saying roughly, "Get away from here," and closed the piano with a bang.

"Brown, come here," was the next order I got from a rough, red-faced woman at the table. "What have you on?" "My clothing," I replied. She lifted my dress and skirts and wrote down one pair of shoes, one pair stockings, one cloth dress, one straw sailor hat and so on.

AT SUPPER

Rancid Butter, Weak Tea and Five Prunes
Her Uninviting Portion

This examination over we heard some one yell, "Go out into the hall." One of the patients kindly explained that this was an invitation to supper. We latecomers tried to keep together, so we entered the hall and stood at the door where all the women had crowded. How we shivered as we stood there! The windows were open and the draft went whizzing through the hall. The patients looked blue with cold, and the minutes stretched into a quarter of an hour. At last one of the nurses went forward and unlocked a door, through which we all crowded to a landing of the stairway. Here again came a long halt directly before an open window. "How very imprudent for the attendants to keep these thinly clad women standing here in the cold," said Miss Neville. I looked at the poor crazy captives shivering and added emphatically, "It's horribly brutal." While they stood there I thought I would not relish supper that night. They looked so lost and hopeless. Some were chattering foolish nonsense to invisible persons, others were laughing or crying aimlessly, and one old gray-haired woman was nudging me, and, with winks and sage noddings of the head and pitiful uplifting of the eyes and hands, was assuring me that I must not mind the poor creatures as they were all mad. "Stop at the heater," was then ordered, "and get in line, two by two." "Mary, get a companion." "How many times must I tell you to keep in line?" "Stand still," and, as the orders were issued, a shove and a push were administered and often a slap on the ears. After this third and final halt we were marched into a long, narrow dining-room, where a rush was made for the table.

The table reached the length of the room and was uncovered and uninviting. Long benches without backs were put for the patients to sit on, and over these they had to crawl in order to face the table. Placed close together all along the table were large dressing bowls filled with a pinkish-looking stuff which the patients called tea. By each bowl was laid a piece of bread, cut thick and buttered. A small saucer containing five prunes accompanied the bread. One fat woman made a rush, and jerking up several saucers from those around her emptied their contents into her own saucer. Then while holding to her own bowl she lifted up another and drained its contents at one gulp. This she did to a second bowl in shorter time than it takes to tell it. Indeed, I was so amused at her successful grabbings that when I looked at my own share the woman opposite, without so much as by your leave, grabbed my bread and left me without any.

Another patient seeing this kindly offered me hers, but I declined with thanks and turned to the nurse and asked for more. As she flung a thick piece down on the table she made some remark about the fact that if I forgot where my home was I had not forgotten how to eat. I tried the bread but the butter was so horrible that one could not eat it. A blue-eyed German girl on the opposite side of the table told me I could have bread unbuttered if I wished, and that very few were able to eat the butter. I turned my attention to the prunes and found that very few of them would be sufficient. A patient near asked me to give them to her. I did so. My bowl of tea was all that was left. I tasted and one taste was enough. It had no sugar and it tasted as if it had been made in copper. It was as weak as water. This was also transferred to a hungrier patient in spite of the protest of Miss Neville. "You must force the food down," she said, "else you will be sick, and who knows but with these surroundings you may go crazy. To have a good brain the stomach must be cared for." "It is impossible for me to eat that stuff," I replied, and despite all her urging I ate nothing that night.

It did not require much time for the patients to consume all that was eatable on the table, and then we got our orders to form in line in the hall. When this was done the doors before us were unlocked and we were ordered to proceed back to the sitting-room. Many of the patients crowded near us, and I was again urged to play, both by them and by the nurses. To please the patients I promised to play and Miss Tillie Mayard was to sing. The first thing she asked me to play was "Rock-a-bye Baby," and I did so. She sang it beautifully.

IN THE BATH

Scrubbed with Soft Soap and Put to Bed in a Wet Gown

A few more songs and we were told to go with Miss Grupe. We were taken into a cold, wet bathroom and I was ordered to undress. Did I protest? Well, I never grew so earnest in my life as when I tried to beg off. They said if I did not they would use force and that it would not be very gentle. At this I noticed one of the craziest women in the ward standing by the filled bathtub with a large discolored rag in her hands. She was chattering away to herself and chuckling in a manner which seemed to me fiendish. I knew now what was to be done with me. I shivered. They began to undress me and one by one they pulled off my clothes. At last everything was gone excepting one garment. "I will not remove it," I said vehemently, but they took it off. I gave one glance at the group of patients gathered at the door watching the scene, and I jumped into the bathtub with more energy than grace.

The water was ice-cold, and I again began to protest. How useless it all was. I begged, at least, that the patients be made to go away, but was ordered to shut up. The crazy woman began to scrub me. I can find no other word that will express it but scrubbing. From a small tin pan she took some soft soap and rubbed it all over me, even all over my face and my pretty hair. I was at last past seeing or speaking, although I had begged that my hair be left untouched. Rub, rub, rub, went the old woman, chattering to herself. My teeth chattered and my limbs were goosefleshed and blue with cold. Suddenly I got, one after the other, three buckets of water over my head— ice-cold water, too—into my eyes, my ears, my nose and my mouth. I think I experienced some of the sensations of a drowning person as they dragged me, gasping, shivering and quaking, from the tub. For once I did look insane, as they put me, dripping wet, into a short canton flannel slip, labelled across the extreme end in large black letters, "Lunatic Asylum, B. I. H. 6." The letters meant Blackwell's Island, Hall 6.

By this time Miss Mayard had been undressed and, much as I hated my recent bath, I would have taken another if by it I could have saved her the experience. Imagine plunging that sick girl into a cold bath when it made me, who have never been ill, shake as if with ague. I heard her explain to Miss Grupe that her head was still sore from her illness. Her hair was short and had mostly come out and she asked that the crazy woman be made to rub more gently, but Miss Grupe said: "There isn't much fear of hurting you. Shut up or you'll get it worse." Miss Mayard did shut up and that was my last look at her for the night.

I was hurried into a room where there were six beds, and had been put into bed when some one came along and jerked me out again, saying: "Nellie Brown has to be put in a room alone tonight, for I suppose she's noisy." I was taken to room 28 and left to try and make an impression on the bed. It was an impossible task. The bed had been made high in the centre and sloping on either side. At the first touch my head flooded the pillow with water and my wet slip transferred some of its dampness to the sheet. When Miss Grupe came in I asked if I could not have a night-gown. "We have no such things in this institution," she said. "I do not like to sleep without," I replied. "Well, I don't care about that," she said. "You are in a public institution now, and you can't expect to get anything. This is charity, and you should be thankful for what you get." "But the city pays to keep these places up," I urged, "and pays people to be kind to the unfortunates brought here." "Well, you don't need to expect any kindness here, for you won't get it," she said, and she went out and closed the door.

A sheet and an oilcloth were under me and a sheet and black wool blanket above. I never felt anything so annoying as that wool blanket as I tried to keep it around my shoulders to stop the chills from getting underneath. When I pulled it up I left my feet bare and when I pulled it down my shoulders were exposed. There was absolutely nothing in the room but the bed and myself. As the door had been locked I imagined I should be left alone for the night, but I heard the sound of the heavy tread of two women down the hall. They stopped at every door, unlocked it and in a few moments I could hear them relock it. This they did without the least attempt at quietness down the whole length of the opposite side of the hall and up to my room. Here they paused. The key was inserted in the lock and turned. I watched those about to enter. In they came, dressed in brown and white striped dresses, fastened by brass buttons, large white aprons, a heavy green cord about the waist, from which dangled a bunch of large keys, and small white caps on their heads. Being dressed as were the attendants of the day, I knew they were nurses. The first one carried a lantern, and she flashed its light into my face while she said to her assistant: "This is Nellie Brown." Looking at her I asked: "Who are you?" "The night nurse, my dear," she replied, and wishing that I would sleep well she went out and locked the door after her. Several times during the night they came into my room, and even had I been able to sleep, the unlocking of the heavy door, their loud talking and heavy tread would have awakened me.

THE HORROR OF FIRE

Escape Practically Impossible in Case the Building Should Burn

I could not sleep, so I lay in bed picturing to myself the horrors in case a fire should break out in the asylum. Every door is locked separately and the windows are heavily barred so that escape is impossible. In the one building alone there are, I think Dr. Ingram[3] told me, some 300 women. They are locked, one to ten to a room. It is impossible to get out unless these doors are unlocked. A fire is not improbable, but one of the most likely occurrences. Should the building burn the jailors or nurses would never think of releasing their crazy patients. This I can prove to you later when I come to tell of their cruel treatment of the poor things intrusted to their care. As I say, in case of fire, not a dozen women could escape. All would be left to roast to death. Even if the nurses were kind, which they are not, it would require more presence of mind than women of their class possess to risk the flames and their own lives while they unlocked the hundred doors for the insane prisoners. Unless there is a change there will some day be a tale of horror never equaled.

In this connection is an amusing incident which happened just previous to my release. I was talking with Dr. Ingram about many things, and at last told him what I thought would be the result of a fire. "The nurses are expected to open the doors," he said. "But you know positively that they would not wait to do that," I said, "and these women would burn to death." He sat silent, unable to contradict my assertion. "Why don't you have it changed?" I asked. "What can I do?" he replied. "I offer suggestions until my brain is tired, but what good does it do. What would you do?" he asked, turning to me, the proclaimed insane girl. "Well, I should insist on them having locks put in, as I have seen in some places, that by turning a crank at the end of the hall you can lock or unlock every door on the one side. Then there would be some chance of escape. Now, every door being locked separately, there is absolutely none." Dr. Ingram turned to me with an anxious look on his kind face as he asked slowly: "Nellie Brown, what institution have you been an inmate of before you came here?" "None. I never was confined in any institution, except boarding-school, in my life." "Where then did you see the locks you have described?" I had seen them in the new Western Penitentiary at Pittsburgh, PA, but I did not dare say so. I merely answered: "Oh, I have seen them in a place I was in—I mean as a visitor." "There is only one place I know of where they have those locks," he said sadly, "and that is at Sing Sing. The inference is conclusive." I laughed very heartily over the implied accusation, and tried to assure him that I had never, up to date, been an inmate of Sing Sing or even ever visited it.

Just as morning began to dawn I went to sleep. It did not seem many moments until I was rudely awakened and told to get up, the window being opened and the clothing pulled off me. My hair was still wet and I had pains all through me, as if I had the rheumatism. Some clothing was flung on the floor and I was told to put it on. I asked for my own, but was told to take what I got and keep quiet by the apparently head nurse, Miss Grady. I looked at it. One underskirt made of coarse dark cotton goods and a cheap white calico dress with a black spot in it. I tied the strings of the skirt around me and put on the little dress. It was made, as are all those worn by the patients, into a straight tight waist sewed on to a straight skirt. As I buttoned the waist I noticed the underskirt was about six inches longer than the upper, and for a moment I sat down on the bed and laughed at my own appearance. No woman ever longed for a mirror more than I did at that moment.

I saw the other patients hurrying past in the hall, so I decided not to lose anything that might be going on. We numbered forty-five patients in Hall 6, and were sent to the bathroom, where there were two coarse towels. I watched crazy patients who had the most dangerous eruptions all over their faces dry on the towels and then saw women with clean skins turn to use them. I went to the bathtub and washed my face at the running faucet and my underskirt did the duty for a towel.

THE FIRST MORNING

Combed with a Public Comb, the Breakfast and the Uniform

Before I had completed my ablutions a bench was brought into the bathroom. Miss Grupe and Miss McCarten came in with combs in their hands. We were told to sit down on the bench, and the hair of forty-five women was combed with one patient, two nurses and six combs. As I saw some of the sore heads combed I thought this was another dose I had not bargained for. Miss Tillie Mayard had her own comb, but it was taken from her by Miss Grady. Oh, that combing! I never realized before what the expression "I'll give you a combing" meant, but I knew then. My hair, all matted and wet from the night previous, was pulled and jerked, and, after expostulating to no avail, I set my teeth and endured the pain. They refused to give me my hairpins, and my hair was arranged in one plait and tied with a red cotton rag. My curly bangs refused to stay back.

After this we went to the sitting-room and I looked for my companions. At first I looked vainly, unable to distinguish them from the other patients, but after a while I recognized Miss Mayard by her short hair. "How did you sleep after your cold bath?" "I almost froze, and then the noise kept me awake. It's dreadful! My nerves were so unstrung before I came here, and I fear I shall not be able to stand the strain." I did the best I could to cheer her. I asked that we be given additional clothing, at least as much as custom says women shall wear, but they told me to shut up; that we had as much as they intended to give us.

We were compelled to get up at 6 o'clock, and at 7.15 we were told to collect in the hall, where the experience of waiting, as on the evening previous, was repeated. When we got into the dining-room at last we found a bowl of cold tea, a slice of buttered bread and a saucer of oatmeal, with molasses on it, for each patient. I was hungry, but the food would not down. I asked for unbuttered bread and was given it. I cannot tell you of anything which is the same dirty black color. It was hard, and in places nothing more than dried dough. I found a spider in my slice, so I did not eat it. I tried the oatmeal and molasses, but it was wretched, and so I endeavored, but without much show of success, to choke down the tea.

After we were back to the sitting-room a number of women were ordered to make the beds, and some of the patients were put to scrubbing and others given different duties which covered all the work in the hall. It is not the attendants who keep the institution so nice for the poor patients, as I had always thought, but the patients, who do it all themselves—even to cleaning the nurses' bedrooms and caring for their clothing.

About 9.30 the new patients, of which I was one, were told to go out to see the doctor. I was taken in and my lungs and my heart were examined by the flirty young doctor who was the first to see us the day we entered. The one who made out the report, if I mistake not, was the Assistant Superintendent, Ingram. A few questions and I was allowed to return to the sitting-room.

I came in and saw Miss Grady with my notebook and long lead pencil, bought just for the occasion. "I want my book and pencil," I said quite truthfully. "It helps me remember things." I was very anxious to get it to make notes in and was disappointed when she said: "You can't have it, so shut up." Some days after I asked Dr. Ingram if I could have it, and he promised to consider the matter. When I again referred to it, he said that Miss Grady said I only brought a book there; that I had no pencil. I was provoked and insisted that I had, whereupon I was advised to fight against the imaginations of my brain.

After the housework was completed by the patients, and as the day was fine, but cold, we were told to go out in the hall and get on shawls and hats for a walk. Poor patients! How eager they were for a breath of air; how eager for a slight release from their prison. They went swiftly into the hall and there was a skirmish for hats. Such hats!

THE VIOLENT PATIENTS

Unspeakable Scenes in the Yard—The Evil of Enforced Idleness

We had not gone many paces when I saw, proceeding from every walk, long lines of women guarded by nurses. How many there were! Every way I looked I could see them in the queer dresses, comical straw hats and shawls, marching slowly around. I eagerly watched the passing lines and a thrill of horror crept over me at the sight. Vacant eyes and meaningless faces, and their tongues uttered meaningless nonsense. One crowd passed and I noted, by nose as well as eyes, that they were fearfully dirty. "Who are they?" I asked of a patient near me. "They are considered the most violent on the island," she replied. "They are from the Lodge, the first building with the high steps." Some were yelling, some were cursing, others were singing or praying or preaching, as the fancy struck them, and they made up the most miserable collection of humanity I had ever seen. As the din of their passing faded in the distance there came another sight I can never forget:

A long cable rope fastened to wide leather belts, and these belts locked around the waists of fifty-two women. At the end of the rope was a heavy iron cart, and in it two women—one nursing a sore foot, another screaming at some nurse, saying: "You beat me and I shall not forget it. You want to kill me," and then she would sob and cry. The women "on the rope," as the patients call it, were each busy on their individual freaks. Some were yelling all the while. One who had blue eyes saw me look at her, and she turned as far as she could, talking and smiling, with that terrible, horrifying look of absolute insanity stamped on her. The doctors might safely judge on her case. The horror of that sight to one who had never been near an insane person before was something unspeakable. "God help them," breathed Miss Neville. "It is so dreadful I cannot look." On they passed, but for their places to be filled by more. Can you imagine the sight? According to one of the physicians there are 1,600 insane women on Blackwell's Island.

I was annoyed a great deal by nurses who had heard my romantic story calling to those in charge of us to ask which one I was. I was pointed out repeatedly.

It was not long until the dinner hour arrived, and I was so hungry that I felt I could eat anything. The same old story of standing for a half and three quarters of an hour in the hall was repeated before we got down to our dinners. The bowls in which we had had our tea were now filled with soup, and on a plate was one cold boiled potato and a chunk of beef, which, on investigation, proved to be slightly spoiled. There were no knives or forks, and the patients looked fairly savage as they took the tough beef in their fingers and pulled in opposition to their teeth. Those toothless or with poor teeth could not eat it. One tablespoon was given for the soup, and a piece of bread was the final entrée. Butter is never allowed at dinner nor coffee or tea. Miss Mayard could not eat, and I saw many of the sick ones turn away in disgust. I was getting very weak from the want of food and tried to eat a slice of bread. After the first few bites hunger asserted itself and I was able to eat all but the crusts of the one slice.

Supt. Dent[4] went through the sitting-room, giving an occasional "How do you do?" "How are you to-day?" here and there among the patients. His voice was as cold as the hall, and the patients made no movement to tell him of their sufferings. I asked some of them to tell how they were suffering from the cold and insufficiency of clothing but they replied that the nurse would beat them if they told.

I was never so tired as I grew sitting on those benches. Several of the patients would sit on one foot or sideways to make a change, but they were always reproved and told to sit up straight. If they talked they were scolded and told to shut up; if they wanted to walk around in order to take the stiffness out of them, they were told to sit down and be still. What, excepting torture, would produce insanity quicker than this treatment? Here is a class of women sent to be cured? I would like the expert physicians who are condemning me for my action, which has proven their ability, to take a perfectly sane and healthy woman, shut her up and make her sit from 6 A.M. until 8 P.M. on straight-back benches, do not allow her to talk or move during these hours, give her no reading and let her know nothing of the world or its doings, give her bad food and harsh treatment, and see how long it will take to make her insane. Two months would make her a mental and physical wreck.

BAD FOOD AND WORSE HELP

When One Falls Ill the Natural Thing Is to Simply Die

I have described my first day in the asylum, and as my other nine were exactly the same in the general run of things it would be tiresome to tell about each. In giving this story I expect to be contradicted by many who are exposed. I merely tell in common words, without exaggeration, of my life in a madhouse for ten days. The eating was one of the most horrible things. Excepting the first two days after I entered the asylum there was no salt for the food. The hungry and even famishing women made an attempt to eat the horrible messes. Mustard and vinegar were put on meat and in soup to give it a taste, but it only helped to make it worse. Even that was all consumed after two days, and the patients had to try to choke down fresh fish, just boiled in water, without salt, pepper or butter; mutton, beef and potatoes without the faintest seasoning. The most insane refused to swallow the food and were threatened with punishment. In our short walks we passed the kitchen where food was prepared for the nurses and doctors. There we got glimpses of melons and grapes and all kinds of fruits, beautiful white bread and nice meats, and the hungry feeling would be increased tenfold. I spoke to some of the physicians, but it had no effect, and when I was taken away the food was yet unsalted.

My heart ached to see the sick patients grow sicker over the table. I saw Miss Tillie Mayard so suddenly overcome at a bite that she had to rush from the dining-room and then got a scolding for doing so. When the patients complained of the food they were told to shut up; that they would not have as good if they were at home, and that it was too good for charity patients.

A German girl, Louise—I have forgotten her last name—did not eat for several days and at last one morning she was missing. From the conversation of the nurses I found she was suffering from a high fever. Poor thing! she told me unceasingly prayed for death. I watched the nurses make a patient carry such food as the well ones were refusing up to Louise's room. Think of that stuff for a fever patient! Of course, she refused it. Then I saw a nurse, Miss McCarten, go to test her temperature, and she returned with the report of it being some 150 degrees. I smiled at the report, and Miss Grupe, seeing it, asked me how high my temperature had ever run. I refused to answer. Miss Grady then decided to try her ability. She returned with the report of 99 degrees.

Miss Tillie Mayard suffered more than any of us from the cold, and yet she tried to follow my advice to be cheerful and try to keep up for a short time. Supt. Dent brought a man in to see me. He felt my pulse and my head and examined my tongue. I told them how cold it was and assured them that I did not need medical aid, but that Miss Mayard did and they should transfer their attentions to her. They did not answer me, and I was pleased to see Miss Mayard leave her place and come forward to them. She spoke to the doctors and told them she was ill, but they paid no attention to her. The nurses came up and dragged her back to the bench, and after the doctors left they said: "After awhile, when you see that the doctors will not notice you, you will quit running up to them." Before the doctors left me I heard one say—I cannot give it in his exact words—that my pulse and eyes were not that of an insane girl, but Supt. Dent assured him in cases such as mine such tests failed. After watching me for a while he said my face was the brightest he had ever seen for a lunatic. The nurses had on heavy undergarments and coats, but the doctors refused to give us shawls.

Nearly all night long I listened to a woman cry about the

cold and beg for God to let her die. Another one yelled: "Murder" at frequent intervals and "Police!" at others until my flesh felt creepy.

The second morning, after we had begun our endless "set" for the day, two of the nurses, assisted by some patients, brought the woman in who had begged the night long for God to take her home. I was not surprised at her prayer. She appeared easily seventy years old and she was blind. Although the halls were freezing cold that old woman had no more clothing on than the rest of us, which I have described. When she was brought into the sitting-room and placed on the hard bench she cried: "Oh, what are you doing with me? I am cold, so cold. Why can't I stay in bed or have a shawl?" and then she would get up and endeavor to feel her way to leave the room. Sometimes the attendants would jerk her back to the bench and again they would let her walk and heartlessly laugh when she bumped against the table or the edge of the benches. At one time she said the heavy shoes which charity provides hurt her feet and she took them off. The nurses made two patients put them on her again, and when she did it several times and fought against having them on, I counted seven people at her at once to put the shoes on. The old woman then tried to lie down on the bench, but they pulled her up again. It sounded so pitiful to hear her cry, "Oh, give me a pillow and pull the covers over me, I am so cold."

At this I saw Miss Grupe sit down on her and run her cold hands over the old woman's face and down inside the neck of her dress. At the old woman's cries she laughed savagely, as did the other nurses, and repeated her cruel action. That day the old woman was carried away to another ward.

MADE MAD BY SURROUNDINGS

The Tragic Case of Miss Tillie Mayard— Very Near to Detection

Miss Tillie Mayard suffered greatly from cold. One morning she sat on the bench next to me and was livid with the cold.

Her limbs shook and her teeth chattered. I spoke to the three attendants who sat with coats on at the table in the centre of the floor. "It is cruel to lock people up and then freeze them," I said. They replied she had on as much as any of the rest, and she would get no more. Just then Miss Mayard took a fit and every patient looked frightened. Miss Neville caught her in her arms and held her, although the nurses roughly said: "Let her fall on the floor and it will teach her a lesson." Miss Neville told them what she thought of their actions, and then I got orders to make my appearance in the office.

Just as I reached there Supt. Dent came to the door and I told them how we were suffering from the cold, and of Miss Mayard's condition. Doubtless I spoke incoherently, for I told of the state of the food, the treatment of the nurses and their refusal to give more clothing, the condition of Miss Mayard, and the nurses telling us, because the asylum was a public institution, we could not expect even kindness. Assuring him that I needed no medical aid I told him to go to Miss Mayard. He did so. From Miss Neville and other patients I learned what transpired. Miss Mayard was still in the fit, and he caught her roughly between the eyebrows or thereabouts, and pinched until her face was crimson from the rush of blood to the head, and her senses returned. All day afterwards she suffered from terrible headache, and from that on she grew worse.

Insane? Yes, insane; and as I watched the insanity slowly creep over the mind that had appeared to be all right I secretly cursed the doctors, the nurses and all public institutions. Some one may say that she was insane at some time previous to her consignment to the asylum. Then if she were, was this the proper place to send a woman just convalescing, to be given cold baths, deprived of sufficient clothing and fed with horrible food?

On this morning I had a long conversation with Dr. Ingram, the assistant superintendent of the asylum. I found that he was kind to the helpless beings in his charge. I began my old complaint of the cold and he called Miss Grady to the office and ordered more clothing given the patients. Miss Grady said if I made a practice of telling it would be a serious thing for me, she warned me in time.

Many visitors looking for missing girls came to see me. Miss Grady yelled in the door from the hall one day, "Nellie Brown, you're wanted." I went to the sitting-room at the end of the hall, and there sat a gentleman who had known me intimately for years. I saw by the sudden blanching of his face and his inability to speak that the sight of me was wholly unexpected and had shocked him terribly. In an instant I determined, if he betrayed me as Nellie Bly, to say I had never seen him before. However, I had one card to play and I risked it. With Miss Grady within touching distance I whispered hurriedly, in language more expressive than elegant, "Don't give me away." I knew by the expression of his eye that he understood, so I said to Miss Grady, "I do not know this man."

"Do you know her?" asked Miss Grady.

"No; this is not the young lady I came in search of," he replied in a strained voice.

"If you do not know her you cannot stay here," she said, and she took him to the door. All at once a fear struck me that he would think I had been sent there through some mistake and would tell my friends and make an effort to have me released. So I waited until Miss Grady had the door unlocked. I knew that she would have to lock it before she could leave, and the time required to do so would give me opportunity to speak, so I called, "One moment, *Señor*." He returned to me and I asked aloud, "Do you speak Spanish, *Señor*?" and then whispered, "It's all right. I'm after an item. Keep still." "No," he said, with a peculiar emphasis, which I knew meant that he would keep my secret.

CHOKINGS AND BEATINGS

The Nurses Amuse Themselves by Worrying Their Helpless Charges

People in the world can never imagine the length of days to those in asylums. They seemed never ending, and we welcomed any event that might give us something to think about as well as talk of. Anxiously the hour was watched for when the boat arrived to see if there were any new unfortunates to be added to our ranks. When they came and were ushered into the sitting-room the patients would express sympathy to one another for them and were anxious to show them little marks of attention. Hall 6 was the receiving hall, so that was how we saw all newcomers.

Soon after my advent a girl called Urena Little-Page was brought in. She was, as she had been born, silly, and her tender spot was, as with many sensible women, her age. She claimed eighteen, and would grow very angry if told to the contrary. The nurses were not long in finding this out, and then they teased her. "Urena," said Miss Grady, "the doctors say that you are thirty-three instead of eighteen," and the other nurses laughed. They kept this up until the simple creature began to yell and cry, saying she wanted to go home and that everybody treated her badly. After they had gotten all the amusement out of her they wanted and she was crying, they began to scold and tell her to keep quiet. She grew more hysterical every moment until they pounced upon her and slapped her face and knocked her head in a lively fashion. This made the poor creature cry the more, and so they choked her. Yes, actually choked her. Then they dragged her out to the closet, and I heard her terrified cries hush into smothered ones. After several hours' absence she returned to the sitting-room, and I plainly saw the marks of their fingers on her throat for the entire day.

This punishment seemed to awaken their desire to administer more. They returned to the sitting-room and caught hold of an old gray-haired woman whom I have heard addressed both as Mrs. Grady and Mrs. O'Keefe. She was insane, and she talked almost continually to herself and to those near her. She never spoke very loud, and at the time I speak of was sitting harmlessly chattering to herself. They grabbed her, and my heart ached as she cried, "For God's sake, ladies, don't let them beat me." "Shut up, you hussy!" said Miss Grady as she caught the woman by her gray hair and dragged her shrieking and pleading from the room. She was also taken to the closet, and her cries grew lower and lower, and then ceased.

The nurses returned to the room and Miss Grady remarked that she had "settled the old fool for awhile." I told some of the physicians of the occurrence, but they did not pay any attention to it.

One of the characters in Hall 6 was Matilda, a little old German who, I believe, went insane over the loss of money. She was small, and had a pretty pink complexion. She was not much trouble, except at times. She would take spells, when she would talk into the steam-heaters or get up on a chair and talk out of the windows. In these conversations she railed at the lawyers who had taken her property. The nurses seemed to find a great deal of amusement in teasing the harmless old soul. One day I sat beside Miss Grady and Miss Grupe and heard them tell her perfectly vile things to call Miss McCarten. After telling her to say these things they would send her to the other nurse, but Matilda proved that she, even in her state, had more sense than they. "I cannot tell you. It is private," was all she would say. I saw Miss Grady, on a pretense of whispering to her, spit in her ear. Matilda quietly wiped her ear and said nothing.

SOME UNFORTUNATES' STORIES

A Few of the Apparently Sane Women Tell of Their Troubles

By this time I had made the acquaintance of the greater number of the forty-five women in Hall 6. Let me introduce a few. Louise, the pretty German girl whom I have spoke of formerly as being sick of fever, had the delusion that the spirits of her dead parents were with her. "I have gotten many beatings from Miss Grady and her assistants," she said, "and I am unable to eat the horrible food they give us. I ought not to be compelled to freeze for want of proper clothing. Oh! I pray nightly that I may be taken to my papa and mamma. One night when Dr. Field came I was in bed and weary of the examination. At last I said, 'I am tired of this. I will talk no more.' 'Won't you?' he said angrily. 'I'll see if I can't make you.' With this he laid his crutch on the side of the bed and, getting up on it, he pinched me very severely in the ribs. I jumped up straight in bed and said, 'What do you mean by this?' 'I want to teach you to obey when I speak to you,' he replied. 'If I could only die and go to papa!'" When I left she was confined to bed with a fever, and maybe by this time she has her wish.

There is a Frenchwoman confined in hall 6, or was during my stay, whom I firmly believe to be perfectly sane. I watched her and talked with her every day, excepting the last three, and I was unable to find any delusion or mania in her. Her name is Josephine Despreau, if that is spelled correctly, and her husband and all her friends are in France. Josephine feels her position keenly. Her lips tremble and she breaks down crying when she talks of her hopeless situation. "How did you get here?" I asked.

"One morning as I was trying to get breakfast I grew deathly sick, and two officers were called in by the woman of the house and I was taken to the station-house. I was unable to understand their proceedings and they paid little attention to my story. Doings in this country were new to me, and before I realized it I was lodged as an insane woman in this asylum. When I first came I cried that I was here without hope of release, and for crying Miss Grady and her assistants choked me until they hurt my throat, for it has been sore ever since."

A pretty young woman spoke so little English I could not get her story except as told by the nurses. They said her name is Sarah Fishbaum, and that her husband put her in the asylum because she had a fondness for other men than himself. Granting that Sarah was insane, and about men, let me tell you how the nurses tried to cure (?)[5] her. They would call her up and say, "Sarah, wouldn't you like to have a nice young man?" "Oh, yes; a young man is all right," Sarah would reply in her few English words. "Well, Sarah, wouldn't you like us to speak a good word to some of the doctors for you? Wouldn't you like to have one of the doctors?" And then they would ask her which doctor she preferred and advise her to make advances to him when he visited the hall, and so on.

I had been watching and talking with a fair-complexioned woman for several days, and I was at loss to see why she had been sent there, she was so sane. "Why did you come here?" I asked her one day, after we had indulged in a long conversation.

"I was sick," she replied. "Are you sick mentally?" I urged. "Oh, no; what gave you such an idea? I had been overworking myself, and I broke down. Having some family trouble and being penniless and nowhere to go, I applied to the Commissioners to be sent to the Poorhouse until I would be able to go to work." "But they do not send poor people here unless they are insane," I said. "Don't you know there are only insane women, or those supposed to be so, sent here?" "I knew after I got here that the majority of these women were insane, but then I believed them when they told me this was the place they sent all the poor who applied for aid as I had done."

"How have you been treated?" I asked. "Well, so far I have escaped a beating, although I have been sickened at the sight of many and the recital of more. When I was brought here they went to give me a bath, and the very disease for which I needed doctoring and from which I was suffering made it necessary that I should not bathe. But they put me in, and my sufferings were increased greatly for weeks thereafter."

A Mrs. McCartney, whose husband is a tailor, seems perfectly rational and has not one fancy. Mary Hughes and Mrs. Louise Schanz showed no obvious traces of insanity.

NURSES WHO SWEAR

Patients Hurried into the Asylum Without Sufficient Examination

One day two newcomers were added to our list. The one was an idiot, Carrie Glass, and the other was a nice-looking German girl—quite young, she seemed, and when she came in all the patients spoke of her nice appearance and apparent sanity. Her name was Gretchen. She told me she had been a cook, and was extremely neat. One day after she had scrubbed the kitchen floor the chambermaids came down and deliberately soiled it. Her temper was aroused and she began to quarrel with them, an officer was called and she was taken to an asylum. "How can they say I am insane, merely because I allowed my temper to run away with me," she complained. "Other people are not shut up for crazy when they get angry. I suppose the only thing to do is to keep quiet and so avoid the beatings which I see others get. No one can say one word about me. I do everything I am told, and all the work they give me. I am obedient in every respect, and I do everything to prove to them that I am sane."

One day an insane woman was brought in. She was noisy, and Miss Grady gave her a beating and blacked her eye. When the doctors noticed it and asked if it was done before she came there the nurses said it was.

While I was in hall 6 I never heard the nurses address the patients except to scold or yell at them, unless it was to tease them. They spent much of their time gossiping about the physicians and about the other nurses in a manner that was not elevating. Miss Grady nearly always interspersed her conversation with profane language, and generally began her sentences by calling on the name of the Lord. The names she called the patients were of the lowest and most profane type. One evening she quarreled with another nurse while we were at supper about the bread, and when the nurse had gone out she called her bad names and made ugly remarks about her.

In the evenings a woman, whom I supposed to be head cook for the doctors, used to come up and bring raisins, grapes, apples and crackers to the nurses. Imagine the feelings of the hungry patients as they sat and watched the nurses eat what was to them a dream of luxury.

One afternoon Dr. Dent was talking to a patient, Mrs. Turney, about some trouble she had had with a nurse or matron. A short time after we were taken down to supper and this woman who had beaten Mrs. Turney, and of whom Dr. Dent spoke, was sitting at the door of our dining-room. Suddenly Mrs. Turney picked up her bowl of tea and, rushing out of the door, flung it at the woman who had beat her. There was some loud screaming and Mrs. Turney was returned to her place. The next day she was transferred to the "rope gang," which is supposed to be composed of the most dangerous and most suicidal women on the island.

At first I could not sleep and did not want to so long as I could hear anything new. The night nurses may have complained of the fact. At any rate one night they came in and tried to make me take a dose of some mixture out of a glass "to make me sleep," they said. I told them I would do nothing of the sort and they left me, I hoped, for the night. My hopes were vain, for in a few minutes they returned with a doctor, the same that received us on our arrival. He insisted that I take it, but I was determined not to lose my wits even for a few hours. When he saw I was not to be coaxed he grew rather rough and said he had wasted too much time with me already. That if I did not take it he would put it into my arm with a needle. It occurred to me that if he put it in my arm I could not get rid of it, but if I swallowed it there was one hope, so I said I would take it. I smelt it and it smelt like laudanum and it was a horrible dose. No sooner had they left the room and locked me in than I tried to see how far down my throat my finger would go.

LAST DAYS

One Good Nurse—Sitting Still for Five Days— Soap Only Once a Week

I want to say that the night nurse, Burns, in hall 6, seemed very kind and patient to the poor, afflicted people. The other nurses made several attempts to talk to me about lovers and asked me if I would not like to have one. They did not find me very communicative on the, to them, popular subject.

Once a week the patients are given a bath, and that is the only time they see soap. A patient handed me a piece of soap one day about the size of a thimble. I considered it a great compliment in her wanting to be kind, but I thought she would appreciate the cheap soap more than I, so I thanked her but refused to take it. On bathing day the tub is filled with water and the patients are washed, one after the other, without a change of water. This is done until the water is really thick, and then it is allowed to run out and the tub is refilled without being washed. The same towels are used on all the women, those with eruptions as well as those without. The healthy patients fight for a change of water, but they are compelled to submit to the dictates of the lazy, tyrannical nurses. The dresses are seldom changed oftener than once a month. If the patient has a visitor I have seen the nurses hurry her out and change her dress before the visitor comes in. This keeps up the appearance of careful and good management.

The patients who are not able to take care of themselves get into beastly conditions and the nurses never look after them, but order some of the patients to do so.

For five days we were compelled to sit in the room all day. I never put in such a long time. Every patient was stiff and sore and tired. We would get in little groups on benches and torture our stomachs by conjuring up thoughts of what we would eat first when we got out. If I had not known how hungry they were and the pitiful side of it, the conversation would have been very amusing. As it was it only made me sad. When the subject of eating, which seemed to be the favorite one, was worn out they used to give their opinions of the institution and its management. The condemnation of the nurses and the eatables was unanimous.

As the days passed Miss Tillie Mayard's condition grew worse. She was continually cold and unable to eat of the food provided. Day after day she sang in order to try to maintain her memory, but at last the nurse made her stop it. I talked with her daily and I grieved to find her grow worse so rapidly. At last she got a delusion. She thought that I was trying to pass myself off for her and that all the people who called to see Nellie Brown were friends in search of her, but that I, by some means, was trying to deceive them into the belief that I was the girl. I tried to reason with her, but found it impossible, so I kept away from her as much as possible, lest my presence should make her worse and feed the fancy.

TRANSFERRED TO ANOTHER WARD

She Is Cursed Before She Leaves and Gets No Better Quarters

When Pauline Moser was brought to the asylum we heard the most horrible screams and an Irish girl, only partly dressed, came staggering like a drunken person up the hall yelling "Hurrah! Three Cheers! I have killed the divil! Lucifer, Lucifer, Lucifer," and so on, over and over again. Then she would pull a handful of hair out, while she exultingly cried, "How I deceived the divils. They always said God made hell, but he didn't." After she had been there an hour or so, Dr. Dent came in, and as he walked down the hall, Miss Grupe whispered to the demented girl, "Here is the devil coming, go for him." Surprised that she would give a mad woman such instructions, I fully expected to see the frenzied creature rush at the doctor. Luckily she did not, but commenced to repeat her refrain of "Oh, Lucifer." After the doctor left, Miss Grupe again tried to excite the woman by saying the pictured minstrel on the wall was the devil, and the poor creature began to scream "You divil. I'll give it to you," so that two nurses had to sit on her to keep her down. The attendants seemed to find amusement and pleasure in exciting the violent patients to do their worst.

I always made a point of telling the doctors I was sane and asking to be released, but the more I endeavored to assure them of my sanity the more they doubted it. "What are you doctors here for?" I asked one whose name I cannot recall. "To take care of the patients and test their sanity," he replied. "Very well," I said. "There are sixteen doctors on this island, and, excepting two, I have never seen them pay any attention to the patients. How can a doctor judge a woman's sanity by merely bidding her good morning and refusing to hear her pleas for release? Even the sick ones know it is useless to say anything, for the answer will be that it is their imagination." "Try every test on me," I have urged others, "and tell me am I sane or insane? Try my pulse, my heart, my eyes; ask me to stretch out my arm, to work my fingers, as Dr. Field did at Bellevue, and then tell me if I am sane." They would not heed me, for they thought I raved.

Again I said to one: "You have no right to keep sane people here. I am sane, have always been so and I must insist on a thorough examination or be released. Several of the women here are also sane. Why can't they be free?" "They are all insane," was the reply, "and suffering from delusions."

After a long talk with Dr. Ingram, he said: "I will transfer you to a quieter ward." An hour later Miss Grady called me into the hall, and, after calling me all the vile and profane names a woman could ever remember, she told me that it was a lucky thing for my "hide" that I was transferred, or else she would pay me for remembering so well to tell Dr. Ingram everything. "You d—n hussy, you forget all about yourself, but you never forget anything to tell the doctor." After calling Miss Neville, whom Dr. Ingram also kindly transferred, Miss Grady took us to the hall above, No. 7.

In hall 7 there are Mrs. Kroener, Miss Fitzpatrick, Miss Finney and Miss Hart. I did not see as cruel treatment as downstairs, but I heard them make ugly remarks and threats, twist the fingers and slap the faces of the unruly patients. The night nurse, Conway I believe her name is, is very cross. In hall 7, if any of the patients possessed any modesty, they soon lost it. Every one was compelled to undress in the hall before their own door, and to fold their clothes and leave them there until morning. I asked to undress in my room, but Miss Conway told me if she ever caught me at such a trick she would give me cause not to want to repeat it.

The first doctor I saw here—Dr. Caldwell—chucked me under the chin, and as I was tired of refusing to tell where my home was, I would only speak to him in Spanish.

THE "RETREAT" AND "ROPE GANG"

Some of the Cruel Atrocities Practiced There—The Last Good-Bye

A Mrs. Cotter told me that for speaking to a man she was sent to the Retreat.[6] "The remembrance of that is enough to make me mad. For crying the nurses beat me with a broom-handle and jumped on me, injuring me internally so that I will never get over it. Then they tied my hands and feet and, throwing a sheet over my head, twisted it tightly around my throat, so I could not scream, and thus put me in a bathtub filled with cold water. They held me under until I gave up every hope and became senseless. At other times they took hold of my ears and beat my head on the floor and against the wall. Then they pulled my hair out by the roots so that it will never grow in again."

Mrs. Cotter here showed me proofs of her story, the dent in the back of her head and the bare spots where the hair had been taken out by the handful. I give her story as plainly as possible: "My treatment was not as bad as I have seen others get in there, but it has ruined my health, and even if I do get out of here I will be a wreck. When my husband heard of the treatment given me he threatened to expose the place if I was not removed, so I was brought here. I am well mentally now. All that old fear has left me, and the doctor has promised to allow my husband to take me home."

I made the acquaintance of Bridget McGuinness, who seems to be sane at the present time. She said she was sent to Retreat 4, and put on the "Rope gang." "The beatings I got there were something dreadful. I was pulled around by the hair, held under the water until I strangled, and I was choked and kicked. The nurses would always keep a quiet patient stationed at the window to tell them when any of the doctors were approaching. It was hopeless to complain to the doctors for they always said it was the imagination of our diseased-brains, and besides we would get another beating for telling. They would hold patients under the water and threaten to leave them to die there if they did not promise not to tell the doctors. We would all promise because we knew the doctors would not help us, and we would do anything to escape the punishment. After breaking a window I was transferred to the Lodge, the worst place on the island. It is dreadfully dirty in there, and the stench is awful. In the summer the flies swarm the place. The food is worse than we get in other wards and we are given only tin plates. Instead of the bars being on the outside, as in this ward, they are on the inside. There are many quiet patients there who have been there for years, but the nurses keep them to do the work. Among other beatings I got there, the nurses jumped on me once and broke two of my ribs.

"While I was there a pretty young girl was brought in. She had been sick and she fought about being put in that dirty place. One night the nurses took her and, after beating her, they held her naked in a cold bath, then they threw her on her bed. When morning came the girl was dead. The doctors said she died of convulsions, and that was all that was done about it.

"They inject so much morphine and chloral that the patients are made crazy. I have seen the patients wild for water from the effect of the drugs, and the nurses would refuse it to them. I have heard women beg for a whole night for one drop and it was not given them. I myself cried for water until my mouth was so parched and dry that I could not speak."

I saw the same thing myself in hall 7. The patients would beg for a drink before retiring, but the nurses—Miss Hart and the others—refused to unlock the bathroom that they might quench their thirst.

Hall 7 looks rather nice to a casual visitor. It is hung with cheap pictures and has a piano, which is presided over by Miss Mattie Morgan, who formerly was in a music store in this city. She has been in the asylum for three years. Miss Mattie has been training several of the patients to sing, with some show of success. The artiste of the hall is Under, pronounced Wanda, a Polish girl. She is a gifted pianist when she chooses to display her ability. The most difficult music she reads at a glance, and her touch and expression are perfect.

On Sunday the quieter patients, whose names have been handed in by the attendants during the week, are allowed to go to church. A small Catholic chapel is on the island, and other services are also held.

A "commissioner" came one day, and made the rounds with Dr. Dent. In the basement they found half the nurses gone to dinner, leaving the other half in charge of us, as was always done. Immediate orders were given to bring the nurses back to their duties until after the patients had finished eating. Some of the patients wanted to speak about their having no salt, but were prevented.

The Insane Asylum on Blackwell's Island is a human rat-trap. It is easy to get in, but once there it is impossible to get out. I had intended to have myself committed to the violent wards, the Lodge and Retreat, but when I got the testimony of two sane women and could give it, I decided not to risk my health—and hair, so I did not get violent.

I had towards the last been shut off from all visitors, and so when the lawyer, Peter A. Hendricks, came and told me that friends of mine were willing to take charge of me if I would rather be with them than in the Asylum, I was only too glad to give my consent. I asked him to send me something to eat immediately on his arrival in the city, and then I waited anxiously for my release.

It came sooner than I had hoped. I was out "in line" taking a walk, and had just gotten interested in a poor woman who had fainted away while the nurses were trying to compel her to walk. "Good-bye; I am going home," I called to Pauline Moser as she went past with a woman on either side of her. Sadly I said farewell to all I knew as I passed them on my way to freedom and life, while they were left behind to a fate worse than death. "Adios," I murmured to the Mexican woman. I kissed my fingers to her, and so I left my companions of hall 7.

I had looked forward so eagerly to leaving the horrible place, yet when my release came and I knew that God's sunlight was to be free for me again, there was a certain pain in leaving. For ten days I had been one of them. Foolishly enough, it seemed intensely selfish to leave them to their sufferings. I felt a Quixotic desire to help them by sympathy and presence. But only for a moment. The bars were down and freedom was sweeter to me than ever.

Soon I was crossing the river and nearing New York. Once again I was a free girl after ten days in the madhouse on Blackwell's Island.

New York World,
OCTOBER 16, 1887

III.

UNDERCOVER AGAIN

THE GIRLS
WHO MAKE BOXES

Bly followed her madhouse performance with a flurry of other impersonations. To expose corrupt practices at employment agencies, she pretended to be a maid looking for work; to document the black market in newborns, she pretended to be an unwed mother looking to sell her baby.[1] Here, she takes a turn as a box factory worker, a venture sensationalized in the headlines as "Nellie Bly Tells How It Feels to Be a White Slave." For most urban dwellers, the "working girl" was a familiar figure. By the turn of the century, five million American women were wage earners, and a quarter of them worked in manufacturing. The number of women factory workers in the United States more than doubled between 1850 and 1880, and it would almost double again by 1900. Women were appealing to employers in part because they were perceived as more docile and easier to manage, but they were also cheaper. Women were almost always hired for the most unskilled jobs and they earned one half to one third the wages of working men. They almost never made what labor advocates referred to as "a living wage."[2] Although the garment industry employed the most women, women also worked in food processing; laundries; and cigar, shoe, metal, and glass factories. Paper box factories like the one where Bly found employment were a small but significant subset of the manufacturing industry; they produced boxes for all kinds of merchandise, including cigarettes, shoes, candy, stationery, jewelry, neckties, feathers, and shirts. According to 1890 census figures, 2,354 women were employed in paper box factories in New York City.

THE GIRLS WHO MAKE BOXES

Nellie Bly Tells How It Feels to Be a White Slave

She Tries Her Hand at Making Paper Boxes—Difficulty in
Getting a Job—Must Work Two Weeks for Nothing—After
One Learns the Trade It Is Hard to Earn a Living—A Fair
Picture of the Work.

Very early the other morning I started out, not with the
pleasure-seekers, but with those who toil the day long that
they may live. Everybody was rushing—girls of all ages and
appearances and hurrying men—and I went along, as one of
the throng. I had often wondered at the tales of poor pay and
cruel treatment that working girls tell. There was one way of
getting at the truth, and I determined to try it: It was becoming myself a Paper Box Factory Girl. Accordingly, I started out
in search of work without experience, reference or aught to
aid me.

It was a tiresome search, to say the least. Had my living depended on it, it would have been discouraging, almost maddening. I went to a great number of factories in and around
Bleecker and Grand streets and Sixth avenue, where the workers number up into the hundreds. "Do you know how to do
the work?" was the question asked by everyone. When I replied that I did not, they gave me no further attention.

"I am willing to work for nothing until I learn," I urged.

"Work for nothing! Why, if you paid us for coming we
wouldn't have you in our way," said one.

"We don't run an establishment to teach women trades,"
said another, in answer to my plea for work.

"Well, as they are not born with the knowledge, how do
they ever learn?" I asked.

"The girls always have some friend who wants to learn. If
she wishes to lose time and money by teaching her, we don't
object, for we get the work the beginner does for nothing."

By no persuasion could I obtain an entree into the larger factories, so I concluded at last to try a smaller one at No. 196
Elm street. Quite unlike the unkind, brusque men I had met at
other factories, the man here was very polite. He said: "If you
have never done the work, I don't think you will like it. It is
dirty work and a girl has to spend years at it before she can
make much money. Our beginners are girls about sixteen years
old, and they do not get paid for two weeks after they come
here."

"What can they make afterwards?"

"We sometimes start them at week work—$1.50 a week.
When they become competent they go on piece-work—that is,
they are paid by the hundred."

"How much do they earn then?"

"A good worker will earn from $5 to $9 a week."

"Have you many girls here?"

"We have about sixty in the building and a number who
take the work home. I have only been in this business for a few
months, but if you think you would like to try it, I shall speak
to my partner. He has had some of his girls for eleven years. Sit
down until I find him."

He left the office and I soon heard him talking outside about
me and rather urging that I be given a chance. He soon returned and with him a small man who spoke with a German
accent. He stood by me without speaking, so I repeated my request.

"Well, give your name to the gentleman at the desk and
come down on Monday morning and we will see what we can
do for you."

And so it was that I started out early in the morning. I had
put on a calico dress to work in and to suit my chosen trade. In
a nice little bundle covered with brown paper with a grease-
spot on the centre of it was my lunch. I had an idea that every
working girl carried a lunch and I was trying to give out the
impression that I was quite used to this thing. Indeed, I considered the lunch a telling stroke of thoughtfulness in my new
role, and eyed with some pride, in which was mixed a little
dismay, the grease-spot, which was gradually growing in size.

Early as it was I found all the girls there and at work. I went through a small wagon-yard, the only entrance to the office. After making my excuses to the gentleman at the desk he called to a pretty little girl, who had her apron full of pasteboard, and said:

"Take this lady up to Norah."

"Is she to work on boxes or cornucopias?" asked the girl.

"Tell Norah to put her on boxes."

Following my little guide I climbed the narrowest, darkest and most perpendicular stair it has ever been my misfortune to see. On and on we went, through small rooms, filled with working girls, to the top floor—fourth or fifth story, I have forgotten which. Anyway I was breathless when I got there.

"Norah, here is a lady you are to put on boxes," called out my pretty little guide.

All the girls that surrounded the long tables turned from their work and looked at me curiously. The auburn-haired girl addressed as Norah raised her eyes from the box she was making and replied:

"See if the hatchway is down, and show her where to put her clothes."

Then the forewoman ordered one of the girls to "get the lady a stool," and sat down before a long table, on which was piled a lot of pasteboard squares, labeled in the center. Norah spread some long slips of paper on the table; then taking up a scrub-brush, she dipped it into a bucket of paste and then rubbed it over the paper. Next she took one of the squares of pasteboard and, running her thumb deftly along, turned up the edges. This done, she took one of the slips of paper and put it quickly and neatly over the corner, binding them together and holding them in place. She quickly cut the paper off at the edge with her thumb-nail and swung the thing around and did the next corner. This I soon found made a box lid. It looked and was very easy, and in a few moments I was able to make one.

I did not find the work difficult to learn, but rather disagreeable. The room was not ventilated and the paste and glue were very offensive. The piles of boxes made conversation impossible with all the girls except a beginner, Therese, who sat by my side. She was very timid at first, but after I questioned her kindly she grew more communicative.

"I live on Eldrige street with my parents. My father is a musician, but he will not go on the streets to play. He very seldom gets an engagement. My mother is sick nearly all the time. I have a sister who works at passementerie.[3] She can earn from $3 to $5 a week. I have another sister who has been spooling silk in Twenty-third street for five years now. She makes $6 a week. When she comes home at night her face and hands and hair are all colored from the silk she works on during the day. It makes her sick, and she is always taking medicine."

"Have you worked before?"

"Oh yes; I used to work at passementerie on Spring street. I worked from 7 until 6 o'clock, piece-work, and made about $3.50 a week. I left because the bosses were not kind and we only had three little oil lamps to see to work by. The rooms were very dark, but they never allowed us to burn the gas. Ladies used to come there and take the work home to do. They did it cheap, for the pleasure of doing it, so we did not get as much pay as we would otherwise."

"What did you do after you left there?" I asked.

"I went to work in a fringe factory on Canal street. A woman had the place and she was very unkind to all the girls. She did not speak English. I worked an entire week, from 8 to 6, with only a half hour for dinner, and at the end of the week she only paid me 35 cents. You know a girl cannot live on 35 cents a week, so I left."

"How do you like the box factory?"

"Well, the bosses seem very kind. They always say good-morning to me, a thing never done in any other place I ever worked, but it is a good deal for a poor girl to give two weeks' work for nothing. I have been here almost two weeks, and I have done a great deal of work. It's all clear gain to the bosses. They say they often dismiss a girl after her first two weeks on the plea that she does not suit. After this I am to get $1.50 a week."

When the whistles of the surrounding factories blew at 12 o'clock the forewoman told us we could quit work and eat our lunch. I was not quite so proud of my cleverness in simulating a working girl when one of them said:

"Do you want to send out for your lunch?"

"No, I brought it with me," I replied.

"Oh!" she exclaimed, with a knowing inflection and amused smile.

"Is there anything wrong?" I asked, answering her smile.

"Oh, no," quickly; "only the girls always make fun of any one who carries a basket now. No working girl will carry a lunch or basket. It is out of style because it marks the girl at once as a worker. I would like to carry a basket, but I don't dare, because they would make so much fun of me."

The girls sent out for lunch and I asked of them the prices. For five cents they get a good pint of coffee, with sugar and milk if desired. Two cents will buy three slices of buttered bread. Three cents a sandwich. Many times a number of the girls will put all their money together and buy quite a little feast. A bowl of soup for five cents will give four girls a taste. By clubbing together they are able to buy warm lunch.

At one o'clock we were all at work again. I having completed sixty-four lids, and the supply being consumed was put at "moulding in." This is fitting the bottom into the sides of the box and pasting it there. It is rather difficult at first to make all the edges come closely and neatly together but after a little experience it can be done easily.

On my second day I was put at a table with some new girls and I tried to get them to talk. I was surprised to find that they are very timid about telling their names, where they live or how. I endeavored by every means a woman knows, to get an invitation to visit their homes but did not succeed.

"How much can girls earn here?" I asked the forewoman.

"I do not know," she said; "they never tell each other, and the bosses keep their time."

"Have you worked here long?" I asked.

"Yes; I have been here eight years, and in that time I have taught my three sisters."

"Is the work profitable?"

"Well, it is steady, but a girl must have many years' experience before she can work fast enough to earn much."

The girls all seem happy. During the day they would make the little building resound with their singing. A song would be begun on the second floor, probably, and each floor would take it up in succession, until all were singing. They were nearly always kind to one another. Their little quarrels did not last long, nor were they very fierce. They were all extremely kind to me, and did all they could to make my work easy and pleasant. I felt quite proud when able to make an entire box.

There were two girls at one table on piece-work who had been in a great many box factories and had had a varied experience.

"Girls do not get paid half enough at any work. Box factories are no worse than other places. I do not know anything a girl can do where by hard work she can earn more than $6 a week. A girl cannot dress and pay her boarding on that."

"Where do such girls live?" I asked.

"There are boarding-houses on Bleecker and Houston, and around such places where girls can get a room and meals for $3.50 a week. The room may be only for two, in one bed, or it may have a dozen, according to size. They have no conveniences or comforts and generally undesirable men board at the same place."

"Why don't they live at these homes that are run to accommodate working women?"

"Oh, those homes are frauds. A girl cannot obtain any more home comforts, and then the restrictions are more than they will endure. A girl who works all day must have some recreation and she never finds it in homes."

"Have you worked in box factories long?"

"For eleven years, and I can't say that it has ever given me a living. On an average I make $5 a week. I pay out $3.50 for board and my wash bill at the least is 75 cents. Can any one expect a woman to dress on what remains?"

"What do you get paid for boxes?"

"I get 50 cents a hundred for one pound candy boxes and 40 cents a hundred for half pound boxes."

"What work do you do on a box for that pay?"

"Everything. I get the pasteboard cut in squares the same as you did. I first 'set up' the lids, then I 'mould in' the bottoms. This forms a box. Next I do the 'trimming,' which is putting the gilt edge around the box lid. 'Cover striping' (covering the edge of the lid) is next, and then comes the 'top label,' which finishes the lid entire. Then I paper the box, do the 'bottom la-beling' and then put in two or four laces (lace paper) on the inside as ordered. Thus you see one box passes through my hands eight times before it is finished. I have to work very hard and without ceasing to be able to make 200 boxes a day, which earns me $1. It is not enough to pay. You see I handle 200 boxes 1,600 times for $1. Cheap labor, isn't it?"

One very bright girl, Maggie, who sat opposite me told a story that made my heart ache.

"This is my second week here," she said, "and, of course, I won't receive any pay until next week, when I expect to get $1.50 for six days work. My father was a driver before he got sick. I don't know what is wrong, but the doctor says he will die. Before I left this morning he said my father will die soon. I could hardly work because of it. I am the oldest child, and I have a brother and two sisters younger. I am sixteen and my brother is twelve. He gets $2 a week for being office-boy at a cigar-box factory."

"Do you have much rent to pay?"

"We have two rooms in a house on Houston street. They are small and have low ceilings, and there are a great many China-men in the same house. We pay for these rooms $14 per month. We do not have much to eat, but then father doesn't mind it because he can't eat. We could not live if father's lodge did not pay our rent."

"Did you ever work before?"

"Yes, I once worked in a carpet factory at Yonkers. I only had to work there one week until I learned, and afterwards I made at piece-work a dollar a day. When my father got so ill my mother wanted me at home, but now when we see I can earn so little they wish I had remained there."

"Why do you not try something else?" I asked.

"I wanted to, but could find nothing. Father sent me to school until I was fourteen, and so I thought I would learn to be a telegraph operator. I went to a place in Twenty-third street, where it is taught, but the man said he would not give me a lesson unless I paid $50 in advance. I could not do that."

I then spoke of the Cooper Institute, which I thought every New Yorker knew was for the benefit of just such cases.[4] I was greatly astonished to learn that such a thing as the Cooper Institute was wholly unknown to all the workers around me.

"If my father knew that there was a free school he would send me," said one.

"I would go in the evenings," said another, "if I had known there was such a place."

Again, when some of them were complaining of unjust wages and some of places where they had been unable to collect the amount due them after working, I spoke of the mission of the Knights of Labor and the newly organized society for women.[5] They were all surprised to hear that there were any means to aid women in having justice. I moralized somewhat on the use of any such societies unless they entered the heart of these factories.

One girl who worked on the floor below me said they were not allowed to tell what they earned. However, she had been working here five years, and she did not average more than $5 a week. The factory in itself was a totally unfit place for women. The rooms were small and there was no ventilation. In case of fire there was practically no escape.

The work was tiresome and after I had learned all I could from the rather reticent girls I was anxious to leave. I noticed some rather peculiar things on my trip to and from the factory. I noticed that men were much quicker to offer their places to the working girls on the cars than they were to offer them to well-dressed women. Another thing quite as noticeable, I had more men try to get up a flirtation with me while I was a box factory girl than I ever had before. The girls were nice in their manners and as polite as ones reared at home. They never forget to thank one another for the slightest service, and there was quite a little air of "good form" in many of their actions. I have seen many worse girls in much higher positions.

New York World,
NOV. 27, 1887

THE KING OF THE LOBBY

Peddling political influence is a time-honored tradition in New York State; the term "lobbyist" is often said to have originated in the 1830s in the lobby of the New York State Capitol, where hopeful "lobby agents" waited long hours for a chance to catch a lawmaker's ear. In this April Fool's Day story, Bly set out to trick an influential Albany lobbyist into exposing his own corruption— and that of the political system in which he operated. Bly chose to approach Edward R. Phelps, a fifty-nine-year-old lobbyist who had been implicated in a bribery scandal seven years earlier.[1] She asked Phelps to ensure the defeat of Assembly Bill 191, a measure that would have outlawed the enormously profitable patent medicine business as it currently existed, by requiring state approval of all medicinal products offered for sale and charging a hefty fine for violations. Bly posed as the timid but determined wife of a patent medicine manufacturer who was so desperate to protect her husband's business that she was willing to pay an exorbitant sum to keep the bill from becoming law. In fact, Bly knew the controversial bill had already died in committee but she pretended ignorance. According to Bly's article, Phelps assured her he could defeat the bill and provided a list of legislators whose votes he could buy. After the article was published, Phelps called Bly "the champion story-teller of the age" and insisted that she had invented "groundless statements" in order "to concoct a sensational romance." Undeterred, the *World* defended Bly's integrity.[2] By mid-April, a grand jury had been convened to investigate the corruption charges. Ultimately the jury decided that there was insufficient evidence to indict any legislators. But Phelps did leave town, at least temporarily. The grand jury thanked the *World* for its efforts, said it was inclined to believe Bly's version of events despite Phelps's denials, and observed, "A professional lobbyist is a plague spot upon the body politic."[3]

THE KING OF THE LOBBY

Edward R. Phelps Caught in a Neatly Laid Trap

NELLIE BLY'S INTERESTING EXPERIENCE IN ALBANY

How the Lobby King Contracts to Kill Bills for Cash

DEALING WITH LEGISLATORS AS WITH PURCHASABLE CHATTELS

Phelps Furnishes "The World" Representative with a List of Assembly Committeemen Who Are Bribable—His Agreement to Kill Assembly Bill No. 191 for $5,000—Afterwards Concludes to Take Less—The Check to Be Made Out to His Side Partner, J. W. Chesbrough[4]—"I Have Control of the House and Can Pass or Kill Any Bill"—A Revelation of Baseness Which Should Fill the State with Indignation—The Watch Here.

> For I'm a Pirate King!
> I'm in the Lobby Ring;
> Oh! what an uproarious,
> Jolly and glorious
> Biz for a Pirate King!

I was a Lobbyist last week. I went up to Albany to catch a professional briber in the act. I did so. The briber, lobbyist and boodler[5] whom I caught was Mr. Ed Phelps. He calls himself "King of the Lobby." I pretended that I wanted to have him help me kill a certain bill. Mr. Phelps was cautious at first and looked carefully into my record. He satisfied himself that I was honest and talked very freely for a King.

He said that he could buy up more than half the members of the Assembly. It was only a question of money. I pretended to doubt his ability to do this. To prove his strength he took out a list of members and put a lead-pencil mark against those he swore he could buy. In his scoundrelly anxiety to prove his strength and to get my money he besmirched the character of many good Assemblymen.

Everybody knows Ed Phelps, the Lobbyist. He has been in trouble before, but his assurance has carried him through. During the celebrated Conkling-Platt Senatorial fight[6] I am told that Phelps, in company with Lo Sessions, was indicted for bribing a member, who took the money up to the Speaker's desk and exposed him. . . .[7]

But enough of Phelps. He is notorious. Anything I can say cannot blacken his character more. I can only tell what I did.

I selected a bill that I pretended to be interested in. It was Assembly bill No. 191. I said that if it passed it would ruin my husband's patent-medicine business. He said he could suppress it. . . .

THE TRIP TO ALBANY

Armed with this little bill and what I had learned, without confiding in any one, I took the train for Albany. The day (last Tuesday) was not bright, so I spent the time reviewing what I had learned. The only thing that amused me was my list of lucky odd numbers. It was the 27th of March, the train was an odd number, my chair was No. 3 and there was an odd number of passengers. Even when I reached Albany this odd streak did not desert me. I walked to Stanwix Hall and was given room No. 15, and there were only three chairs in the room. I did not look any further for odds.

The next day about noon I made my appearance at the Kenmore Hotel, where Mr. Phelps resides and keeps his legislative office. A half-grown boy in uniform met me at the door and politely escorted me through the lobby of the hotel to the elevator. A number of men who sat around glanced at me curiously.

"I want to see Mr. Phelps, please," I said as the boy started the elevator on its upward flight.

"Do you want to send your card up?" he asked. I had

intended to send up a card—not Nellie Bly's of course—until the boy unwittingly let me know that it was possible to get in without the use of that modern passport. I immediately decided to storm his castle.

I followed Buttons along the softly carpeted halls until he stopped at a door which bore on a little china plate the number 98.

At the boy's second knock an invitation to enter was given in a gruff voice. I stood at the half-opened door and saw a gray-haired man busily writing at a desk which occupied the centre of the room.

"He's in the other room," he replied to Buttons's inquiry for Mr. Phelps without lifting his head. The boy knocked on the door which separated the two rooms, as he said, "A lady to see you, Mr. Phelps."

"Very well, show her to the other door," was the answer, delivered in a rather smooth and not disagreeable voice.

THE MEETING WITH PHELPS

"Are you Mr. Phelps?" I asked, only to make him confess the fact.

"Yes, madam," he replied, smiling slightly, while he offered me a chair, with the request to "please be seated."

I sat down and looked about me. This was not what I had pictured to myself. This self-possessed, smiling man could not be the vampire I had been made to believe him. As he sat in the chair close by me with a reassuring smile on his face he did not look more than fifty-five years old. He is not a robust man, yet he is not of delicate build. He was dressed plainly, but with taste. There was nothing gaudy or loud about him, as one might imagine from his position. His hair and his side whiskers are gray. His upper lip and chin are clean shaven and he has something of the parson in his appearance.

The room in which we sat was comfortably furnished. It was apparently fitted up for an office; the only piece of furniture which looked out of place was a wardrobe which stood against the centre wall.

I thought my surest bait for this occasion was assumed innocence and a natural ignorance—not entirely assumed—as to how such affairs are conducted.

"Mr. Phelps, I came to consult you on a matter of importance," I began nervously, as if afraid of my position. "I—I hope no one can overhear us?" and I looked at him imploringly.

WINNING HER CONFIDENCE

"Oh no; you are safe to speak here," he assured me with a pleasant smile. He drew his chair closer to me and adjusted his glasses carefully on his nose, meanwhile looking over me critically.

"I have come to see you about a bill," I began to explain. His face lighted up as a girl's will over strawberry soda on an August day. He smiled encouragingly and rubbed his hands together gently.

"What bill is it?" he asked eagerly.

"A bill about patent medicines," I answered. "My husband is ill and he sent me to New York from Philadelphia to place some advertisements and a friend, who also has a patent medicine, told me of this bill, so I came up to see if anything could be done."

"Have you the bill with you?" he asked in a low tone.

"Yes, my friend gave it to me when he told me about it," I replied. He got up and walked over to the door, as if to be positive it was tightly closed. Then he came back, and taking the bill, which I held in my hand, he quickly scanned it.

"Do you think you can kill it?" I asked, with a proper amount of enthusiasm.

"Oh, yes," he responded heartily. "Never fear, I'll have it killed."

Excusing himself he went to the other room. When he came back he had a large ledger in his hand and a large smile on his face. He sat down and, resting the book on his knee, he ran his finger down the alphabet. He turned to a page which was filled with data of bills—a sort of a memorandum. He grew very

happy after this and closed the book in order to pay all attention to the poor little lamb who had come to be fleeced.

"What made you come to me?" he asked. I hardly knew
what was my best reply, so I said:

"Well, I had often read of you, you know; so when my friend
told me about the bill I did not want to place the advertisements and so lose all my money. If that bill passes you know it
will ruin our business."

"That is true," he assented warmly. "It will kill patent medicines. But who sent you to me?" he still urged.

"My friend said I might consult Mr. Phelps," I answered
evasively.

"Who is he?" he asked sharply.

"I would not like to give his name without his authority," I
said, while I wondered what I would do if he pressed the
subject.

"I only wanted to know, because we have had lots of people
up here paying to have that bill killed. Do you know Pierce of
Buffalo?[8] He is trying to get it killed," he said.

"I never heard of the bill until yesterday," which was true.
"I concluded not to go home, so I telegraphed my husband and
came on here."

"Where are you from?" he asked.

"Philadelphia. We make a patent medicine there, but it sells
all over New York State. Do you think you can kill the bill?"

IT WILL TAKE MONEY

"Oh, yes; I assure you of that. Now you keep up your nerve,"
he said, seeing my assumed nervousness. "I'll kill that bill. It
will take money, you know."

It was a shock, this cool assertion. I clutched at my umbrella.

"I am willing to pay anything up to $2,000," I said faintly,
"if you assure me it will be stopped."

"I can assure you that," he replied confidently. "Of course
you don't need to talk of $2,000. You see there will be my ex-
penses, and then I will have to pay some Assemblymen."

He went to the end of the room and took from there some pages containing the names and classifications of Assembly-men and Senators—a list of committees. Under the title of "Affairs of Cities" he showed me the twelve names of the men who he said would kill or save the bill.

"Mr. Crosby, of New York,[9] is a rich man, and can't be bought," he said, calmly. "But we can buy Gallagher, of Erie; Tallmadge, of Kings; Prime, of Essex; De Witt, of Ulster; Hagan, of New York, and McLaughlin, of Kings.[10] The rest are no good."

Oh, Mr. Phelps, I thought sadly, you are into the trap with both feet, for he had marked with his lead-pencil the names as he read them off.

"But if the rest are opposed?" I urged quietly.

"The majority gains," he said sweetly. "There are six out of eleven I can buy."

"How much will it take for them?" I asked, innocently.

"You can get the lot for $1,000."

Great goodness! just imagine, the whole lot for $1,000!

"I must never be known as connected with this," I began to cry. "It frightens me. I wouldn't have it known for anything; though," I added, "I'm willing to pay all it may cost to have the bill killed."

"That is nothing," he said lightly. "That's my business. I just stay here to watch bills for railroad presidents, insurance com-panies, &c. I'm kept here just to do this," he said firmly. "There is a lawyer of the name of Bates in New York who is also assisting me in getting people who want to fight this same bill you are here about. I've had my agents send out hundreds of copies of it."

SHE CAME TO THE RIGHT MAN

I felt inclined to ask if it were to bleed the public, but I was afraid. I had not finished yet, so I said, "I thought when I came up that I would go to see Mr. J. W. Smith,[11] who introduced the bill, but I did not know where to find him, so I came direct to you."

"It's a good thing you did," he said warmly. I wondered if he would feel so sure of that in a few days. "Smith is a dissipated and unprincipled fellow. He would have taken your money and given you no returns. You came just to the right one to help you this time."

"You are sure then for about $2,000—which I would rather spend this way than lose it in advertising—you can kill the bill?"

"I can have it killed for that amount or near it," he replied confidently. "Now, where can I see you again to make final arrangements?"

"Any place you state," I replied.

"Well, when you come from Philadelphia—could you come Friday? Well, you telegraph me to meet you at your hotel in New York. Where do you stop?"

"Sometimes at the Sturtevant and again at the Gilsey," I answered. "But then I dread exposure in this affair. Could you not appoint a place where it would attract less attention? Have you no place I could see you?"

"You might come to my office," he said, falling easily into the trap I had laid for him. That's just where, of all places, I wanted to go, but I said with well-feigned surprise:

"Oh, you have an office in New York also?"

"Yes, in the Borie Building. Do you know where that is? Well, when you cross the Cortlandt Street Ferry you cross to Broadway, and it is about two blocks below. No. 115, room 97. Wait, I'll write it here for you on the bill." And he thereupon took the bill and wrote on the margin, "E. R. Phelps, 115 Broadway, room 97, Borie Building."

"How very kind of you," I said.

"Now you come down Friday; meet me there between 12 and 1. If I'm not in when you arrive wait for me. I'll be there as soon as possible. I live out of the city. Come down prepared to make final arrangements (this meant pay the price) and I assure you I'll kill the bill afterwards."

"Then I can place my advertisements on Friday, on your assurance that the bill will be killed?" I asked.

"Don't place them until you see me." This was for fear I would resent the price after my sham advertisements were safely placed. "I assure you, after you see me you can safely place them. The bill will then be dead, or just as good, it will be harmless."

TRYING TO GET RID OF HER

"Why stay in Albany any longer?" he asked. "Why not take the 1.30 train for New York?" It was close on to that time, and I wanted my dinner, so I told him.

"They carry an eating car," he urged. "Take that train; it will get you in at 5 o'clock."

"That will allow me to go on to Philadelphia," I said, apparently falling into his plans, while I had no intentions of going.

"There is no use in waiting any longer," he urged. "You'll be seen, and that will raise comment. You might as well go now, and be sure to meet me Friday." I began to suspect that he feared if I remained longer some other boodler would get hold of me and rob him of his prey, or that I would discover that which I already knew, i. e., that the patent-medicine bill was really dead and had been for some time. So I promised to go.

"I'll take that list home to show my husband," I said, as I reached for the list he had marked of buyable Assemblymen.

"Give it to me," he exclaimed hurriedly, as he took it from my grasp. "Your husband may know some of these men and may tell them. It wouldn't look well for me to cross off those that can be bought. I'll cross out all the names."

THE LIST OF HONEST MEN

My heart sank. I really believe if hearts could faint mine fainted. Here was my only clue to those who, Mr. Phelps alleged, could be bought. If he crossed out all I could not tell one from the other. I shut my eyes and thought of several nasty things against cunning men and odd numbers. Then I opened them and looked blankly as he started to destroy my clue. He placed the sheet on a book on his desk and made crosses against the remaining names, excepting Mr. Crosby's, and then he handed it to me. I glanced at it, and with a prayer of thanks folded it hurriedly and placed it in my purse.

The rough covering of the book had caused the lead pencil to make a peculiar spotted line against the second lot of names marked by Mr. Phelps.

When marking the original ones the committee list was on a flat, smooth surface, and so it happens that the lines are as distinctly recognizable as though they were in different colors. . . .[12]

After dining at my hotel I started for the city. I had told Mr. Phelps that the name I gave him—Miss Consaul—was an assumed one, taken because my own and my husband's name was so familiar everybody would recognize it at once. So I went under my maiden name.

As soon as I got to New York I sent a telegram to a friend in Philadelphia, instructing him to forward it from there to Mr. Phelps. It was done to ease any doubts he might have. This ran as follows:

PHILADELPHIA, March 28.
E. R. Phelps, Room 98 Kenmore,
Albany, N. Y.
Have made satisfactory
arrangements with husband.   Will see
you as agreed.   MISS CONSAUL.

THE SECOND MEETING

Friday came and with it the disquieting intelligence that the bill I professed to be interested in had been reported adversely by the Committee on Thursday. Would my story be without a climax? How would Mr. Phelps act under this news? However, I borrowed a long sealskin dolman to give me a matronly look, and hiring a hansom I was driven to No. 115 Broadway, the Borie Building.

Mr. Phelps's name was on the door of No. 97, and before I could knock the door was opened, and he, smiling sweetly, stood before me and invited me in. "My son," he said, introducing a rather handsome young man who sat behind the solitary desk the office contained.¹³ I was wondering how Mr. Phelps knew I was at the door, when I glanced out and saw that from his window he could see everybody who came up on the elevator. The door of the office was darkened.

"I suppose you know about the bill?" he inquired sharply.

"Oh, no," I said, in assumed voice of alarm and ignorance. "Can't it be killed?"

"Yes, that's it," he said, smiling, "it has been killed."

"So soon. How clever you must be!" I remarked flatteringly.

"Well, I saw that you were anxious to kill the bill and I told you that it should be killed. It's done. That will never bother you again." Mr. Phelps's son here took his silk hat and left the room.

"How did you ever manage it?" I asked simply, with a world of admiration in my eyes.

HOW CLEVER MR. PHELPS WAS

"Why, you see"—he talked in a confiding whisper—"I went to work on it right away. You see I had it transferred from the committee that first had it. As I told you, Mr. Crosby could not be bought, and I knew he and some others determined to pass it, so I went to the ones I told you I could get and told them I wanted that bill killed. They said they were anxious to get rid of it, so I had it reported back to the Committee on Public Health. I knew I could get them easier."

"Oh, how very clever!" I breathed rapturously, "and they did not refuse?"

"No, they asked me what it was worth," he said boldly, "and I told them $1,000, and so they promised to do it."

"They did not dare refuse," I murmured again.

"No; I should say they did not," he said laughingly. "You see that's my business. I'm the head of the Lobby."

"Oh, indeed! What a good thing I went to you. How can you ever do all the work?"

"Why, I keep a lot of runners who watch and know everything that happens. I am head. They report to me, and I have books in my rooms where entries are made of every bill and notes of every incident connected with it. You noticed when you gave me the bill in the Kenmore I went into another room and got a large book? Well, by that book I at once saw all about the bill and knew just what to say to you."

"What did you say to the committee about the bill?" I asked, curiously.

"I just told them the bill had to be killed, and I told them it was worth $1,000. I had to give my check for it right off, but I told you that I could have it done for $1,000 for the committee, with my expenses extra."

"My husband could not understand how you could buy the whole Committee for $1,000. It seems so little," I suggested.

"I couldn't if that was my only case, but you see this is my business. I spend all my time at it. I pay these men heavily on other bills, so that makes some bills more moderate."

"Then you can have any bill killed?"

HE OWNS THE HOUSE

"*I have control of the House and can pass or kill any bill that so pleases me,*" was Mr. Phelps's astounding reply.

"Next week," he continued, "I am going to pass some bills and I'll get $10,000 for it. I often get that and more to pass or kill a bill."

I was stricken dumb. I did not know what to say. The brazen effrontery of this appalled me.

"You can take this," handing me the Albany *Journal*, "to show your husband that the bill was killed. You will also see an account of it in today's WORLD."

"I would like you to tell me who sent you to me," continued Mr. Phelps. "Not that I want to pry into your affairs, but it may be one of my agents and I want to pay him."

The only agent had been my own sweet self, so I demurred and said I feared to give the name without the man's authority.

"I have to pay the money for killing the bill to the committee this week," Mr. Phelps began, returning to the subject of money, "and as I got it done so quickly I thought I would deal honestly with you and only charge you $250 for my expenses. That will make a total of $1,250. Could you write out a check here for the amount?" he asked boldly.

FENCING ABOUT THE MONEY

"I—, Oh, dear, I'm dreadfully frightened," I exclaimed, to give myself time to think. He smiled, as if well pleased. "You see, my husband told me not to do anything that would connect me with this affair." I breathed easier. "For that reason I do not want to give a check."

"Well, you could write out a check payable to J. F. Chesbrough. He is a relative of mine, and it's just the same as giving it to me; or you could make it out in my son's name."

"No; I don't want it made out to Phelps, I'm afraid," I said; "but if you send your son up to the St. James Hotel, where I am stopping, I will give it to him there."

"That will do," he said, carelessly, and then he called, "Johnny, Johnny!"

"Aha! Johnny is waiting on the outside," I thought, and comes at the call when the poor lamb is fleeced. I began to fear that really, somehow, they would compel me to pay the money.

"I'd rather make out a check," I began, hastily.

"Very well, I'll write the name for you," and suiting the action to the word he took from his desk a white envelope, smaller than the ordinary envelope, and wrote across it the name I was to make the check payable to.[14] He then wrote in the corner the amount, $1,250.

"My son will go up with you and get the check," he said, and again began to call "Johnny."

"Oh, then I might just as well get the money and hand it to him," in half hopes of getting him to abandon the idea of sending some one with me. I wanted a chance to escape. He took the envelope from me and tore the ends and back off it. I wanted to save that name, so I said quickly: "Give me that, I'll write the check after all and give it to your son."

He handed it back. The name was yet clear, but the numbers were partially torn away, only "50" remained. . . .

Mr. Phelps showed me the telegram, which purported to come from me in Philadelphia, after he had called his son in to tell him to accompany me to my hotel.

SUCH AN HONEST LITTLE WOMAN

"I felt queer about you at first," he said confidingly. "It is the most unusual thing in the world for a woman to come to me for such work. First I thought it was a trap to catch me." I looked at him and then at his son in a hurt manner. "But then I saw how innocent you were and how honest. I must say I was surprised though."

"Well, you see, I did not know what to do," I urged, as if I had blundered. "I was so ignorant of it all."

Mr. Phelps, jr., leaned on the desk and glanced at me admiringly. My cheeks began to burn and I began to long for freedom. Would I never escape them?

"Madam is going up to the St. James," Phelps, sr., explained to Phelps, jr., "and you are to go with her. She will give you a check there for some work I have been doing for her."

"Can't you come along?" I asked Mr. Phelps, sr.; "I hate to have your son connected with this, besides I am better acquainted with you." I was getting deeper and deeper into it and I didn't know what to do.

"Father, you go," urged the young man. "You might as well. You would leave the office in a half hour, anyway."

I said I had a cab at the door, but that I would not like to be seen taking Mr. Phelps away in it. They urged, but I was firm, and at last Mr. Phelps said his father would go up on the Elevated Railway and would get there about the same time I would.

FAREWELL WORDS

"He can wait for me in the parlor," I began, joyously, now that I could escape. Wait for me? Well, he would wait years before I would come. "I'll get the money, and when I go in the parlor I will hand it to you. No one will see me there." He could be sure, no one would ever see me give him money.

"Where will you get the money?" he asked, impudently.

"Father, that's nothing to you, so she gets it," the young man remarked, for which I looked my heartfelt thanks.

"In a half hour, in the parlors of the St. James Hotel?" said Mr. Phelps, as I arose to start.

"Yes," I replied, and walked smilingly with the young man to the elevator.

"I was extremely nervous over this," I said, half apologizing for my hesitating manner.

"You'll get over that by the time you have had more bills to kill," he said, encouragingly. I laughed and said that I thought I should.

I got into cab 922, gave the driver instructions to go a thousand different ways and to stop at THE WORLD office, where I could write my story. He was a man who knew his business and I felt confident in a short time that I was not followed.

So far as I personally know, Mr. Phelps is still waiting my arrival in the parlor of the St. James Hotel.[15]

from "THE KING OF THE LOBBY,"
The New York World, APRIL 1, 1888

IV.

THE WOMAN
QUESTION

WOMAN'S PART
IN POLITICS

In the course of her career, Bly interviewed a range of public officials, prisoners, celebrities, and activists. Her subjects included labor activist Eugene V. Debs, champion prizefighter John L. Sullivan, and Laura Bridgman, famed as the first deaf and blind person in America to communicate using sign language.[1] Bly's interview with U.S. presidential candidate Belva Lockwood offers a sympathetic portrait of a women's rights pioneer and showcases Bly's skills as an interviewer. Bly's interviews tended to quote her subjects at length, allowing them to address readers in their own words, but she also included details about her own feelings about her subjects, and she almost always found a way to mention what they thought about *her*. As this interview suggests, Bly, a longtime advocate for women—especially women's right to work—admired Lockwood's courage. Lockwood (1830–1917) was a feminist attorney, politician, peace activist, and educator. In 1879, she became the first woman admitted to practice before the Supreme Court, and shortly after, she became the first woman to argue at the Court. Years later, when she was in her seventies, she advocated on behalf of Cherokees who had been removed from their ancestral lands without just compensation and won a multimillion-dollar settlement. Lockwood was also a pioneer in flexible work arrangements for working mothers. Her home in Washington, D.C., served as both her office and a permanent residence for her extended family, which included two families with small children whose mothers worked in the law office. Lockwood first ran for president in 1884, when she became the first woman to appear on official ballots, decades before women gained the right to vote. Lockwood received a few thousand votes, although the precise number was disputed. When the Equal Rights party nominated her for president again in 1888—the year Bly interviewed her—she struggled to gain national attention; although she campaigned up until the eve of the election, no votes for her appear to have been recorded. Nonetheless, Lockwood articulated her goals succinctly for Bly when she spoke of the need to "educate people to the idea" of a woman president of the United States—an idea that, more than a century later, remains just that.

WOMAN'S PART IN POLITICS

Mrs. Belva A. Lockwood Talks About Herself to Nellie Bly

The Feminine Candidate for the Presidency of This Great Country Thinks She Has a Fighting Chance—Mrs. Cleveland, [2] However, Is Stronger—Something About Her Home Life—Her Washington Office.

Equal Rights.—We, the undersigned, citizens of the State of New York, believe in woman suffrage, prohibition, arbitration, money and labor reform and the control of railroads and telegraphs by the Government.

This is the platform, as well as the plank, on which Mrs. Belva A. Lockwood stands during her campaign for the Presidency of the United States. Does she really expect to be elected? Certainly; why shouldn't she? Remember the old adage about certain folks falling out, in which event Mrs. Lockwood might reasonably expect to get her just dues.[3]

The other day I called to see Mrs. Lockwood at the home of Mrs. Leonard,[4] No. 136 West Twenty-third street. Mrs. Lockwood had come from Washington, D.C., on the Saturday previous to lecture in Brooklyn and New York. A girl—pretty and plump—invited me to enter an artistic parlor, where portraits of Lillian Russell[5] predominated. I was lost in the contemplation of Lillian's beauty in various poses and costumes when a lady entered noiselessly, gracefully, and with an ease few women acquire. Her hand clasped mine and held it while she asked if I had called to see her, and I replied that if she was Mrs. Lockwood, I had.

"What is your name?" she asked easily.

"Bly," I replied hurriedly.

"Nellie Bly!" she exclaimed. "My goodness! sit down. I'm glad to see you."

How much there is in a handshake! It bespeaks every passion known to the human mind. I verily believe a handclasp can make or unmake a man. Now Mrs. Lockwood's handshake was delightful. Her hand closed around mine firmly, softly, warmly, not with the vulgar shake, as if testing the strength of the arm, but with a clasp. It seemed to rouse and inspire one with good humor, strength and good-fellowship. If Candidate Harrison's[6] handshake can be compared to Mrs. Lockwood's one might safely bet on him.

"I am very sorry you did not come sooner, Miss Bly," Mrs. Lockwood said, as she leaned back in her chair. "I had a visitor I would have liked you to meet, Sister Agnes, as her name is, came here and founded a school. When it became prosperous it was taken from her, and when she tried to regain it she was sent to an insane asylum. Not being insane she was at length discharged from the asylum. I advised her to go to *The World*, as it always stands ready to defend the oppressed."

"Do you have many such visitors?"

"Numbers of them," she replied with a smile. "I have been overrun with visitors wanting advice since I came here. One of the most prominent was a man who came to consult me in regard to the Panama Canal."[7]

"Do you really expect to be elected President?" I asked curiously.

"Certainly," she replied, as she looked at me with an amused smile which allowed several interpretations of her answer.

There have been worse looking Presidents, or I might say,

there have been few as fine looking. There is one thing, if Belva Lockwood gains the day she will go into the White House with a reputation that will bear discussion in the family circle.

Mrs. Lockwood does not look like the cuts newspapers have published of her, still less does she answer to descriptions of her. She is a womanly woman; what greater praise can one give her. She is firm and intelligent, without being manly; and gentle and womanly without being frivolous. She is the beau ideal of a woman with a brain. She is of good height, neither tall nor short, and of strong, but not flabby, build. She wore a blue tricot skirt, braided in black up the sides. The drapery was not conspicuous for bustle, nor for the ugly flatness which follows the absence of one. A fine white muslin house sacque looked comfortable and was becoming. A certain trimness about the waist proved that Belva Lockwood, Presidential candidate, has not abolished stays. Six large diamonds, set in a square, caught a webby lace scarf about her throat, and from the coils of gray hair glistened a diamond comb. Her curly bang allows a space of broad forehead to show between it and her sparkling brown eyes. A few pinks and sprigs of mignonette were pinned close to her throat.

AN INTERESTING TICKET

As she talked with me, twirling her black-rimmed eye-glasses, her changing expression echoing her conversation was interesting. I dislike to talk to people with dead faces! It always struck me as uncanny for a tongue to be running inside an unchanging face.

"Isn't this the second time that you have been nominated for President?" I asked.

"Yes. I was ill in Washington at the time," she answered. "The convention which was held in Des Moines, Ia., was attended by some six hundred people, among whom were as many men as women."

"I suppose you depend entirely on the vote of the men to put you in office?"

"Certainly, women have no vote," she replied with a smile. "We are coming to it, though. It is the universal opinion of all thinking men that women will eventually vote. I delivered a lecture not long ago at the Delaware Institution, Franklin, N. Y., in reference to women voting. President Cleveland, in congratulating me afterwards, said, 'It has got to come; we all recognize that.'"

"Have you any regular course of canvass?"

"Oh, yes, we would accomplish little without plans. We have both men and women to lecture. What women? Well, there is Mrs. Nettie Sanford Chapin, Marshalltown, Ia.; Mrs. Catherine Denning Clark, Lexington, Ky.; Mary Ata L. Stowe, San Francisco, Cal.; Mrs. Mary Anna Munger, Worcester, Mass.; Dr. Rachel Davidson, Flint, Mich.; Margaret Berg, Chattanooga, Tenn.; Alma M. Mitchell, Salem, Ia.; Mrs. Emma Beckwith and Mrs. Cynthia Leonard, of New York. Dr. J. G. Lamber, of Chattanooga, is one of the men who is to lecture and—as I cannot easily recall strange names, I can only say the others are prominent men from Alabama, Mississippi, New York, Vermont and Tennessee."

"Have you any newspapers devoted to your cause?"

"No, not that I know of. There is nothing to make it worth their while," she said with a jolly laugh. "However, I am Vice-President of the Woman's National Press Association, of Washington, and the members are united in favoring me. They will help all they can in their correspondence, but they can't vote. I had been nominated as delegate to the Union Labor party," she continued, "and expected to leave for Cincinnati to lecture the very day Mrs. N. S. Chapin, Chairman of the National Committee, notified me of my renomination for President."

"Have you had any money offered for the aid of your campaign?"

"We receive many private donations, besides having an offer of $25,000 to carry on the campaign; but you know, as we have no big places to offer, we'd not get the help other political parties get. I have just received correspondence which may show you how our work is starting."

BOURBON, IND., 7, 2, '88.
Hon. Belva A. Lockwood.

DEAR MADAM: Your standard was thrown to the breeze this
P.M. by our citizens, 'mid wild huzzas of enthusiastic votes.
From now to November the good work will go forward until
the vote for fair citizenship shall be counted, when you may
expect to hear from old Bourbon.

With prayers for your success and the triumphant victory of
the cause we all hold sacred, I am, very respectfully yours.

A. C. MATCHETTE, M. D.

"Mrs. Lockwood, if you do not reach the White House this
time," I said, "what good do you expect to result from your
campaign?"

"It educates the people to the idea," she replied. "If we always talk and never work we will not accomplish anything.
Men always say, 'Let's see what you can do.' Now we are trying to show them."

"What class of women support you in your Equal Rights
ideas?"

"Thinking women and working women. Society women
never go outside of society. It is all in all to them, so they give
us no support, and the very poor—the masses—are no better.
One is the slave, the other the doll, and equally useless to us."

"Do you mind telling me something of your home life?" It's
a question I always feel delicate about asking, but it's always
the most interesting thing about prominent people.

"Certainly not," she replied without hesitation, "but it is
a little like a writer once calling to get something from my
mother to write about me—something I had done in my baby
days; but mother said I never did anything. Rather rough on
me, wasn't it? I live in Washington, at No. 619 F street Northwest. My mother, my daughter, my granddaughter, my niece
and my grand-niece all occupy the same house. This is my
card." She handed me the following business-like card:

BELVA A. LOCKWOOD & CO.,
ATTORNEYS AND SOLICITORS,
NO. 619 F STREET, NORTHWEST,
WASHINGTON, D.C.

*Practice before the United States Supreme Court
and Court of Claims. Pension and
Bounty Claims a specialty.
Patents obtained.*

HER LAW BUSINESS

"My husband, Dr. Lockwood, was an invalid," she continued, "and so I taught school for fifteen years. It was very poor pay and hard work. I had my family to support, besides the niece I have spoken of, whom I adopted and raised. There were then no respectable paying positions open to women as there are now, so I began to read law. I was admitted to the Bar in September, 1879, and have been in active practice for fifteen years. My husband died in 1877."

"Have you made much money?"

"Well I have run a large house and kept a large family.[8] I never make less than $3,000 a year. Lura M. Ormes, my daughter, is a skilled lawyer. She takes charge in my absence. She also manages the house and looks after her three-year-old daughter, Inez Ormes, who is a wonderfully clever child. Lura likes to do fancy cooking, but none of us waste time scrubbing or making beds. Yes, I can work. I was once a good chambermaid and seamstress. Why don't I do housework? Because servants are cheap and I can earn more in a month at my desk than I could at housework in years. My niece, Clara B. Harrison, is also a lawyer, but her regular duties are attending to the correspondence, at which she is very skillful, and keeping the accounts. She is a widow, with one boy, four years old, Warren L. Harrison. My daughter's husband is interested in getting up a stock company in New York for the telautograph.[9] My office is in the first floor of my house."

"Do you feel encouraged in your work—political work, I mean?"

"Yes, we are making great progress. It is only by practical work that we can show what we can do. People are less wedded to party, and do some thinking. Once it was considered a disgrace to change one's party; now it is a sign of progress. If I don't gain the Presidency, we expect to get in as Governors and legislators. Linda Gilbert, the great prison worker, was nominated for Lieutenant-Governor of New York, in Brooklyn, Saturday night."[10]

"Do you expect to carry any State?"

"Yes, Iowa," she replied.

"Do you favor tariff?" I asked.

POLITICAL VIEWS

"I favor a reduced tariff.[11] A great number of American industries need protection," she answered positively. "I don't believe in the absence of tariff of the Democratic platform, nor the high tariff of the Republicans. What do I think of immigration? I heretofore thought that America should be the asylum for all foreigners, but now, since they have made our land a dumping ground for paupers and criminals, I think it is the President's duty to suggest reform. What of the Chinese? Their labor is not more harmful than that of the other foreigners. Keep one nation out, do the same with all."[12]

"What exercise would you suggest as best for women?" I asked.

"Tricycle, by all odds," she answered. "I rode one for five years, and there is nothing that can equal it for healthful exercise."

"What do you think of Harrison's chances?"

"Well," she mused, smilingly, "if every man who shakes hands with him is going to vote for him—but that's what you can't tell."

"What are Cleveland's chances?"

"Cleveland?" in surprise, "he is not a candidate. It's Mrs. Cleveland."

"What is your latest work?" I asked, curious to know all that this woman with a mother's face and a man's intellect is doing.

"I am interested in trying to establish a court of international arbitration between America and foreign lands. The trouble over the fisheries treaty with Canada helps to prove how much we have need of it. I am beginning with France—others will come later—and have just sent some papers on the subject from Washington to the Peace Minister of France."

"So, Mrs. Lockwood," I said, "you expect to be elected President of the United States?"

"I do," she answered.

"Next to you, who stands the best chance for the Presidency?"

"Frances Folsom Cleveland."[13]

The New York World,
AUGUST 12, 1888

SHOULD WOMEN PROPOSE?

Nellie Bly Advances Arguments in the Affirmative

She Thinks It Is Not Fair for Women to Have to Sit Around and Wait for a Proposal—Mr. Depew Agrees, with His Characteristic Courtesy—Mrs. Frank Leslie Scouts the Idea as Preposterous.

Should women propose?

Leap year is rapidly nearing its end. The unlucky girl who does not win her other soul—her mate—before midnight of Dec. 31 will have to wait three weary years for the right to propose.[1] Is it just? In this day of almost equal rights, when women fill the same positions—yes, and ably, too—which were considered man's and man's alone, is it just that women shall not have the right to propose?

Is it just that an able (woman) lawyer shall be allowed to plead for everything except the hand of the man she loves? Is it just that a skillful (woman) surgeon shall dress all wounds except those to her own feelings? Or set all fractures save those of her own heart? Is it just that an eloquent (woman) minister shall teach the way to paradise to others and yet not make a way for herself to woman's heaven? Shall a (woman) dentist fill your teeth and not ask to fill some good man's home and life? Shall a (woman) artist have no right to paint her portrait on some man's heart? Shall (a woman) sculptor not model a Cupid to do her bidding? Shall (women) writers only woo imaginary people in their studies—propose only in stories?

In the days of barbarism, when men stood off and made their selections and afterwards consummated the bargain with the father; or even in the days of our gentle great and great-great grandmothers, whose golden chains and rings were fit emblems of their slavery—when women were animated dolls, having no will but their lords', having no thoughts of their own—when they were dressed, curled, driven, then it would have been sheer folly to ask such a question.

Women are not confined to their homes now, lamentable or otherwise as different persons may deem the fact. They are in the world—are of it. They write, think, drive and work like men. Should they not, then, have an equal right to propose marriage?

THE PRESIDENT OF THE HOUSEHOLD

What gives a man the sole right to ask the one he loves to wed him? Does merely being a man make him the more fitted to ask such a question? When one sifts the subject one finds that the greater responsibilities of a home rest on the woman. Should not this fact alone grant her the right to do what she can to secure the man of her choice to share her domestic throne? She is the hub of the wheel in every home. She has charge of the cook, she economizes, she bears the children, watches over their thousand wants, not little ones either; she makes her boys a credit to her family and honorable citizens, or otherwise; the future of her daughters is in her hands; her husband's happiness, his buttons and his comfort generally are under her control. She is the president of the household, her husband the secretary of the treasury. With all this in mind, who shall say that women should not have the right to propose?

Everything in life, and some say afterwards, hinges on love. "Love is life's end; an end, but never ending."[2] It's the mainspring to everything, from a tragedy to a bonnet, and it often even flavors our soup. Shall a woman love and die of love and dare not breath it, or shall she woo? Many women have died old maids because some man courted too long, kept others away and did not propose marriage himself. Such cases are frequent and the girl is always the one who suffers therefrom. If every woman were as straightforward as Juliet, and when men began to pay her idle compliments brought them up to a standstill with a "If thou lovest, pronounce it faithfully," and if he thinks her "too quickly won" she'll "frown and be perverse, else not for the world,"[3] people would be better and happier. The rules which govern women in love teach them deceit and to deceive. They debase all that is lovely in woman's character for that very reason. The social rules which govern love teach a girl to hide every sincere feeling and to pretend what she does not feel, yet those who would be first to cry "Shame!" at a woman for deceit would be the first to cry "Bold!" if she gave evidence of her true feelings.

There would be fewer unhappy marriages, fewer divorces and fewer melancholy women if women had the right to propose. I remember when I attended Sunday-school that I was taught "Ask and it shall be given unto you,"[4] but I don't know that it was meant for women. I decided to ask the opinion of several people on the subject and then leave the question open to the readers of *The World*.

WHAT CHAUNCEY DEPEW THINKS

First I went to see Mr. Chauncey M. Depew[5] at the Grand Central Depot. I sent my card in and in a few moments was requested to "step this way." I did so and found myself in a room furnished comfortably, but in business-like fashion. Not quite in the centre of the room, but standing distinct and alone, was a desk. In a chair before it, swung half facing the door, sat Chauncey M. Depew, whose handsome, genial face is as familiar to the reading public as that of any President of the United States. Of all the men in public life this noted after-dinner speaker is recognized as the most courteous to newspaper people. I don't think Mr. Depew could be rude or unkind if he wished to.

"And this is Nellie Bly?" he asked, arising from his chair and taking both my hands in a cordial grasp.

I admitted that I was responsible for that person, and continued:

"I have just come to get your opinion on a certain subject which doubtless you will think very silly. It is this"—I took a long breath—"should women propose?"

Mr. Depew gazed at me a moment with a look of surprise in which I detected a faint trace of alarm, then he burst into a hearty laugh. He bent over, lacing his hands on his knees, and laughed until his gold eyeglasses tumbled off. A man sitting on the other side of the room with a large book on his knee joined in, and somehow I began to feel awkward.

"I am not going to propose," I made haste to add, "but really, now, when we have women who do everything as ably as men, don't you think that they should have the right to propose?"

"I do indeed," he replied earnestly, straightening up. "But there are prejudices against it which will not likely be overcome."

"You do not entertain any?"

"No, no; certainly not"—still smiling.

"Then you believe in women proposing?"

"I do." His eyes twinkled, but his tone was serious. "Proposing cost me ten years of my life. I would have lived just ten years longer if I had not proposed. It took me a year to get my courage up to the point. I most certainly believe in women taking that privilege from the men."

"I suppose you feel happy over the election?"[6] I said, forgetting for an instant the main subject of the interview.

"Oh, yes, yes," he replied, pleasantly. "Why don't you telegraph Gen. Harrison[7] and ask him if women should propose?"

"He would be too busy just now answering congratulations to find time to answer my question," I said. "Now, if women would propose," going back to the old subject, "do you think the men would be so ungenerous as to laugh at them or to refuse them?"

MR. DEPEW ILLUSTRATES WITH A STORY

"Oh, no; they would never do that." His eyes gleamed roguishly. "That reminds me of a friend of mine—I never tell stories, but I'll tell this one. He was lecturing in some small town out West. In the midst of his talk a number of young girls in the back part of the house began to giggle and laugh; so one of the men, who was conducting the meeting, arose and requested them to please keep better order in the back part of the room. A young man who was sitting by the girls got up and said, 'Please excuse the girls, they couldn't help laughing, 'cause a hornet has just stung me.' Now if the hornet had stung the girls the men would not have laughed, but would have applied the remedies usual in such cases."

Somehow, when I went out, and especially as I had never been stung by a hornet, I wondered what the remedies were for such wounds.

Mrs. Frank Leslie[8] was resting her elbow on a desk, which is thoroughly businesslike in every respect, when I entered her private office. I said:

"Mrs. Leslie, we are going to discuss a question in *The World*, and I would like to have your opinion on the subject."

"Yes; I was just reading a lot of clippings containing my opinions on various subjects, and here is one," lifting up one from the desk, "which describes what my mouth is like."

"This question is quite important in this day of almost equal rights," I continued. "Should women propose?"

"Oh!" she exclaimed, and then she laughed. "What an idea! Brigham Young[9] once said that he wished all women had the right to propose."

"And what do you think?"

"Well, I don't think so," she replied, slowly. "The more womanly a woman is, the sweeter she is. Let the men keep that right. It is much easier to use the right of refusal or acceptance than that of proposing."

"Don't you think a woman has as much right as a man to woo?" I urged.

MRS. LESLIE DISCRIMINATES

"Yes," with a smile, "and she can do it with her eyes and with the thousand little ways she knows so well how to employ, but let her lips be silent."

"But don't you think if women could propose they would more often get those they love?"

"Doubtless, but they must not do it, for it means death," she said earnestly.

"How so?"

"Why, if a man should refuse a woman she would never be

satisfied until she killed him. I know I would not," with a tap of her tiny foot.

"Would he dare—would he have the courage to refuse her?" I asked.

"I don't think he would," she smiled. "Then think how wretched a woman would be. She would always fear that he wanted to refuse but did not dare."

We both laughed at this view of the question, and then I said again:

"So you do not believe in a woman having that right?"

"No; let her be as womanly as she can," she said, firmly. "If I had my life to live over, and I know if you had the choosing of yours, we would both prefer a quiet home, obscurity, no knowledge of the world, and no rights except those of a mother and a wife."

I had nothing more to say.

MAYOR-ELECT GRANT FRIGHTENED

Mr. Hugh J. Grant,[10] the new Mayor, is a tall, handsome man, blessed with all the qualities which endear men to women, yet he is a bachelor. I believe it is only because he is too bashful to propose even if he were in love. I met him in his office two days after his election.

"Before you go," I began, "I want to ask you—Do you think that women should propose?" He almost fell back against the bookcase and his face flushed so red that I was frightened at my own boldness.

"I have often wondered why some one did not propose to me," he said, still flushing deeply.

"Oh, you are not married," I exclaimed. I never knew it until then.

"No," he said, making his way to the door, and I was just as frightened over it as he was.

I went to the stage door of Palmer's Theatre and gave my card to a man who was sitting in a little dimly lighted box to take to Mr. W. H. Gillette.[11] I thought I would like to have the opinion of America's most successful playwright on the subject.

"Miss Bly," I heard called. I looked, and I saw Mr. Gillette leaning on the partition at the head of the uncarpeted stairs. "Will you come up here, or shall I go down?"

"Oh, I will go up," I replied.

"I just wrote you a note," he said, pointing the way to his room, "telling you that I had a long wait later in the evening when you might come, but that I was never interviewed. I always interview. But sit down. You take the chair. I'll sit on this trunk."

"I have come just to ask you one little question," I said, shortly. "Should women propose?"

"It depends on what they propose," he said, crossing one leg over the other and smiling as if he had me cornered.

"Marriage, of course. Should a woman have the right to propose marriage?"

"Yes," with a drawl, "I think she should do the proposing."

"Really?"

"Yes, really."

MEN ARE NEVER MEAN

"Do you think the men would be mean enough to say to her afterwards, 'Well, you married me, I didn't marry you,' and all that sort of thing."

"No, no man would ever be so mean," he said, with a laugh.

"Well I am glad you think so and I'm glad you say women should propose."

"Do you want my candid opinion?" he said. "Do you want me to tell you what I really believe?"

"I do, indeed."

"Well, I'll tell you my candid opinion if you will promise to ask me no more questions," I promised.

"You know the story of the one-armed man who worked around a railroad station. Everybody annoyed him by asking him how he lost his arm, so one day he said to a questioner, 'I'll tell you how I lost my arm if you promise to ask me no more questions.' The man promised. 'It was bit off,' he said."

"Then what is your candid opinion?" I asked, answering his smile.

"There should be no such thing—there should be no proposing."

Hum! I bit my lips. He had my promise and I was helpless.

So it rests. Shall women propose, or shall they always tune their harps and sing:

> "Never wedding, ever wooing,
> Still a lovelorn heart pursuing.
> Read you not the wrong you're doing
> In my cheek's pale hue?
> All my life with sorrow strewing;
> Wed, or cease to woo."[12]

The New York World,
NOV. 11, 1888

SUSAN B. ANTHONY

Bly's admiring interview with venerable suffragist Susan B. Anthony (1820–1906) was featured in *The New York World* in 1896, just a few days after the paper had published Bly's detailed coverage of the National Woman Suffrage Convention in Washington, D.C. The interview is remarkable for its candor. Although Anthony was a recognizable public figure who spoke out tirelessly to promote equal rights for women, she was rarely so forthcoming about her personal life.

CHAMPION OF HER SEX: MISS SUSAN B. ANTHONY

Miss Susan B. Anthony Tells the Remarkable Story of Her Life to "Nellie Bly"

WOMAN SUFFRAGE MUST COME

Interesting Views, Ideas, and Opinions on All the Live Questions of the Hour

---

ADVANCED THEORIES ABOUT MARRIAGE

Perfectly Proper for Women to Propose Now That They Are Independent Wage-Earners

---

Susan B. Anthony! She was waiting for me. I stood for an instant in the doorway and looked at her. She made a picture to remember and to cherish.

She sat in a low rocking chair, an image of repose and restfulness. Her well-shaped head, with its silken snowy hair combed smoothly over her ears, rested against the back of the chair. Her shawl had half-fallen from her shoulders and her soft black silk gown lay in gentle folds about her. Her slender hands lay folded idly in her lap, and her feet, crossed, just peeped from beneath the edge of her skirt. If she had been posed for a picture, it could not have been done more artistically or perfectly.

"Do you know the world is a blank to me," she said after we had exchanged greetings. "I haven't read a newspaper in ten days and I feel lost to everything. Tell me about Cuba! I am so interested in it. I would postpone my own enfranchisement to see Cuba free."[1]

I had gone to talk to her of her own great self, not Cuba, so after I told her briefly how matters stood, I instantly followed it up with a question about herself.

"Tell me, what was the cause of your being a suffragist? How did you begin?" I asked.

"My being a suffragist resulted from many other things that happened to me early in my life," she answered, unclasping her hands and resting them on the arms of her chair. "I remember the first time I heard of suffragists I was bored and complained because my family were so intensely interested in the subject. 'Can't you find anything else to talk about?' I asked my sisters in disgust. That was over fifty years ago."

HER FAMILY HISTORY

"Let me tell you of my family, and then you can understand it better," she continued. "I was born in South Adams, Mass. My mother and my father were born in the same town. My father was a Quaker and my mother was a Methodist, so you see at once began the question of the education of the children. There were four girls and two boys in the family. My father was a practical man. He believed in the equality of his daughters even in those days. One of my sisters was a splendid businesswoman and was a great assistance to my father. He said he would put Anthony & Daughters on his business house if he hadn't known that such a move would kill him. People were very narrow in those days.

"My family were my strong supporters when I first started out," she said earnestly. "I don't think I could ever have done my public work, Nellie, if I had had opposition at home. My youngest sister, who taught school twenty-six consecutive years, superintended everything I wore, and I was relieved of every home responsibility. Before I would go to a town to speak, ministers would preach against me. They would say I was a member of the Quaker Friends and, while we were good people morally, we had no orthodox religion. When I went home disheartened and told my father, he would say, 'My child, you should have thought of such a text to quote against them.' And he could always furnish me with some text that aptly replied to my enemies."

"But what gave you the idea of becoming a suffrage leader?" I urged.

HER FIRST IDEA OF SUFFRAGE

"Many people will tell you," she answered, smiling, "that from their earliest days they cherished the ideas that eventually became their life work. I won't. As a little girl my highest ideal was to be a Quaker minister. I wanted to be inspired by God to speak in church. That was my highest ambition. My father believed in educating his girls so they could be self-supporting if necessary. In olden times there was only one avenue open to women. That was teaching. So every one of us girls took turns at teaching. I began when I was fifteen and taught until I was thirty.

"I think the first seed for thought was planted during my early days as a teacher. I saw the injustice of paying stupid men double or treble women's wages for teaching merely because they were men. . . ."

"Tell me about your first school," I pleaded. "Were you frightened?"

Susan B. Anthony leaned on the arm of the chair and smiled at me.

USED TO THINK SHE KNEW IT ALL

"I wasn't a bit timid," she said frankly. "I was only fifteen, but I thought I was the wisest girl in all the world. I knew it all. No one could make me think anything else. The first time I taught was in 1835. An old Quaker lady came to our house for a teacher for her children and several of her neighbors', making in all a class of eight. I accepted the position. I lived in her family, and for teaching the children three hours before dinner and three hours after, I got $1 a week and my board.

"After that, as I wanted to finish my own studies, I taught in the summer and went to school in the winter. And my father was the richest man in the county, too. For several terms I taught district school and boarded among my pupils. My pay was $1.50 a week. In 1837 I gave up teaching and came to Philadelphia to a boarding school."

"Did you ever whip any of your scholars?" I inquired anxiously.

"Oh, my, yes!" she laughed. "I whipped lots of them. I recall one pupil I had. I was very young at the time, I had been warned that he had put the last master out of the window and that he would surely insult me. I went into that school boy when he began on me, I made him take off his coat and I gave him a good whipping with a stout switch. He was twice as large as I, but he behaved after that.

"In those days," she said, "we did not know any other way to control children. We believed in the goodness of not sparing the rod. As I got older I abolished whipping. If I couldn't manage a child, I thought it my ignorance, my lack of ability as a teacher. I always felt less the woman when I struck a blow.

"You spoke in your article the other day[2] about the way some of our women dress," Miss Anthony observed, suddenly changing the topic. "Forty-five years ago I tried a reform dress. But I gave it up. People couldn't see a great intellect under grotesque clothes. Although I saw Horace Greeley[3] go before an audience once with one trouser leg inside his boot and one outside!" . . .

"For whom were you named?" I asked.

"I was named Susan after my father's sister and after my grandmother on my mother's side. My grandmother's name was Susannah, but they never put the ah on me. When I was a young woman there came a great craze for middle initials. We girls scratched our heads to find one. The aunt who named me afterwards married a man named Brownell, and I decided to take her initials for mine. So you see I named myself. And I am always glad I did. There might be a thousand Susan Anthonys, but the B. makes it distinctive."

EQUAL RIGHTS WITH MEN

"Now you want to know when I first heard of woman suffrage," she resumed. "I will tell you. In 1848 I came home at the end of my school term to visit my family. Mrs. Stanton and Mrs. Mott had just been in Rochester,[4] and my family could talk of nothing else. I didn't understand suffrage, but I knew I wanted equal wages with men teachers. However, I had no idea between voting and equality. I went back to my school and forgot all about it.

"In 1849 I heard Abby Kelley Foster,[5] the Quaker Abolitionist, and I read the reports of a great convention that gave me the first clear statement of the underlying principles of woman suffrage. The next year I went to an abolition meeting at Seneca Falls where I met Mrs. Stanton, who was head of the Daughters of Temperance society.[6] As I was a schoolmarm, I was asked to make a speech. I've got the yellow manuscript now of that speech. There was nothing to it. I never could think of points, and I can't write a speech out. I must have an audience to inspire me. When I am before a house filled with people I can speak, but to save my life I couldn't write a speech.

"A little later the Sons of Temperance held a convention at Albany, and they invited the Daughters to send delegates. I was one of the delegates. They were assembled in the hall and something was under discussion when I arose to address the Grand Worthy Master. 'The sister will allow me to say,' he shouted to me, 'that we invited them here to look and learn, but not to speak.'

"I instantly left the hall, and Lydia Mott, cousin of Mrs. Mott's husband,[7] followed me. We hired a hall, and got Thurlow Weed[8] to announce in his paper, the Evening Journal, that the Woman's Temperance Society would hold a meeting that evening.

"Hon. David Wright[9] and Rev. Samuel J. May, father of Rev. Joseph May, of Philadelphia,[10] came to our meeting, and dear Rev. May taught us how to preside. I was made Chairwoman of the committee, and the first thing I did was to call a state convention. I got the call signed by such distinguished men as Horace Greeley and Henry Ward Beecher.[11] We held a two days' convention and Mrs. Stanton was made President and I was Secretary. And it all came out of the men refusing to let me speak."

SECRET OF HER WORK

"The secret of all my work," she said, "is that when there is something to do, I do it. I rolled up a mammoth temperance petition of 28,000 names and it was presented to the Legislature.[12] When it came up for discussion one man made an eloquent speech against it. 'And who are these,' he asked, 'who signed the petition? Nothing but women and children.' Then I said to myself, 'Why shouldn't women's names be as powerful as men's? They would be if women had the power to vote. Then that man wouldn't have been so eloquent against temperance, for he would have known that the women would vote his head off.' I vowed there and then women should be equal. Women could not respect themselves or get men to respect them as equal until they had the power to vote. . . .'"

"Are you afraid of death?"

"I don't know anything about Heaven or hell," she answered, "or whether I will ever meet my friends again or not. But as no particle of matter is ever lost, I have a feeling that no particle of mind is ever lost. The thought doesn't bother me. I feel that nothing is lost and that the hereafter will be managed as this life is managed now."

"Then you don't find life tiresome?"

"Oh mercy, no! I don't want to die just as long as I can work. The minute I can't, I want to go. I dread the thought of being enfeebled. I find the older I get the greater power I have to help the world. I feel like a snowball—the further I am rolled the more I gain. When my powers begin to lessen, I want to go. But," she added, significantly, "I'll have to take it as it comes. I'm just as much in the hands of eternity now as when the breath goes out of my body."

SOME IDEAS ON PRAYER AND MARRIAGE

"Do you pray?"

"I pray every single second of my life. I never get on my knees or anything like that, but I pray with my works. My prayer is to lift women to equality with men. Work and worship are one with me." . . .

"Do you think women should propose?"

"Yes!" very decidedly. "If she can see a man she can love. She has the right to propose today that she did not have some years ago because she has become a bread winner. Once a proposal from a woman would have meant, 'Will you please support me, sir?' And I think woman will make better choices than man. She'll know quicker what man will suit her and whether he loves her and she loves him." . . .

"Let me tell you what I think of bicycling," Miss Anthony said, leaning forward and laying a slender hand on my arm. "I think it has done more to emancipate women than anything else in the world. I stand and rejoice every time I see a woman ride by on a wheel. It gives woman a feeling of freedom and self-reliance. It makes her feel as if she were independent. The moment she takes her seat she knows she can't get into harm unless she gets off her bicycle, and away she goes, the picture of free, untrammeled womanhood."

"And bloomers?" I suggested, quietly.

"Are the proper thing for wheeling," added Miss Anthony promptly. "It is as I have said—dress to suit the occasion. A woman doesn't want skirts and flimsy lace to catch in the wheel. Safety, as well as modesty, demands bloomers or extremely short skirts. You know women only wear foolish articles of dress to please men's eyes anyway."

WHAT WILL THE NEW WOMAN BE?

"What do you think the new woman will be?"

"She'll be free," said Miss Anthony. "Then she'll be whatever her best judgment wants to be. We can no more imagine what the true woman will be than we can what the true man will be." . . .

"Who is the greatest woman of our time?"

"Elizabeth Cady Stanton. She is a philosopher, a statesman, and a prophet. She is wonderfully gifted—more gifted than any person I ever knew, man or woman—had she possessed the privileges of a man her fame would have been world-wide and she would have been the greatest person of her time."

"And now," I said, approaching a very delicate subject on tip-toes, "tell me one thing more. Were you ever in love?"

"In love?" she laughed merrily. "Bless you, Nellie, I've been in love a thousand times!"

"Really?" I gasped, taken aback by this startling confession.

"Yes, really!" nodding her snowy head. "But I never loved any one so much that I thought it would last. In fact I never felt I could give up my life of freedom to become a man's housekeeper. When I was young, if a girl married poor, she became a housekeeper and a drudge. If she married wealth she became a pet and a doll. Just think, had I married at twenty, I would have been either a drudge or a doll for fifty-five years. Think of it!

"I want to add one thing," she said. "Once men were afraid of women with ideas and a desire to vote. Today our best suffragists are sought in marriage by the best class of men." . . .

Susan B. Anthony is all that is best and noblest in woman. She is ideal and if we will have in women who vote what we have in her, let us all help to promote the cause of woman suffrage.

from "SUSAN B. ANTHONY," *The New York World,*
FEB. 2, 1896

V.

GLOBETROTTER

In the heyday of stunt journalism, assigning a reporter to break the record for the fastest trip around the world was a good idea. Assigning the task to a woman was an even better one. Respectable women rarely traveled alone, and even if they did, convention dictated that they bring a lot of luggage with them. It was especially noteworthy, then, that when Nellie Bly set out to circumnavigate the globe in November 1889, she went unchaperoned and she carried only a single bag she could grip with one hand. Her goal was to beat the fictional record set by Phileas Fogg, the British hero who circled the globe in Jules Verne's popular novel *Around the World in Eighty Days*. Bly was in Hong Kong and more than halfway through her journey before she realized that she had a real-life competitor as well. A rival New York publication, *Cosmopolitan* magazine, had sent its own newspaperwoman, Elizabeth Bisland, off to race in the opposite direction, hoping to beat Bly home. Bly won the race, and the *World*'s venture attracted as much attention as her editors could have possibly hoped for: It gave Joseph Pulitzer's famously self-promoting newspaper a spectacular opportunity to fund, execute, and celebrate its very own unique historical phenomenon.

Bly's trip transformed her from celebrity journalist to American icon, an emblem of boldness and imagination in a modern world crisscrossed by steamships and transcontinental railroads. This single American woman, who traveled 21,700 miles without an extra dress, made the entire globe seem more accessible to everyone. Yet the success of Bly's stunt depended at least as much on editorial spin as it did on steamship captains and railroad engineers. She dashed off an occasional cable while she was traveling, but time pressure and the limits of technology made it impossible for her to share much of anything with her readers until after she was back in New York. Still, the *World* found a way to mention Bly's trip in every edition of the newspaper from the day she left until the day she came home. The paper published updates on Bly's itinerary, commentary about her trip from other newspapers, and letters from readers about the stunt. Examples of the newspaper updates about Bly's trip are interspersed in the text reprinted below. In what turned out to be a brilliant marketing move, the paper sponsored a Nellie Bly Guessing Contest: entrants had to estimate, down to the second, how long it would take Bly to circle the globe. The grand prize was a trip to Europe, hotel accommodations for a week each in London and Paris, and 50 pounds of spending money. The *World* allowed people to enter as many times as they wished, as long as they bought an extra edition of the Sunday paper and used the special coupon printed inside. By the time Bly was close enough to home that the paper stopped accepting entries, they had received 927,433 coupons.[1] The winner, a handsome young New Yorker named F. W. Stevens, was closest to Bly's actual time of 72 days, 6 hours, 11 minutes, and 14 seconds.[2] When she entered the final phase of her trip—a dash from San Francisco to New Jersey on the fastest train the *World* could arrange—she was met by crowds of well-wishers at every stop. The *World* published a full-page Nellie Bly board game, a spiral of seventy-two illustrated squares with instructions like "Indian Mail Accident/Go Back 5 Spaces" and "Malacca Straits/Go Ahead 1 Day."

Plenty of women had traveled the world before Bly. None, however, had sought or attained her level of celebrity. The gleeful *World* printed a letter from one Bly enthusiast with some wry advice: "The next time Nellie Bly encircles the globe it would be advisable for you to issue papers enough to supply your customers. I had to travel a mile and a half in Brooklyn this morning before I could get a *World*, and then I had to borrow one" (*The New York World*, Jan. 28, 1890). The image of Bly in her traveling outfit—a cap, a high-necked blue jacket and skirt, and a long wool coat in a bold checked pattern—was so popular that women copied the uniform for more than decade. Bly's account of her trip, published in four installments in the *World* and later reprinted as *Nellie Bly's Book: Around the*

World in Seventy-Two Days, showcased some of her most appealing traits: her daring, her determination, her willingness
to laugh at herself. It also exposed a less appealing side, such
as her relative lack of interest in cultures different from her
own and her racist views, especially of Chinese and South
Asians. When she was delayed for five days in Ceylon (now
Sri Lanka), a tropical island so beautiful that both Muslim
and Christian accounts have suggested it could have been the
original Garden of Eden, she produced some lyrical passages,
but for the most part, she found relatively little of interest in
the natural landscape, ancient palaces, or Hindu and Buddhist
temples. Some parts of Bly's travelogue—such as her visit to a
leper colony in China, and her bemused account of the Malaysian laborers who, after loading coal onto the ship, struggled
to return to shore in rough seas—are startling in their lack of
empathy and understanding. She never inquired, either, into
the inhuman conditions faced by the stokers who shoveled coal
into the furnaces of the great steamships that were bearing her
so swiftly through the waves. Preoccupied by her own itinerary, she skimmed along the surface of the world, her reporto-
rial instincts blunted by either the grandness of her ambition
or the sheer magnitude of the undertaking. Yet her travelogue
still stands as a matchless record of a young woman charging
through the world, more entranced by her own sense of purpose than by anything she might see along the way. Bly cap-
tures most effectively the restless spirit of her starting place, a
nation on the brink of becoming a world power.

FROM *AROUND THE WORLD IN SEVENTY-TWO DAYS*

(New York: Pictorial Weeklies Company, 1890)

CHAPTER I

A Proposal to Girdle the Earth

What gave me the idea?

It is sometimes difficult to tell exactly what gives birth to an idea. Ideas are the chief stock in trade of newspaper writers and generally they are the scarcest stock in market, but they do come occasionally.

This idea came to me one Sunday. I had spent a greater part of the day and half the night vainly trying to fasten on some idea for a newspaper article. It was my custom to think up ideas on Sunday and lay them before my editor for his approval or disapproval on Monday. But ideas did not come that day and three o'clock in the morning found me weary and with an aching head tossing about in my bed. At last tired and provoked at my slowness in finding a subject, something for the week's work, I thought fretfully:

"I wish I was at the other end of the earth!"

"And why not?" the thought came: "I need a vacation; why not take a trip around the world?"

It is easy to see how one thought followed another. The idea of a trip around the world pleased me and I added: "If I could do it as quickly as Phileas Fogg[3] did, I should go."

Then I wondered if it were possible to do the trip in eighty days and afterwards I went easily off to sleep with the determination to know before I saw my bed again if Phileas Fogg's record could be broken.

I went to a steamship company's office that day and made a selection of timetables. Anxiously I sat down and went over them and if I had found the elixir of life I should not have felt better than I did when I conceived a hope that a tour of the world might be made in even less than eighty days.

I approached my editor rather timidly on the subject. I was afraid that he would think the idea too wild and visionary.

"Have you any ideas?" he asked, as I sat down by his desk.

"One," I answered quietly.

He sat toying with his pens, waiting for me to continue, so I blurted out:

"I want to go around the world!"

"Well?" he said, inquiringly looking up with a faint smile in his kind eyes.

"I want to go around in eighty days or less. I think I can beat Phileas Fogg's record. May I try it?"

To my dismay he told me that in the office they had thought of this same idea before and the intention was to send a man. However he offered me the consolation that he would favor my going, and then we went to talk with the business manager about it.

"It is impossible for you to do it," was the terrible verdict. "In the first place you are a woman and would need a protector, and even if it were possible for you to travel alone you would need to carry so much baggage that it would detain you in making rapid changes. Besides you speak nothing but English, so there is no use talking about it; no one but a man can do this."

"Very well," I said angrily, "Start the man, and I'll start the same day for some other newspaper and beat him."

"I believe you would," he said slowly. I would not say that this had any influence on their decision, but I do know that before we parted I was made happy by the promise that if any one was commissioned to make the trip, I should be that one.

After I had made my arrangements to go, other important projects for gathering news came up, and this rather visionary idea was put aside for a while.

One cold, wet evening, a year after this discussion, I received a little note asking me to come to the office at once. A summons, late in the afternoon, was such an unusual thing to me that I was to be excused if I spent all my time on the way to the office wondering what I was to be scolded for.

I went in and sat down beside the editor waiting for him to speak. He looked up from the paper on which he was writing and asked quietly: "Can you start around the world day after tomorrow?"

"I can start this minute," I answered, quickly trying to stop the rapid beating of my heart.

"We did think of starting you on the City of Paris tomorrow morning, so as to give you ample time to catch the mail train out of London. There is a chance if the Augusta Victoria, which sails the morning afterwards, has rough weather of your failing to connect with the mail train."

"I will take my chances on the Augusta Victoria, and save one extra day," I said.

The next morning I went to Ghormley, the fashionable dressmaker, to order a dress. It was after eleven o'clock when I got there and it took but very few moments to tell him what I wanted.

I always have a comfortable feeling that nothing is impossible if one applies a certain amount of energy in the right direction. When I want things done, which is always at the last moment, and I am met with such an answer: "It's too late. I hardly think it can be done;" I simply say:

"Nonsense! If you want to do it, you can do it. The question is, do you want to do it?"

I have never met the man or woman yet who was not aroused by that answer into doing their very best.

If we want good work from others or wish to accomplish anything ourselves, it will never do to harbor a doubt as to the result of an enterprise.

So, when I went to Ghormley's, I said to him: "I want a dress by this evening."

"Very well," he answered as unconcernedly as if it were an everyday thing for a young woman to order a gown on a few hours' notice.

"I want a dress that will stand constant wear for three months," I added, and then let the responsibility rest on him.

Bringing out several different materials he threw them in artistic folds over a small table, studying the effect in a pier glass before which he stood.

He did not become nervous or hurried. All the time that he was trying the different effects of the materials, he kept up a lively and half humorous conversation. In a few moments he had selected a plain blue broadcloth and a quiet plaid camel's-hair as the most durable and suitable combination for a traveling gown.

Before I left, probably one o'clock, I had my first fitting. When I returned at five o'clock for a second fitting, the dress was finished. I considered this promptness and speed a good omen and quite in keeping with the project.

After leaving Ghormley's I went to a shop and ordered an ulster. Then going to another dressmaker's, I ordered a lighter dress to carry with me to be worn in the land where I would find summer.

I bought one handbag with the determination to confine my baggage to its limit.

That night there was nothing to do but write to my few friends a line of farewell and to pack the handbag.

Packing that bag was the most difficult undertaking of my life; there was so much to go into such little space.

I got everything in at last except the extra dress. Then the question resolved itself into this: I must either add a parcel to my baggage or go around the world in and with one dress. I always hated parcels so I sacrificed the dress, but I brought out a last summer's silk bodice and after considerable squeezing managed to crush it into the handbag.

I think that I went away one of the most superstitious of girls. My editor had told me the day before the trip had been decided upon of an inauspicious dream he had had. It seemed that I came to him and told him I was going to run a race. Doubting my ability as a runner, he thought he turned his back so that he should not witness the race. He heard the band play, as it does on such occasions, and heard the applause that greeted the finish. Then I came to him with my eyes filled with tears and said: "I have lost the race."

"I can translate that dream," I said, when he finished; "I will start to secure some news and some one else will beat me."

When I was told the next day that I was to go around the world I felt a prophetic awe steal over me. I feared that Time would win the race and that I should not make the tour in eighty days or less.

Nor was my health good when I was told to go around the world in the shortest time possible at that season of the year. For almost a year I had been a daily sufferer from headache, and only the week previous I had consulted a number of eminent physicians fearing that my health was becoming impaired by too constant application to work. I had been doing newspaper work for almost three years, during which time I had not enjoyed one day's vacation. It is not surprising then that I looked on this trip as a most delightful and much needed rest.

The evening before I started I went to the office and was given £200 in English gold and Bank of England notes. The gold I carried in my pocket. The Bank of England notes were placed in a chamois-skin bag which I tied around my neck. Besides this I took some American gold and paper money to use at different ports as a test to see if American money was known outside of America.

Down in the bottom of my handbag was a special passport, number 247, signed by James G. Blaine, Secretary of State.[4] Someone suggested that a revolver would be a good companion piece for the passport, but I had such a strong belief in the world's greeting me as I greeted it, that I refused to arm myself. I knew if my conduct was proper I should always find men ready to protect me, let them be Americans, English, French, German or anything else.

It is quite possible to buy tickets in New York for the entire trip, but I thought that I might be compelled to change my route at almost any point, so the only transportation I had provided on leaving New York was my ticket to London.

When I went to the office to say good-bye, I found that no itinerary had been made of my contemplated trip and there was some doubt as to whether the mail train which I expected to take to Brindisi,[5] left London every Friday night. Nor did we know whether the week of my expected arrival in London was the one in which it connected with the ship for India or the ship for China. In fact when I arrived at Brindisi and found the ship was bound for Australia, I was the most surprised girl in the world.

I followed a man who had been sent to a steamship company's office to try to make out a schedule and help them arrange one as best they could on this side of the water.[6] How near it came to being correct can be seen later on.

I have been asked very often since my return how many changes of clothing I took in my solitary handbag. Some have thought I took but one; others think I carried silk which occupies but little space, and others have asked if I did not buy what I needed at the different ports.

One never knows the capacity of an ordinary hand-satchel until dire necessity compels the exercise of all one's ingenuity to reduce every thing to the smallest possible compass. In mine I was able to pack two traveling caps, three veils, a pair of slippers, a complete outfit of toilet articles, ink-stand, pens, pencils, and copy-paper, pins, needles and thread, a dressing gown, a tennis blazer, a small flask and a drinking cup, several complete changes of underwear, a liberal supply of handkerchiefs and fresh ruchings and most bulky and uncompromising of all, a jar of cold cream to keep my face from chapping in the varied climates I should encounter.

That jar of cold cream was the bane of my existence. It seemed to take up more room than everything else in the bag and was always getting into just the place that would keep me from closing the satchel. Over my arm I carried a silk waterproof, the only provision I made against rainy weather. Afterexperience showed me that I had taken too much rather than too little baggage. At every port where I stopped at I could have bought anything from a ready-made dress down, except possibly at Aden,[7] and as I did not visit the shops there I cannot speak from knowledge. . . .

So much for my preparations. It will be seen that if one is traveling simply for the sake of traveling and not for the purpose of impressing one's fellow passengers, the problem of baggage becomes a very simple one. On one occasion—in Hong Kong, where I was asked to an official dinner—I regretted not having an evening dress with me, but the loss of that dinner was a very small matter when compared with the responsibilities and worries I escaped by not having a lot of trunks and boxes to look after.

CHAPTER II

The Start

On Thursday, November 14, 1889, at 9.40.30 o'clock, I started on my tour around the world.

Those who think that night is the best part of the day and that morning was made for sleep, know how uncomfortable they feel when for some reason they have to get up with—well, with the milkman.

I turned over several times before I decided to quit my bed. I wondered sleepily why a bed feels so much more luxurious, and a stolen nap that threatens the loss of a train is so much more sweet, than those hours of sleep that are free from duty's call. I half promised myself that on my return I would pretend sometime that it was urgent that I should get up so I could taste the pleasure of a stolen nap without actually losing anything by it. I dozed off very sweetly over these thoughts to wake with a start, wondering anxiously if there was still time to catch the ship.

Of course I wanted to go, but I thought lazily that if some of these good people who spend so much time in trying to invent flying machines would only devote a little of the same energy towards promoting a system by which boats and trains would always make their start at noon or afterwards, they would be of greater assistance to suffering humanity.

I endeavored to take some breakfast, but the hour was too early to make food endurable. The last moment at home came. There was a hasty kiss for the dear ones, and a blind rush downstairs trying to overcome the hard lump in my throat that threatened to make me regret the journey that lay before me.

"Don't worry," I said encouragingly, as I was unable to speak that dreadful word, good-bye; "only think of me as having a vacation and the most enjoyable time in my life."

Then to encourage myself I thought, as I was on my way to the ship: "It's only a matter of 28,000 miles, and seventy-five days and four hours, until I shall be back again."

A few friends who were told of my hurried departure were there to say good-bye. The morning was bright and beautiful, and everything seemed very pleasant while the boat was still; but when they were warned to go ashore, I began to realize what it meant for me.

"Keep up your courage," they said to me while they gave my hand the farewell clasp. I saw the moisture in their eyes and I tried to smile so that their last recollection of me would be one that would cheer them.

But when the whistle blew and they were on the pier, and I was on the Augusta Victoria, which was slowly but surely moving away from all I knew, taking me to strange lands and strange people, I felt lost. My head felt dizzy and my heart felt as if it would burst. Only seventy-five days! Yes, but it seemed an age and the world lost its roundness and seemed a long distance with no end, and—well, I never turn back.

I looked as long as I could at the people on the pier. I did not feel as happy as I have at other times in life. I had a sentimental longing to take farewell of everything.

"I am off," I thought sadly, "and shall I ever get back?"

Intense heat, bitter cold, terrible storms, shipwrecks, fevers, all such agreeable topics had been drummed into me until I felt much as I imagine one would feel if shut in a cave of midnight darkness and told that all sorts of horrors were waiting to gobble one up.

The morning was beautiful and the bay never looked lovelier. The ship glided out smoothly and quietly, and the people on deck looked for their chairs and rugs and got into comfortable positions, as if determined to enjoy themselves while they could, for they did not know what moment someone would be enjoying themselves at their expense.

NELLIE BLY IS OFF

She Takes the World in Her Great Race Against Time Around the Globe

---

WILL SHE BEAT THE RECORD?

The Plucky Newspaper Globe-Trotter Sailed at 9.40 A. M. Yesterday

---

SHE CARRIES BUT ONE GOWN

The Leader of a Host of Imitators Was in Good Spirits as the Augusta Victoria Sailed Down the Bay—Already Another Globe-Trotter Has Started Westward and May Meet Miss Bly Coming Home[8]—Travellers Here and in Other Big Cities Are Intensely Interested in the Trip—Dr. Chauncey Depew Says That It May Cause a Social Revolution in the East—"Jules Verne's Pace Is Too Slow for 'The World,'" Says a Thoughtful Westerner.

Miss Bly, when this page reaches its readers, will be far out at sea, just about a day on her way round the globe. If a good beginning is half the struggle, then the intrepid, petticoated traveller has nothing to complain of. A finer morning for a start on a sea trip could not have been chosen, and the crisp November air freshened her fair young cheeks as she stood blushingly in the centre of a group of admiring and rather envious gentlemen and chatted first with one, then another, and then all together. There was not a wince of fear or trepidation, and no youngster just let loose from school could have been more merry and light-hearted.

She came, bright and early, to the steamer, having taken an affectionate farewell of her mother after a hearty breakfast. Then grasping that not over-bulky gripsack, all in its bright, clean newness, she took a democratic horsecar down to Christopher street ferry, took her chances of getting across the river by that uncertain route, lay locked in the New York berth while a great, long White Star steamer rested across the mouth of the slip, then lay in midstream until a great rumbling mass of coal barges had lazily crawled by the Hoboken slip to the Lackawanna docks besides, and finally found herself within the broad domain set apart to the uses of the Hamburg-American Company. She was quickly under the escort of General Passenger Agents O. L. Richard and Emil L. Boas, who paid her particular attention. Commander Albers[9] was presented to the pretty passenger and assured her that he would do all he could to see that the initial part of her complex voyage by sea and land was a complete success. The popular commander felt certain that he could be able to put her ashore in Southampton Thursday evening, and that she could take a quiet night's sleep in a hotel and be up in time for any one of a dozen trains which would run her up to Lunnen[10] over the two-hours' schedule of running time between the Channel seaport and the city on the Thames.

"I won't take any sleep until I am in London and made sure of my place in that bakers' dozen who go from Victoria Station on Friday night," said the globe trotter, and got a smile of approval from the captain of the big Augusta Victoria.

FROM *The New York World*, NOV. 15, 1889

———

When the pilot went off everybody rushed to the side of the ship to see him go down the little rope ladder. I watched him closely, but he climbed down and into the rowboat, that was waiting to carry him to the pilot boat, without giving one glance back to us. It was an old story to him, but I could not help wondering if the ship should go down, whether there would not be some word or glance he would wish he had given.

"You have now started on your trip," someone said to me. "As soon as the pilot goes off and the captain assumes command, then, and only then our voyage begins, so now you are really started on your tour around the world."

Something in his words turned my thoughts to that demon of the sea—seasickness.

Never having taken a sea voyage before, I could expect nothing else than a lively tussle with the disease of the wave.

"Do you get seasick?" I was asked in an interested, friendly way. That was enough; I flew to the railing.

Sick? I looked blindly down, caring little what the wild waves were saying, and gave vent to my feelings.

People are always unfeeling about seasickness. When I wiped the tears from my eyes and turned around, I saw smiles on the face of every passenger. I have noticed that they are always on the same side of the ship when one is taken suddenly, overcome, as it were, with one's own emotions.

The smiles did not bother me, but one man said sneeringly: "And she's going around the world!"

I too joined in the laugh that followed. Silently I marveled at my boldness to attempt such a feat wholly unused, as I was, to sea-voyages. Still I did not entertain one doubt as to the result.

Of course I went to luncheon. Everybody did, and almost everybody left very hurriedly. I joined them, or, I don't know, probably I made the start. Anyway I never saw as many in the dining room at any one time during the rest of the voyage.

When dinner was served I went in very bravely and took my place on the Captain's left. I had a very strong determination to resist my impulses, but yet, in the bottom of my heart was a little faint feeling that I had found something even stronger than my will power.

Dinner began very pleasantly. The waiters moved about noiselessly, the band played an overture, Captain Albers, handsome and genial, took his place at the head, and the passengers who were seated at his table began dinner with a relish equaled only by enthusiastic wheelmen when roads are fine. I was the only one at the Captain's table who might be called an amateur sailor. I was bitterly conscious of this fact. So were the others.

I might as well confess it, while soup was being served, I was lost in painful thoughts and filled with a sickening fear. I felt that everything was just as pleasant as an unexpected gift on Christmas, and I endeavored to listen to the enthusiastic remarks about the music made by my companions, but my thoughts were on a topic that would not bear discussion.

I felt cold, I felt warm; I felt that I should not get hungry if I did not see food for seven days; in fact, I had a great, longing desire not to see it, nor to smell it, nor to eat of it, until I could reach land or a better understanding with myself.

Fish was served, and Captain Albers was in the midst of a good story when I felt I had more than I could endure.

"Excuse me," I whispered faintly, and then rushed, madly, blindly out. I was assisted to a secluded spot where a little reflection and a little unbridling of pent up emotion restored me to such a courageous state that I determined to take the Captain's advice and return to my unfinished dinner.

"The only way to conquer seasickness is by forcing one's self to eat," the Captain said, and I thought the remedy harmless enough to test.

They congratulated me on my return. I had a shamed feeling that I was going to misbehave again, but I tried to hide the fact from them. It came soon, and I disappeared at the same rate of speed as before.

Once again I returned. This time my nerves felt a little unsteady and my belief in my determination was weakening. Hardly had I seated myself when I caught an amused gleam of a steward's eye, which made me bury my face in my handkerchief and choke before I reached the limits of the dining hall.

The bravos with which they kindly greeted my third return to the table almost threatened to make me lose my bearings again. I was glad to know that dinner was just finished and I had the boldness to say that it was very good!

I went to bed shortly afterwards. No one had made any friends yet, so I concluded sleep would be more enjoyable than sitting in the music hall looking at other passengers engaged in the same first-day-at-sea occupation.

SHE WILL HAVE TO HUSTLE

Can Old Sol Make 75 Laps Around the Earth to Nellie Bly's One?

A CALIFORNIAN FIGURES THAT THE TRIP CAN BE MADE IN 72 DAYS

But the Figuring Is Done on Paper and Doesn't Count for Much in a Race Against Time—"The World's" Latest Has Set Globe-Trotters to Thinking—Many Wagers Being Made on the Result.

[SPECIAL TO THE WORLD.]

San Francisco, Nov. 15.—Miss Nellie Bly's globe-trotting enterprise is being made the subject of numerous bets here, and opinion is about equally divided as to whether or not she can complete the circuit on time. There will be many persons watching as the time rolls around for the steamer on which the adventurous young woman should reach this point. Those who ought to know say that barring accidents Miss Nellie should be able to circumnavigate the globe in seventy-five days and have time to spare to write interesting letters to The World, as well as to be examined for insanity by doctors in Brindisi and Yokohama.[11] The time she will spend in transit on steamers and railroads should not be more than sixty-one days.

FROM *The New York World*, NOV. 16, 1889

I went to bed shortly after seven o'clock. I had a dim recollection afterwards of waking up enough to drink some tea, but beyond this and the remembrance of some dreadful dreams, I knew nothing until I heard an honest, jolly voice at the door calling to me.

Opening my eyes I found the stewardess and a lady passenger in my cabin and saw the Captain standing at the door.

"We were afraid that you were dead," the Captain said when he saw that I was awake.

"I always sleep late in the morning," I said apologetically.

"In the morning!" the Captain exclaimed, with a laugh, which was echoed by the others, "It is half-past four in the evening!"

"But never mind," he added consolingly, "as long as you slept well it will do you good. Now get up and see if you can't eat a big dinner."

I did. I went through every course at dinner without flinching, and stranger still, I slept that night as well as people are commonly supposed to sleep after long exercise in the open air.

The weather was very bad, and the sea was rough, but I enjoyed it. My seasickness had disappeared, but I had a morbid, haunting idea, that although it was gone, it would come again, still I managed to make myself comfortable. . . .

NELLIE BLY'S TRIP

Confidence in a Woman's Ability Is All That Is Wanted

No doubt about it. The *World*, in sending its bright little correspondent upon such a novel, yet hazardous mission, has with one unique stroke accomplished more for my sex than could have been achieved in any other way in a decade. The long-felt want of confidence in woman's ability to dare and to do has kept many struggling souls upon the very lowest round of the ladder.

This odd but clever departure from every rule that has heretofore governed the newspaper kingdom is a stirring editorial upon woman's pluck and woman's energy and swings wide open the door that leads to success in every branch of the world of letters. It also goes a long way toward proving that the gentler sex, released from depreciating influences and given a sound body to cooperate with the divine inspiration of the mind, may compete most successfully with the brightest men of the day.

DOROTHY MADDOX[12]

FROM *The Philadelphia Inquirer*, NOV. 18, 1889

Many were the discussions about the erroneous impression entertained by most foreigners about Americans and America. Some one remarked that the majority of people in foreign lands were not able to tell where the United States is.

"There are plenty of people who think the United States is one little island, with a few houses on it," Captain Albers said. "Once there was delivered at my house, near the wharf, in Hoboken, a letter from Germany, addressed to,

'CAPTAIN ALBERS,
FIRST HOUSE IN AMERICA.'"

"I got one from Germany once," said the most bashful man at the table, his face flushing at the sound of his own voice, "addressed to,

'HOBOKEN, OPPOSITE THE UNITED STATES.'"

While at luncheon on the 21st of November, some one called out that we were in sight of land. The way everyone left the table and rushed on deck was surely not surpassed by the companions of Columbus when they discovered America. I cannot give any good reason for it, but I know that I looked at the first point of bleak land with more interest than I would have bestowed on the most beautiful bit of scenery in the world.

We had not been long in sight of land until the decks began to fill with dazed-looking, wan-faced people. It was just as if we had taken on new passengers. We could not realize that they were from New York and had been enjoying (?)[13] a season of seclusion since leaving that port.

Dinner that evening was a very pleasant affair. Extra courses had been prepared in honor of those that were leaving at Southampton. I had not known one of the passengers when I left New York seven days before, but I realized, now that I was so soon to separate from them, that I regretted the parting very much.

Had I been traveling with a companion I should not have felt this so keenly, for naturally then I would have had less time to cultivate the acquaintance of my fellow passengers.

They were all so kind to me that I should have been the most ungrateful of women had I not felt that I was leaving friends behind. Captain Albers had served many years as commander of a ship in Eastern seas, and he cautioned me as to the manner in which I should take care of my health. As the time grew shorter for my stay on the Augusta Victoria, some teased me gently as to the outcome of my attempt to beat the record made by a hero of fiction, and I found myself forcing a false gaiety that helped to hide my real fears.

The passengers on the Augusta Victoria all stayed up to see us off. We sat on deck talking or nervously walking about until half-past two in the morning. Then some one said the tugboat had come alongside, and we all rushed over to see it. After it was made secure we went down to the lower deck to see who would come on and to get some news from land.

One man was very much concerned about my making the trip to London alone. He thought as it was so late, or rather so early, that the London correspondent, who was to have met me, would not put in an appearance.

"I shall most certainly leave the ship here and see you safely to London, if no one comes to meet you," he protested, despite my assurances that I felt perfectly able to get along safely without an escort.

More for his sake than my own, I watched the men come on board, and tried to pick out the one that had been sent to meet me. Several of them were passing us in a line just as a gentleman made some remark about my trip around the world. A tall young man overheard the remark, and turning at the foot of the stairs, looked down at me with a hesitating smile.

"Nellie Bly?" he asked inquiringly.

"Yes," I replied, holding out my hand, which he gave a cordial grasp, meanwhile asking if I had enjoyed my trip, and if my baggage was ready to be transferred.

The man who had been so fearful of my traveling to London alone, took occasion to draw the correspondent into conversation. Afterwards he came to me and said with the most satisfied look upon his face:

"He is all right. If he had not been so, I should have gone to London with you anyway. I can rest satisfied now for he will take care of you."

I went away with a warm feeling in my heart for that kindly

man who would have sacrificed his own comfort to insure the safety of an unprotected girl.

A few warm handclasps, and interchanging of good wishes, a little dry feeling in the throat, a little strained pulsation of the heart, a little hurried run down the perpendicular plank to the other passengers who were going to London, and then the tug cast off from the ship, and we drifted away in the dark.

CHAPTER III

Southampton to Jules Verne's

"Mr. & Mrs. Jules Verne have sent a special letter asking that if possible you will stop to see them," the London correspondent said to me, as we were on our way to the wharf.

"Oh, how I should like to see them!" I exclaimed, adding in the same breath, "Isn't it hard to be forced to decline such a treat?"

"If you are willing to go without sleep and rest for two nights, I think it can be done," he said quietly.

"Safely? Without making me miss any connections? If so, don't think about sleep or rest."

"It depends on our getting a train out of here to-night. All the regular trains until morning have left, and unless they decide to run a special mail train for the delayed mails, we will have to stay here all night and that will not give us time to see Verne. We shall see when we land what they will decide to do."

The boat that was landing us left much to be desired in the way of comfort. The only cabin seemed to be the hull, but it was filled with mail and baggage and lighted by a lamp with a smoked globe. I did not see any place to sit down, so we all stood on deck, shivering in the damp, chilly air, and looking in the gray fog like uneasy spirits.

The dreary, dilapidated wharf was a fit landing place for the antique boat. I silently followed the correspondent into a large empty shed, where a few men with sleep in their eyes and uniforms that bore ample testimony to the fact that they had slept in their clothes, were stationed behind some long, low tables.

"Where are your keys?" the correspondent asked me as he sat my solitary bag down before one of these weary looking inspectors.

"It is too full to lock," I answered simply.

"Will you swear that you have no tobacco or tea?" the inspector asked my escort lazily.

"Don't swear," I said to him; then turning to the inspector I added: "It's my bag."

He smiled and putting a chalk mark upon the bag freed us. . . .

Passing through the custom house we were made happy by the information that it had been decided to attach a passenger coach to the special mail train to oblige the passengers who wished to go to London without delay. The train was made up then, so we concluded to get into our car and try to warm up.

A porter took my bag and another man in uniform drew forth an enormous key with which he unlocked the door in the side of the car instead of the end, as in America. I managed to compass the uncomfortable long step to the door and striking my toe against some projection in the floor, went most ungracefully and unceremoniously on to the seat.

My escort after giving some order to the porter went out to see about my ticket, so I took a survey of an English railway compartment. The little square in which I sat looked like a hotel omnibus and was about as comfortable. The two red leather seats in it run across the car, one backing the engine, the other backing the rear of the train. There was a door on either side and one could hardly have told that there was a dingy lamp there to cast a light on the scene had not the odor from it been so loud. I carefully lifted the rug that covered the thing I had fallen over, curious to see what could be so necessary to an English railway carriage as to occupy such a prominent position. I found a harmless object that looked like a bar of iron and had just dropped the rug in place when the door opened and the porter, catching the iron at one end, pulled it out, replacing it with another like it in shape and size.

"Put your feet on the foot warmer and get warm, Miss," he said, and I mechanically did as he advised.

My escort returned soon after, followed by a porter who

carried a large basket which he put in our carriage. The guard came afterwards and took our tickets. Pasting a slip of paper on the window, which backwards looked like "etavirP," he went out and locked the door.

"How should we get out if the train ran the track?" I asked, not half liking the idea of being locked in a box like an animal in a freight train.

"Trains never run off the track in England," was the quiet, satisfied answer.

"Too slow for that," I said teasingly, which only provoked a gentle inquiry as to whether I wanted anything to eat.

With a newspaper spread over our laps for a tablecloth, we brought out what the basket contained and put in our time eating and chatting about my journey until the train reached London.

As no train was expected at that hour, Waterloo Station was almost deserted. It was some little time after we stopped before the guard unlocked the door of our compartment and released us. Our few fellow-passengers were just about starting off in shabby cabs when we alighted. Once again we called goodbye and good wishes to each other, and then I found myself in a four-wheeled cab, facing a young Englishman who had come to meet us and who was glibly telling us the latest news.

I don't know at what hour we arrived, but my companions told me that it was daylight. I should not have known it. A gray, misty fog hung like a ghostly pall over the city. I always liked fog, it lends such a soft, beautifying light to things that otherwise in the broad glare of day would be rude and commonplace.

"How are these streets compared with those of New York?" was the first question that broke the silence after our leaving the station.

"They are not bad," I said with a patronizing air, thinking shamefacedly of the dreadful streets of New York, although determined to hear no word against them.

Westminster Abbey and the Houses of Parliament were pointed out to me, and the Thames, across which we drove. I felt that I was taking what might be called a bird's-eye view of

London. A great many foreigners have taken views in the same rapid way of America, and afterwards gone home and written books about America, Americans, and Americanisms.

We drove first to the London office of the New York *World*. After receiving the cables that were waiting for my arrival, I started for the American Legation to get a passport as I had been instructed by cable.

Mr. McCormick, Secretary of the Legation, came into the room immediately after our arrival, and after welcoming and congratulating me on the successful termination of the first portion of my trip, sat down and wrote out a passport.

My escort was asked to go into another part of the room until the representative could ask me an important question. I had never required a passport before, and I felt a nervous curiosity to know what secrets were connected with such proceedings.

"There is one question all women dread to answer, and as very few will give a truthful reply, I will ask you to swear to the rest first and fill in the other question afterwards, unless you have no hesitancy in telling me your age."

"Oh, certainly," I laughed. "I will tell you my age, swear to it, too, and I am not afraid; my companion may come out of the corner."[14]

"What is the color of your eyes?" he asked.

"Green," I said indifferently.

He was inclined to doubt it at first, but after a little inspection, both the gentlemen accepted my verdict as correct.

It was only a few seconds until we were whirling through the streets of London again. This time we went to the office of the Peninsular and Oriental Steamship Company,[15] where I bought tickets that would cover at least half of my journey. A few moments again and we were driving rapidly to the Charing Cross station.[16]

I was faint for food, and while my companion dismissed the cab and secured tickets, I ordered the only thing on the Charing Cross bill of fare that was prepared, so when he returned, his breakfast was ready for him. It was only ham and eggs, and coffee, but what we got of it was delicious. I know we did not get much, and when we were interrupted by the announcement that our train was starting, I stopped long enough to take another drink of coffee and then had to run down the platform to catch the train.

There is nothing like plenty of food to preserve health. I know that cup of coffee saved me from a headache that day. I had been shaking with the cold as we made our hurried drive through London, and my head was so dizzy at times that I hardly knew whether the earth had a chill or my brains were attending a ball. When I got comfortably seated in the train I began to feel warmer and more stable.

The train moved off at an easy-going speed, and the very jog of it lulled me into a state of languor.

"I want you to see the scenery along here; it is beautiful," my companion said, but I lazily thought, "What is scenery compared with sleep when one has not seen bed for over twenty-four hours?" so I said to him, very crossly:

"Don't you think you would better take a nap? You have not had any sleep for so long and you will be up so late to-night, that, really, I think for the sake of your health you would better sleep now."

"And you?" he asked with a teasing smile. I had been up even longer.

"Well, I confess, I was saying one word for you and two for myself," I replied, with a laugh that put us at ease on the subject.

"Honestly, now, I care very little for scenery when I am so sleepy," I said apologetically. "Those English farm houses are charming and the daisy-dotted meadows (I had not the faintest conception as to whether there were daisies in them or not), are only equaled by those I have seen in Kansas, but if you will excuse me?—" and I was in the land that joins the land of death.

I slept an easy, happy sleep, filled with dreams of home until I was waked by the train stopping.

"We change for the boat here," my companion said catching up our bags and rugs, which he hauled to a porter.

A little walk down to the pier brought us to the place where a boat was waiting. Some people were getting off the boat, but a larger number stood idly about waiting for it to move off.

The air was very cold and chilly, but still I preferred the deck to the close, musty-smelling cabin beneath. . . .

There has been so much written and told about the English Channel, that one is inclined to think of it as a stream of horrors. It is also affirmed that even hardy sailors bring up the past when crossing over it, so I naturally felt that my time would come.

All the passengers must have been familiar with the history of the channel, for I saw everyone trying all the known preventives of seasickness. The women assumed reclining positions and the men sought the bar.

I remained on deck and watched the seagulls, or what I thought were these useful birds—useful for millinery purposes—and froze my nose. It was bitterly cold, but I found the cold bracing until we anchored at Boulogne, France.[17] Then I had a chill.

At the end of this desolate pier, where boats anchor and where trains start, is a small, dingy restaurant. While a little English sailor, who always dropped his h's and never forgot his "sir," took charge of our bags and went to secure accommodations for us in the outgoing train, we followed the other passengers into the restaurant to get something warm to eat.

I was in France now, and I began to wonder now what would have been my fate if I had been alone as I had expected. I knew my companion spoke French, the language that all the people about us were speaking, so I felt perfectly easy on that score as long as he was with me.

We took our places at the table and he began to order in French. The waiter looked blankly at him until, at last, more in a spirit of fun than anything else, I suggested that he give the order in English. The waiter glanced at me with a smile and answered in English.

We traveled from Boulogne to Amiens in a compartment with an English couple and a Frenchman. There was one footwarmer and the day was cold. We all tried to put our feet on the one foot-warmer and the result was embarrassing. The Frenchman sat facing me and as I was conscious of having tramped on someone's toes, and as he looked at me angrily all the time above the edge of his newspaper, I had a guilty feeling of knowing whose toes had been tramped on.

During this trip I tried to solve the reason for the popularity of these ancient, incommodious railway carriages. I very shortly decided that while they may be suitable for countries where little traveling is done, they would be thoroughly useless in thinly populated countries where people think less of traveling 3,000 miles than they do about their dinner. I also decided that the reason why we think nothing of starting out on long trips, is because our comfort is so well looked after, that living on a first-class railway train is as comfortable as living at a first-class hotel. The English railway carriages are wretchedly heated. One's feet will be burning on the foot-warmer while one's back will be freezing in the cold air above. If one should be taken suddenly ill in an English railway compartment, it would be a very serious matter.

Still, I can picture conditions under which these ancient railway carriages might be agreeable, but they are not such as would induce a traveler to prefer them to those built on the American model.

Supposing one had the measles or a black eye, then a compartment in a railway carriage, made private by a tip to the porter, would be very consoling.

Supposing one was newly wed and was bubbling over in ecstasy of joy, then give one an English railway compartment, where two just made one can be secluded from the eyes of a cold, sneering public, who are just as great fools under the same conditions, although they would deny it if one told them so.

But talk about privacy! If it is privacy the English desire so much, they should adopt our American trains, for there is no privacy like that to be found in a large car filled with strangers. Everybody has, and keeps his own place. There is no sitting for hours, as is often the case in English trains, face to face and knees to knees with a stranger, offensive or otherwise, as he may chance to be.

Then too, did the English railway carriage make me understand why English girls need chaperones. It would make any American woman shudder with all her boasted self-reliance, to think of sending her daughter alone on a trip, even of a few hours' duration, where there was every possibility that during those hours she would be locked in a compartment with a stranger.

Small wonder the American girl is fearless. She has not been used to so called private compartments in English railway carriages, but to large crowds, and every individual that helps to swell that crowd is to her a protector. When mothers teach their daughters that there is safety in numbers, and that numbers are the body-guard that shield all woman-kind, then chaperones will be a thing of the past, and women will be nobler and better.

As I was pondering over this subject, the train pulled into a station and stopped. My escort looking out, informed me that we were at Amiens. We were securely locked in, however, and began to think that we would be carried past, when my companion managed to get his head out of the window and shouted for the guard to come to our release. Freed at last, we stepped out on the platform at Amiens.

CHAPTER IV

Jules Verne at Home

M. Jules Verne and Mme. Verne, accompanied by Mr. R. H. Sherard,[18] a Paris journalist, stood on the platform waiting our arrival.

When I saw them I felt as any other woman would have done under the same circumstances. I wondered if my face was travel-stained, and if my hair was tossed. I thought regretfully, had I been traveling on an American train, I should have been able to make my toilet *en route*, so that when I stepped off at Amiens and faced the famous novelist and his charming wife, I would have been as trim and tidy as I would had I been receiving them in my own home.

There was little time for regret. They were advancing towards us, and in another second I had forgotten my untidiness in the cordial welcome they gave me. Jules Verne's bright eyes beamed on me with interest and kindliness, and Mme. Verne greeted me with the cordiality of a cherished friend. There were no stiff formalities to freeze the kindness in all our hearts, but a cordiality expressed with such charming grace that before I had been many minutes in their company, they had won my everlasting respect and devotion.

M. Verne led the way to the carriages which waited our coming. Mme. Verne walked closely by my side, glancing occasionally at me with a smile, which said in the language of the eye, the common language of the whole animal world, alike plain to man and beast:

"I am glad to greet you, and I regret we cannot speak together." M. Verne gracefully helped Mme. Verne and myself into a coupé, while he entered a carriage with the two other gentlemen. I felt very awkward at being left alone with Mme. Verne, as I was altogether unable to speak to her.

Her knowledge of the English language consisted of "No" and my French vocabulary consisted of "Oui," so our conversation was limited to a few apologetic and friendly smiles interluded with an occasional pressure of the hand. Indeed, Mme. Verne is a most charming woman, and even in this awkward position she made everything go most gracefully.

It was early evening. As we drove through the streets of Amiens I got a flying glimpse of bright shops, a pretty park, and numerous nursemaids pushing baby carriages about.

When our carriage stopped I got out and gave my hand to Mme. Verne to help her alight. We stood on a wide, smooth pavement, before a high stone wall, over the top of which I could see the peaked outlines of the house.

M. Verne was not long behind us. He hurried up to where we were standing and opened a door in the wall. Stepping in I found myself in a small, smoothly paved courtyard, the wall making two sides and the house forming the square.

A large, black shaggy dog came bounding forward to greet me. He jumped up against me, his soft eyes overflowing with affection, and though I love dogs and especially appreciated this one's loving welcome, still I feared that his lavish display of it would undermine my dignity by bringing me to my knees at the very threshold of the home of the famous Frenchman.

M. Verne evidently understood my plight, for he spoke shortly to the dog, who, with a pathetic droop of his tail, went off to think it out alone.

We went up a flight of marble steps across the tiled floor of a beautiful little conservatory that was not packed with flowers but was filled with a display just generous enough to allow one to see and appreciate the beauty of the different plants. Mme. Verne led the way into a large sitting-room that was dusky with the early shade of a wintry evening. With her own hands she touched a match to the pile of dry wood that lay in the wide open fireplace.

Meanwhile M. Verne urged us to remove our outer wrappings. Before this was done a bright fire was crackling in the grate, throwing a soft, warm light over the dark room. Mme. Verne led me to a chair close by the mantel, and when I was seated she took the chair opposite. Cheered by the warmth I looked quietly on the scene before me.

The room was large and the hangings and paintings and soft velvet rug, which left visible but a border of polished hard wood, were richly dark. On the mantel, which towered above Mme. Verne's head, were some fine pieces of statuary in bronze and, as the fire gave frequent bright flashes as the flames greedily caught fresh wood, I could see another bronze piece on a pedestal in a corner. All the chairs artistically upholstered in brocaded silks, were luxuriously easy. Beginning at either side of the mantel they were placed in a semi-circle around the fire, which was only broken by a little table that held several tall silver candlesticks.

A fine white Angora cat came rubbing up against my knee, then seeing its charming mistress on the opposite side, went to her and boldly crawled up in her lap as if assured of a cordial welcome.

Next to me in this semi-circle sat Mr. Sherard. M. Jules Verne was next to Mr. Sherard. He sat forward on the edge of his chair, his snow-white hair rather long and heavy, was standing up in artistic disorder; his full beard, rivaling his hair in snowiness, hid the lower part of his face and the brilliancy of his bright eyes that were overshadowed with heavy white brows, and the rapidity of his speech and the quick movements of his firm white hands all bespoke energy—life—with enthusiasm.

The London correspondent sat next to Jules Verne. With a smile on her soft rosy lips, Mme. Verne sat nursing the cat which she stroked methodically with a dainty, white hand, while her luminous black eyes moved alternately between her husband and myself.

She was the most charming figure in that group around the wood fire. Imagine a youthful face with a spotless complexion, crowned with the whitest hair, dressed in smooth, soft folds on the top of a dainty head that is most beautifully poised on a pair of plump shoulders. Add to this face pretty red lips, that opened disclose a row of lovely teeth, and large, bewitching black eyes, and you have but a faint picture of the beauty of Mme. Verne.

This day when she met me she wore a sealskin jacket and carried a muff, and on her white head was a small black velvet bonnet. On taking her wraps off in the house I saw she wore a watered-silk skirt, laid in side plaits in the front with a full straight black drapery, that was very becoming to her short, plump figure. The bodice was of black silk velvet.

Mme. Verne is, I should judge, not more than five feet two in height; M. Verne about five feet five. M. Verne spoke in a short, rapid way, and Mr. Sherard in an attractive, lazy voice translated what was said for my benefit.

"Has M. Verne ever been to America?" I asked.

"Yes, once;" the answer came translated to me. "For a few days only, during which time I saw Niagara. I have always longed to return, but the state of my health prevents my taking any long journeys. I try to keep a knowledge of everything that is going on in America and greatly appreciate the hundreds of letters I receive yearly from Americans who read my books. There is one man in California who has been writing to me for years. He writes all the news about his family and home and country as if I were a friend and yet we have never met. He has urged me to come to America as his guest. I know of nothing that I long to do more than to see your land from New York to San Francisco."

"How did you get the idea for your novel, 'Around the World in Eighty Days?'" I asked.

"I got it from a newspaper," was his reply. "I took up a copy of *Le Siécle* one morning, and found in it a discussion and some calculations showing that the journey around the world might be done in eighty days. The idea pleased me, and while thinking it over it struck me that in their calculations they had not called into account the difference in the meridians and I thought what a denouement such a thing would make in a novel, so I went to work to write one. Had it not been for the denouement I don't think that I should ever have written the book.

"I used to keep a yacht, and then I traveled all over the world studying localities; then I wrote from actual observation. Now, since my health confines me to my home, I am forced to read up descriptions and geographies."

M. Verne asked me what my line of travel was to be, and I was very happy to speak one thing that he could understand, so I told him.

"My line of travel is from New York to London, then Calais, Brindisi, Port Said, Ismailia, Suez, Aden, Colombo, Penang, Singapore, Hong Kong, Yokohama, San Francisco, New York."

"Why do you not go to Bombay as my hero Phileas Fogg did?" M. Verne asked.

"Because I am more anxious to save time than a young widow,"[19] I answered.

"You may save a young widower before you return," M. Verne said with a smile.

I smiled with a superior knowledge, as women, fancy free, always will at such insinuations.

I looked at the watch on my wrist and saw that my time was getting short. There was only one train that I could take from here to Calais, and if I missed it I might just as well return to New York by the way I came, for the loss of that train meant one week's delay.

NELLIE BLY'S TRIP

How She Skimmed Like a Swallow Through England, France, and Italy to Brindisi

---

A WILD RACE AGAINST TIME!

Had to Overtake a Fast Steamer a Week Ahead of Her

JULES VERNE'S FRIENDLY INTEREST

Strong Men Might Well Shrink from the Fatigues and Anxieties Cheerfully Faced by This Young American Girl— Through London Without Seeing It—Food and Sleep Hastily Caught on Flying Trains—Everybody Interested and Willing to Lend a Hand and Speed Her on Her Way.

[SPECIAL CORRESPONDENT OF THE WORLD][20]

London, Nov. 28. Nellie Bly will have her own story to tell of her arrival in England. This letter is not intended in any way to anticipate it, but merely to put on record a few events of this interesting trip which Miss Bly is not likely to mention, principally because she doesn't know anything about them. If she attempts any description at all of what she saw in England, it will be much the same as a man describing Broadway if he were shot through a pneumatic tube from the Western Union Building to the Twenty-Third Street Uptown Office. Nellie Bly landed at Southampton in the dark, was rushed through London in a thick fog and did not see a gleam of sunshine until the coast of France was in sight from the deck of a Calais boat.

In the first place the Augusta Victoria was late. She met with stormy seas and head-winds. She should have been reported at The Lizard[21] before I started from Southampton, but she was not. When I reached Southampton I was told that she passed The Lizard at 1.15 o'clock on Thursday (the 21st), exactly seven days from the time she left New York. Things began to look exciting. If the vessel beat her previous record from The Lizard to Hurst Castle²² the World's globe-trotter would arrive in Southampton in time to catch the regular train at 1 o'clock Friday morning for London, and to make connections all right for Amiens to see Jules Verne. If she missed that train nothing would do but a "special." It is not so easy to get a special train here as it is in America. A great deal of red tape is necessary. But before leaving London I had seen Mr. Verinder, the extremely courteous Superintendent of the London and Southwestern Railway, and had thoroughly interested him in Miss Bly's trip. He at once notified Mr. Winchester, the Divisional Superintendent at Southampton, to have an engine "fired" ready to start the instant Miss Bly required it. Mr. Winchester was on hand when I arrived at Southampton, and he became very much interested in the journey too.

"Have no fear," he said, "Miss Bly shall get to London in time if she goes on a cyclone." . . .

England, at Last!

The hours drag along very wearily until nearly midnight, when we receive a message that the Augusta has been sighted off Hurst Castle. . . . Late as it is all the passengers are on deck, fully as eager to ascertain whether Nellie Bly is going to make her connections to London as they are sorry to see her leave the ship. When the gangplank is run aboard the Augusta Nellie Bly is waiting for it, satchel in hand, surrounded with fellow-voyagers bidding her farewell. The important-looking sacks, stuffed with mail matter, are stacked against the rail and in less than ten minutes are transferred to the tender. A shriek of the whistle which is almost drowned by a chorus of "Good-bye, Nellie; good luck to you," and we are off. The clock has passed the half hour after 2 before we are made fast to the wharf at Southampton, and the special mail train backs down from the central station to meet us. Ten minutes more and we are flying over the rails to London. . . .

The conversation in the drawing room between Jules Verne and the World's traveller has already been printed. But while Mme. Verne was showing Nellie some of her household treasures I had a talk with the novelist. . . .

"What do you think," I asked, "of this idea of a young girl endeavoring to beat your fictitious record in a journey around the world?"

"I think it is extremely original," he answered, "even for Americans."

FROM *The New York World,* DEC. 8, 1889

———

"If M. Verne would not consider it impertinent I should like to see his study before I go," I said at last.

He said he was only too happy to show it me, and even as my request was translated Mme. Verne sprang to her feet and lighted one of the tall wax candles.

She started with the quick, springy step of a girl to lead the way. M. Verne, who walks with a slight limp, the result of a wound, followed, and we brought up the rear. We went through the conservatory to a small room up through which was a winding stair, or, more properly speaking, a spiral staircase. Mme. Verne paused at every curve to light the gas.

Up at the top of the house and along a hall that corresponded in shape to the conservatory below, M. Verne went, Mme. Verne stopping to light the gas in the hall. He opened a door that led off the hall and I stepped inside after him.

I was astonished. I had expected, judging from the rest of the house, that M. Verne's study would be a room of ample proportions and richly furnished. I had read so many descriptions of the studies of famous authors, and have dwelt with something akin to envy (our space is so limited and expensive in New York) on the ample room, the beautiful hand-carved desks filled with costly trinkets, the rare etchings and paintings that covered the walls, the rich hangings, and, I will confess it, I have thought it small wonder that amid such surroundings authors were able to dream fancies that brought them fame.

But when I stood in M. Verne's study I was speechless with surprise. He opened a latticed window, the only window in the room, and Mme. Verne, hurrying in after us, lighted the gas jet that was fastened above a low mantel.

The room was very small; even my little den at home was

almost as large. It was also very modest and bare. Before the window was a flat-topped desk. The usual litter that accompanies and fills the desks of most literary persons was conspicuously absent, and the waste-basket that is usually filled to overflowing with what one very often considers their most brilliant productions, in this case held but a few little scraps.

On the desk was a neat little pile of white paper, probably 8x10 in size. It was part of the manuscript of a novel that M. Verne is engaged on at present. I eagerly accepted the manuscript when he handed it to me, and when I looked at the neat penmanship, so neat in fact that had I not known it was prose I should have thought it was the work of a poet, I was more impressed than ever with the extreme tidiness of this French author. In several places he had most effectually blotted out something that he had written, but there was no interlining, which gave me the idea that M. Verne always improved his work by taking out superfluous things and never by adding.

One bottle of ink and one penholder was all that shared the desk with the manuscript. There was but one chair in the room, and it stood before the desk. The only other piece of furniture was a broad, low couch in the corner, and here in this room with these meagre surroundings, Jules Verne has written the books that have brought him everlasting fame.

I leaned over the desk and looked out of the little latticed window which he had thrown open. I could see through the dusk the spire of a cathedral in the distance, while stretching down beneath me was a park, beyond which I saw the entrance to a railway tunnel that goes under M. Verne's house, and through which many Americans travel every year, on their way to Paris.

Leading off from the study, is an enormous library. The large room is completely lined with cases from ceiling to floor, and these glass-doored cases are packed with handsomely bound books which must be worth a fortune.

While we were examining the wealth of literature that was there before us, M. Verne got an idea. Taking up a candle and asking us to follow, he went out into the hall; stopping before a large map that hung there, holding up with one hand the candle, he pointed out to us several blue marks. Before his words were translated to me, I understood that on this map he had, with a blue pencil, traced out the course of his hero, Phileas Fogg, before he started him in fiction to travel around the world in eighty days. With a pencil he marked on the map, as we grouped about him, the places where my line of travel differed from that of Phileas Fogg.

Our steps lagged as we descended the winding stair again. It had come time to take farewell, and I felt as if I was separating from friends. Down in the room where we had been before, we found wine and biscuit on the little table, and M. Jules Verne explained that, contrary to his regular rules, he intended to take a glass of wine, that we might have the pleasure of drinking together to the success of my strange undertaking.

They clinked their glasses with wine, and wished me "Godspeed."

"If you do it in seventy-nine days, I shall applaud with both hands," Jules Verne said, and then I knew he doubted the possibility of my doing it in seventy-five, as I had promised. In compliment to me, he endeavored to speak to me in English, and did succeed in saying, as his glass tipped mine:

"Good luck, Nellie Bly."

Mme. Verne was not going to be outdone by her gallant husband in showing kindness to me. She told Mr. Sherard that she would like to kiss me good-bye, and when he translated her kind request, he added that it was a great honor in France, for a woman to ask to kiss a stranger.

I was little used to such formalities, or familiarities, as one may deem them, but still I had not one thought of refusing such delicate attention, so I gave her my hand and inclined my head, for I am taller than she, and she kissed me gently and affectionately on either check. Then she put up her pretty face for me to kiss. I stifled a strong inclination to kiss her on the lips, they were so sweet and red, and show her how we do it in America. My mischievousness often plays havoc with my dignity, but for once I was able to restrain myself, and kissed her softly after her own fashion.

With uncovered heads, and despite our protestations, they

followed us out into the cold courtyard, and as far as I could see I saw them standing at the gate waving farewell to me, the brisk winds tossing their white hair.

CHAPTER V

On to Brindisi

When M. and Mme. Verne were no longer visible, my thoughts turned to my trip. I feared that the enjoyment of my visit to their home had jeopardized the success of my tour.

The driver had been told to make the best speed back to the station, but the carriage seemed to be rolling along so quietly that I could not rest until it was urged again upon the coachman to reach the station in the shortest possible time.

Some few moments after we reached there the train came in. Bidding a hearty good-bye to Mr. Sherard, I started again on my tour of the world, and the visit to Jules Verne was a thing of the past. I had gone without sleep and rest; I had traveled many miles out of my way for the privilege of meeting M. and Mme. Verne, and I felt that if I had gone around the world for that pleasure, I should not have considered the price too high.

The train which carried us to Calais is, I infer from what I have heard, the pride of France. It is called the Club train, and is built on the plan of the vestibule trains in America. The carriages are so narrow, that after having been accustomed to wide ones, the Club train seems like a toy.

I have been curious to know why this train is called the Club train. I had a foolish idea at first that it was the private property of some club, run for the special benefit of its members, and I felt some hesitancy about traveling on a train devoted to the use of men. However, the presence of a number of women put me at ease, and though I made many inquiries about the train, all I could learn was that it was considered quite the finest equipped train in Europe.

The car in which we sat, as I said before, contained some women, and was besides liberally filled with men passengers. Shortly after we left Amiens, a porter announced that dinner was served in a front car. Everybody at once filed out and into the dining car. I have thought since that probably the train carried two dining cars, because the dinner, and an excellent one it proved to be, was served *table d'hôte*, and there seemed to be accommodations for all.

After we had our cheese and salad, we returned to our drawing-room car, where we were served with coffee, the men having the privilege of smoking with it. I thought this manner of serving coffee a very pleasing one, quite an improvement on our own system, and quite worthy of adoption.

When I reached Calais, I found that I had two hours and more to spend in waiting. The train that I intended to take for Brindisi is a weekly mail train that runs to accommodate the mails and not passengers. It starts originally from London, at eight o'clock Friday evening of each week. The rule is that the persons desiring to travel on it must buy their tickets twenty-four hours in advance of the time of its departure. The mail and passengers are carried across the channel, and the train leaves Calais at 1.30 in the morning.

There are pleasanter places in the world to waste time in than Calais. I walked down along the pier and looked at the lighthouse, which I am told is one of the most perfect in the world, throwing its light farther away than any other. It is a revolving light, and it throws out long rays that seem so little above our heads that I found myself dodging to avoid being struck. Of course, that was purely imaginary on my part, for the rays are just the opposite to being near the ground, but they spread between the ground and the sky like the laths of an unfinished partition. I wonder if the people of Calais ever saw the moon and stars.

There is a very fine railway station built near the end of the pier. It is of generous size, but seemed, as far as I could judge, at this hour of the night, quite empty. There is a smoothly tiled enclosed promenade on the side of the station facing the pier that I should say would prove quite an attraction and comfort for passengers who were forced to wait in that place.

My escort took me into the restaurant where we found something to eat, which was served by a French waiter who could speak some English and understand more. When it was announced that the boat from England was in we went out and saw the be-bundled and be-baggaged passengers come ashore and go to the train which was waiting alongside. One thousand bags of mail were quickly transferred to the train, and then I bade my escort good-bye, and was shortly speeding away from Calais.

There is but one passenger coach on this train. It is a Pullman Palace sleeping-car with accommodations for twenty-two passengers, but it is the rule never to carry more than twenty-one, one berth being occupied by the guard.

The next morning, having nothing else to occupy my time, I thought that I would see what my traveling companions looked like. I had shared the stateroom at the extreme end of the car with a pretty English girl who had the rosiest cheeks and the greatest wealth of golden brown hair I ever saw. She was going with her father, an invalid, to Egypt, to spend the winter and spring months. She was an early riser, and before I was awake had gotten up and joined her father in the other part of the car.

When I went out so as to give the porter an opportunity to make up my stateroom, I was surprised at the strange appearance of the interior of the car. All the head- and footboards were left in place, giving the impression that the coach was divided into a series of small boxes. Some of the passengers were drinking, some were playing cards, and all were smoking until the air was stifling. I never object to cigar smoke when there is some little ventilation, but when it gets so thick that one feels as if it is molasses instead of air that one is inhaling, then I mildly protest. It was soon this occasion, and I wonder what would be the result in our land of boasted freedom if a Pullman car should be put to such purposes. I concluded it is due to this freedom that we do not suffer from such things. Women travelers in America command as much consideration as men.

I walked down the car looking in the "boxes" only to find them all occupied by unsocial looking men. When I reached the middle of the car my little English roommate, who was sitting with her father, saw me and kindly asked me to sit down with them.

Her father I remember as a cultured, broad-minded man, with a sense of humor that helped me to hear with less dread the racking cough that frequently stopped all speech and shook his thin frame as though he had the ague.

"Father," the little English girl said in a clear, musical voice, "the clergyman sent you his large prayer-book just before our departure, and I put it in your bag."

"My daughter is very thoughtful," he said to me, then turning to her he added, with a smile in his eye, "Please take the first opportunity to return the prayer-book to the clergyman, and tell him, with my compliments, that he might have saved himself that trouble; that I was grieved to deprive him of his book for so long."

The young girl's face settled into a look that spoke disapproval of her father's words, and a determination not to return the prayer-book. She held, clasped to her breast, a large prayer-book, and when her father jokingly told her she had bought the largest one she could find, which he looked on as wasting valuable packing space, when she could have carried a small one that would have been of as much service, I was actually startled by the hard, determined light on her face. In everything else she was the sweetest, most gentle girl I ever met, but her religion was of the hard, uncompromising kind, that condemns everything, forgives nothing, and swears the heathen is forever damned because he was not born to know the religion of her belief.

She spent all the afternoon trying to implant the seeds of her faith in my mind, and I listened, thinking from her words that if she was not the original Catherine Elsmere, she at least could not be more like that interesting character.[23]

For the first day food was taken on the train at different stations, and the conductor, or guard, as they called him, served it to the passengers. A dining car was attached in the evening but I was informed by the women that it was not exactly the thing for us to eat in a public car with men, so we continued to be served in our state rooms.

I might have seen more while traveling through France if the car windows had been clean. From their appearance I judged that they had never been washed. We did not make many stops. The only purpose of stopping was for coal or water, as passengers are not taken on or off this train between Calais and Brindisi.

In the course of the afternoon we passed some high and picturesque mountains that were covered with a white frost. I
found that even wearing my ulster and wrapped in a rug I was
none too warm. About eight o'clock in the morning we reached
Modena. The baggage was examined there and all the passengers were notified in advance to be prepared to get out and unlock the boxes that belonged to them. The conductor asked me
several times if I was quite certain that I had no more than the
handbag with me, telling me at the same time if any boxes
were found locked, with no owner to open them, they would
be detained by the custom inspectors. When partly assured
that I had no trunks he said that it was not necessary to get out
with my handbag, as no one would think it necessary to examine it.

Half an hour later we were in Italy. I was anxiously waiting
to see that balmy, sunny land, but though I pressed my face
close to the frosty windowpane bleak night denied me even
one glimpse of sunny Italy and its dusky people. I went to bed
early. It was so very cold that I could not keep warm out of
bed, and I cannot say that I got much warmer in bed. The
berths were provided with only one blanket each. I piled all
my clothing on the berth and spent half the night lying awake
thinking how fortunate the passengers were the week previous
on this train. Just in the very same place that we were traveling
through Italian bandits had attacked the train and I thought,
with regretful envy, if the passengers then felt the scarcity of
blankets they at least had some excitement to make their blood
circulate.

When I got awake in the morning I hastily threw up the
window shade and eagerly looked out. I fell back in surprise,
wondering, if for once in my life I had made a mistake and
waked up early. I could not see any more than I had the night
before on account of a heavy gray fog that completely hid everything more than a yard away. Looking at the watch on my
wrist I found that it was ten o'clock, so I dressed with some
haste determined to find the guard and demand an explanation of him.

"It is a most extraordinary thing," he said to me; "I never
saw such a fog in Italy before."

There was nothing for it except to sit quietly counting the days I had been away from New York, subtracting them from the number that must elapse before my return. When this grew monotonous I carefully thought over the advisability of trying to introduce brown uniforms for railroad employees in the United States. I thought with wearied frenzy of the universal employment of navy-blue uniforms in America, and I turned with rest to the neat brown uniforms brightened with a touching of gold braid on the collars and cuffs, that adorned the conductor and porter of the India mail. . . .

All day I traveled through Italy—sunny Italy, along the Adriatic Sea. The fog still hung in a heavy cloud over the earth, and only once did I get a glimpse of the land I had heard so much about. It was evening, just at the hour of sunset, when we stopped at some station. I went out on the platform, and the fog seemed to lift for an instant, and I saw on one side a beautiful beach and a smooth bay dotted with boats bearing oddly-shaped and brightly-colored sails, which somehow looked to me like mammoth butterflies, dipping, dipping about in search of honey. Most of the sails were red, and as the sun kissed them with renewed warmth, just before leaving us in darkness, the sails looked as if they were composed of brilliant fire.

A high rugged mountain was on the other side of the train. It made me feel dizzy to look at the white buildings perched on the perpendicular side. I noticed the road that went in a winding line up the hill had been built with a wall on the ocean side; still I thought I would not care to travel up it.

I got out for a few minutes at the next station where we stopped to take our dinners. I walked into a restaurant to look about. It was very neat and attractive. Just as I stepped inside a little girl with wonderful large black eyes and enormous gold hoop-rings in her ears, ran forward to me with the fearless boldness of a child. I touched her pretty black hair, and then naturally felt in my pocket for something to give her. Just as I drew forth a large copper coin—the less the value of a coin generally, the larger its size—a small man with a delicately re-fined face, flashing black eyes, wide expanse of white shirt front, broken by a brilliant diamond, came up and spoke to the baby. In the way she drew back from me, although her little hand had been stretched out expectantly before, I knew he had told her not to accept anything from me.

I felt on first impulse like boxing his ears, he was so tiny and impudent. The guard coming in search of me, found us at this critical moment.

"You have insulted him," he said to me, as if I was not conscious of it! "The Italians are the poorest and proudest people on earth. They hate the English."

"I am an American," I said bluntly and abruptly. At this a waiter who had been standing close by apparently not listening, but catching every word just the same, came up and spoke to me in English. Then I determined to remedy the fault I had committed, but nevertheless I had a dogged determination that the child should yet take the coin.

"What a beautiful restaurant!" I exclaimed. "I am passing hurriedly through Italy and in my desire to see, judging from the samples of good cooking I have had *en route*, Italian eating houses are excellent. I hope I have not put you to any inconvenience. I almost forgot the restaurant when I saw that lovely baby. What exquisitely beautiful eyes! Exactly the same as her father's, at least I judge from the similarity of their eyes that he is her father, though he looks so young."

The waiter smiled and bowed and translated. I knew he would, and that is why I said it all. Then the little man's pride melted away, and a smile replaced the frown on his face. He spoke to the baby who came up and shook hands with me. I gave her the coin and our peace was sealed. Then the little father brought forth a bottle of wine, and with the most cordial smiles and friendliest words, begged me to accept it. I did not intend to be out-done, so I told the waiter that I must take some wine with me, insisted on paying for it, and with low bows and sweet smiles we took leave of one another, and I rushed after the guard to the train, boarding it just as the horn blew for it to continue on its way.

We arrived at Brindisi two hours late. When the train stopped, our car was surrounded with men wanting to carry us as well as our baggage to the boats. Their making no mention of hotels led me to wonder if people always passed through

Brindisi without stopping. All these men spoke English very well, but the guard said he would get one omnibus and escort the English women, the invalid man and his daughter, and myself to our boats, and would see that we were not charged more than the right fare.

We drove first to the boat bound for Alexandria, where we took leave of my roommate, and her father. Then we drove to the boat that we expected to sail on.

I alighted from the omnibus, and followed my companions up the gangplank. I dreaded meeting English people with their much-talked-of prejudices, as I knew I would shortly have to do. I was earnestly hoping that everybody would be in bed. As it was after one in the morning, I hardly expected the trial of facing them at once. The crowds of men on the deck dispelled my fond hope. I think every man on board that boat was up waiting to see the new passengers. They must have felt but ill-paid for their loss of sleep, for besides the men who came on board, there were only the two large English women and my own plain, uninteresting self.

These women were more helpless than I. As they were among their own people, I waited for them to take the lead; but after we had stood at the foot of the stairs for some time, gazed at by the passengers, and no one came forward to attend to our wants, which were few and simple, I gently asked if that was the usual manner of receiving passengers on English boats.

"It is strange, very strange. A steward, or some one should come to our assistance," was all they could say.

At last a man came down below, and as he looked as if he was in some way connected with the boat, I ventured to stop him and inquire if it was expecting too much to ask if we might have a steward to show us to our cabins. He said there should be some about, and began lustily to call for one. Even this brought no one to us, and as he started to find one himself, I started in the opposite direction. . . .

I put my bag down and returned to the guard who was waiting to take me to the cable office. I stopped to ask the purser if I had time to make the trip, to which he replied in the affirmative, with the proviso, "If you hurry." The two women who had traveled with me from Calais, had by this time found their way to the purser's office, and I heard them telling that they had come away from home and left their purse and tickets lying on the table in the sitting-room, they had started in such a rush!

The guard took me down the gangplank, and along several dark streets. At last, coming to a building where a door stood open, he stopped and I followed him in. The room in which we stood was perfectly bare and lighted by a lamp whose chimney was badly smoked. The only things in the room were two stationary desks. On the one lay a piece of blank paper before an ancient ink well and a much-used pen.

I thought that everybody had retired for the night, and the cable would have to wait until I reached the next port, until the guard explained to me that it was customary to ring for the operator, who would get up and attend to the message for me. Suiting the action to the words, the guard pulled at a knob near a small closed window, much like a postage stamp window. The bell made quite a clatter, still I had begun to think that hopeless, when the window opened with a clink, and a head appeared at the opening. The guard spoke in Italian, but hearing me speak English, the operator replied in the same language.

I told him I wanted to send a cable to New York. He asked me where New York was! I explained as best I could; then he brought out a lot of books, through which he searched first, to know by which line he could send the message; at least, so he explained; then what it would cost. The whole thing was so new and amusing to me that I forgot all about the departure of the boat until we had finished the business and stepped outside.

A whistle blew long and warningly. I looked at the guard, the guard looked at me. It was too dark to see each other, but I know our faces were the picture of dismay. My heart stopped beating and I thought with emotions akin to horror, "My boat was gone—and with it my limited wardrobe!"

"Can you run?" the guard asked in a husky voice. I said I could, and he taking a close grasp of my hand, we started down the dark street with a speed that would have startled a deer. Down the dark streets, past astonished watchmen and late pedestrians, until a sudden bend brought us in full view of my ship still in port. The boat for Alexandria had gone, but I was saved.

CHAPTER VI

An American Heiress

I had not been asleep long, it seemed to me, until I waked to find myself standing upright beside my berth. It required but a second, a glance at my drenched self, and the sounds of vigorous scrubbing on the deck above to explain the cause of my being out of bed before I knew it. I had gone to sleep with the porthole open, and as my berth was just beneath it, I received the full force of the scrub-water as it came pouring over the sides. I managed to let the heavy window down and went back to bed, wet, but confident that I would not again be caught napping under such circumstances.

I had not been asleep many moments until I heard a voice call: "Miss, will you have your tea now?" I opened my eyes and saw a steward standing at the door awaiting a reply. I refused the tea, as did the English girl on the other side of my cabin, managing to answer her bright smile with a very tired one, and then I was off to sleep again.

"Miss, will you have your bath now?" a voice broke in on my slumbers shortly afterwards. I looked up in disgust at a little white-capped woman who was bending over me, tempted to say I had just had my bath, a shower-bath, but thought better of it before speaking. I know I said something about "in a few minutes," and then I was asleep again.

"Well, you are a lazy girl! You'll miss your bath and breakfast if you don't get up the instant," was my third greeting. My surprise at the familiarity of the remark got the better of my sleepiness, and I thought:

"Well, by all that is wonderful, where am I? Am I in school again that a woman dare assume such a tone to me?" I kept my thoughts to myself, and said stiffly:

"I generally get up when I feel so inclined."

I saw my roommate was missing, but I felt like sleeping and I decided to sleep; whether it pleased the stewardess or not, it mattered little to me. The steward was the next one to put in an appearance.

"Miss, this ship is inspected every day and I must have this cabin made up before they come," he said complainingly. "The captain will be here presently."

There was nothing to do but to get up, which I did. I found my way to the bathroom, but soon saw that it was impossible for me to turn on the water, as I did not understand the mechanism of the faucet. I asked a steward I saw outside the door, the whereabouts of the stewardess, and was simply amazed to hear him reply:

"The stewardess is taking a rest and cannot be disturbed."

After dressing I wandered up on the next deck and was told that breakfast was over long ago. I went out on deck, and the very first glimpse of the lazy looking passengers in their summer garments, lounging about in comfortable positions, or slowly promenading the deck, which was sheltered from the heat of the sun by a long stretch of awnings, and the smooth, velvety looking water, the bluest I had ever seen, softly gurgling against the side of the ship as it almost imperceptibly steamed on its course, and the balmy air, soft as a rose leaf, and just as sweet, air such as one dreams about but seldom finds; standing there alone among strange people, on strange waters, I thought how sweet life is!

Before an hour had passed I was acquainted with several persons. I had thought and expected that the English passengers would hold themselves aloof from a girl who was traveling alone, but my cabin-companion saw me before I got away from the door, and came forward to ask me to join herself and friends. We first had an amusing search for the steamer-chair which I had told the guard to buy at Brindisi and send on before our departure. There were over three hundred passengers on the ship, and I suppose they averaged a chair apiece, so it can easily be pictured the trouble it would be to find a chair among that number. I asked where the deck-stewards were when at last I felt the search was useless, and was surprised to learn that a deck-steward was an unknown commodity on the P. and O. line. . . .

Notwithstanding all annoying trifles it was a very happy life we spent in those pleasant waters. The decks were filled all the day, and when the lights were put out at night the passengers reluctantly went to their cabins. The passengers formed two striking contrasts. There were some of the most refined and lovely people on board, and there were some of the most ill-bred and uncouth. Most of the women, whose acquaintance I formed, were very desirous of knowing all about American women, and frequently expressed their admiration for the free American woman, many going so far as to envy me, while admiring my unfettered happiness. Two clever Scotch women I met were traveling around the world, but are taking two years at it. One Irishwoman, with a laugh that rivaled her face in sweetness, was traveling alone to Australia. My cabin-mate was bound for New Zealand, but she was accompanied by her brother, a pleasant young Englishman, who insisted on relinquishing his place at first dinner in my favor, and who stayed away despite my protests and my determination not to deprive him of a warm dinner.

In the daytime the men played cricket and quoits.[24] Sometimes, in the evenings, we had singing, and other times we went to the second-class deck and listened to better music given by second-class passengers. When there were no chairs we would all sit down on the deck, and I remember nothing that was more enjoyable than these little visits. There was one little girl with a pale, slender face, who was a great favorite with us all, though none of us ever spoke to her. She sang in a sweet, pathetic voice a little melody about "Who'll buy my silver herrings?" until, I know, if she had tried to sell any, we should all have bought. The best we could do was to join her in the refrain, which we did most heartily.

Better than all to me, it was to sit in a dark corner on deck, above where the sailors had their food, and listen to the sounds of a tom-tom and a weird musical chanting that always accompanied their evening meal. The sailors were Lascars. They were not interesting to look at, and doubtless, if I could have seen as well as heard them at their evening meal, it would have lost its charm for me. They were the most untidy looking lot of sailors I ever saw. Over a pair of white muslin drawers they wore a long muslin slip very like in shape to the old-time nightshirt. This was tied about the waist with a colored handkerchief, and on their heads they wore gaily colored turbans, which are really nothing but a crown of straw with a scarf-shaped piece of bright cloth, often six feet in length, wound about the head. Their brown feet are always bare. They chant, as all sailors do, when hoisting sails, but otherwise are a grim, surly looking set, climbing about over the ship like a pack of monkeys. . . .

A GUESS THAT WILL PAY

Somebody Will Figure Out
Miss Nellie Bly's Precise Time

AND HAVE A FREE TRIP TO EUROPE AS A REWARD

Great Popular Interest in the Guessing Contest—Everybody Who Reads the "Sunday World" May Enter the Lists—A Number of Guessers Sharpening Their Intellects for the Fray—Some Important Questions Concerning the Match Answered in This Column—The Sensation of the Day.

Thousands of "mind's eyes" are now following Nellie Bly in her trip around the world. Interest in her race with the sun has been increased by The World's offer to furnish a first-class trip to Europe, with about a week each in the English and French capitals, and perhaps a run down to historic Rome, all free of cost, to the person who sends to The World on Sunday World blanks the nearest guess to the exact time in days, hours, minutes, and seconds that are required for her globe-girdling tour.

Nellie Bly's trip is the sensation of the day. Everybody is wondering what manner of young woman this is, who takes a small grip in her hand and with but the one dress to her back starts out to dim the lustre of romance by making the reality more wonderful than the dream. All are anxious to see her brave attempt crowned with success. A new zest has been added by the guessing match. Anybody can guess. The single condition is that a blank, which will be printed in the Sunday World, must be used in recording the guess. Only one guess can be written on one blank. Those who wish to guess more than once must equip themselves with a number of the Sunday World blanks. Miss Bly's time may be figured out from the time-tables if the guesser wants to be carefully exact. The blank will be printed in the Sunday World tomorrow.

FROM *The New York World*, NOV. 30, 1889

———

I had not been on the Victoria many days until some one who had become friendly with me, told me it was rumored on board that I was an eccentric American heiress, traveling about with a hair brush and a bank book. I judged that some of the attention I was receiving was due to the story of my wealth. I found it convenient, later on, to correct the report when a young man came to me to say that I was the kind of a girl he liked, and as he was the second son and his brother would get both the money and the title, his sole ambition was to find a wife who would settle £1,000 a year on him.

There was another young man on board who was quite as unique a character and much more interesting to me. He told me that he had been traveling constantly since he was nine years old, and that he had always killed the desire to love and marry because he never expected to find a woman who could travel without a number of trunks, and bundles innumerable. I noticed that he dressed very exquisitely and changed his apparel at least three times a day, so my curiosity made me bold enough to ask how many trunks he carried with him.

"Nineteen," was the amazing reply. I no longer wondered at his fears of getting a wife who could not travel without trunks.

CHAPTER VII

"Two Beautiful Black Eyes"

It was in the afternoon when the Victoria anchored at Port Said.[25] We were all on deck eagerly watching for the first sight of land, and though that sight showed us a wide, sandy beach, and some uninteresting two-storied white houses with arcade fronts, still it did not lessen our desire to go ashore. I suppose that would have been the result under the circumstances had Port Said been the most desolate place on earth. I know everybody was experiencing a slight weariness, though we should all have stoutly denied such a reflection on our constant companions, and gladly welcomed the change of a few hours on shore, where at least we might see new faces. A more urgent reason still, for our going to land, was the fact that this was a coaling port for the Victoria, and I never knew of anything that would make one more quickly feel that there are things in life much worse than death, if I may use the expression, than to have to stay on board a ship during the coaling operation.

Before the boat anchored the men armed themselves with canes, to keep off the beggars they said; and the women carried parasols for the same purpose. I had neither stick nor umbrella with me, and refused all offers to accept one for this occasion, having an idea, probably a wrong one, that a stick beats more ugliness into a person than it ever beats out.

Hardly had the anchor dropped than the ship was surrounded with a fleet of small boats, steered by half-clad Arabs, fighting, grabbing, pulling, yelling in their mad haste to be first. I never in my life saw such an exhibition of hungry greed for the few pence they expected to earn by taking the passengers ashore. Some boatmen actually pulled others out of their boats into the water in their frantic endeavors to steal each other's places. When the ladder was lowered, numbers of them caught it and clung to it as if it meant life or death to them, and here they clung until the captain was compelled to order some sailors to beat the Arabs off, which they did with long poles, before the passengers dared venture forth. This dreadful exhibition made me feel that probably there was some justification in arming one's self with a club.

Our party were about the first to go down the ladder to the boats. It had been our desire and intention to go ashore together, but when we stepped into the first boat some were caught by rival boatmen and literally dragged across to other boats. The men in the party used their sticks quite vigorously; all to no avail, and although I thought the conduct of the Arabs justified this harsh course of treatment, still I felt sorry to see it administered so freely and lavishly to those black, half-clad wretches, and marveled at their stubborn persistence even while cringing under the blows. Having our party divided there was nothing to do under the circumstances but to land and reunite on shore, so we ordered the Arabs to pull away. Midway between the Victoria and the shore the boatmen stopped and demanded their money in very plain and forcible English. We were completely at their mercy, as they would not land us either way until we paid what they asked. One of the Arabs told me that they had many years' experience in dealing with the English and their sticks, and had learned by bitter lessons that if they landed an Englishman before he paid they would receive a stinging blow for their labor.

Walking up the beach, sinking ankle deep in the sand at every step, we came to the main street. Almost instantly we were surrounded by Arab boys who besought us to take a ride on the burros that stood patiently beside them. There were burros of all colors, sizes and shapes, and the boys would cry out, most beseechingly, "Here's Gladstone! Take a ride; see Gladstone with two beautiful black eyes."[26]

This they would cry in such a soft plaintive way that one felt the "two beautiful black eyes" made the animals irresistible.

If one happened to be of a different political belief and objected to riding the Gladstone hobby, as it were, a choice could be made of almost any well-known, if not popular name. There were Mrs. Maybricks, Mary Andersons, Lillie Langtrys,[27] and all the prominent men of the time.

I knew all about burros, having lived for some time in Mexico, but they proved to be quite a novelty to many of the passengers, almost all of whom were anxious to take a ride before returning to the boat. So, as many as could find animals to ride, mounted and went flying through that quaint, sleeping town, yelling with laughter, bouncing like rubber balls on their saddles, while half-naked Arab boys goaded the burros on by short, urgent hisses, and by prodding them from behind with a sharp stick.

After seeing about fifty of our passengers started off in this happy manner, a smaller number of us went to a gambling house, and in a short time were deep in the sport of placing our English gold on colors and numbers and waiting anxiously for the wheel to go 'round to see the money at last swept in by the man at the table. I do not think that any one of us knew anything about the game, but we recklessly put our money on the table and laughed to see it taken in by the man who gave the turn to the wheel.

There was another attraction in this place which helped to win a number of young men from that very expensive table. It was an orchestra composed of young women, some of whom were quite pleasing both in looks and manners.

The longer we remained at this gambling house the less money we had to spend in the shops. I went ashore with the determination not to buy anything as I was very anxious not to increase my baggage. I withstood the tempting laces which were offered at wonderfully low prices, the quaint Egyptian curios, and managed to content myself by buying a sun hat, as everybody else did; and a pugaree[28] to wind about it, as is customary in the East.

Having bought a hat and seen all I cared to of the shops I went strolling about with some friends feasting my eyes on what were to me peculiarities of a peculiar people. I saw old houses with carved-wood fronts that would have been worth a fortune in America occupied by tenants that were unmistakably poor. The natives were apparently so accustomed to strangers that we attracted very little, if any attention, except from those who hoped to gain something from our visit. Unmolested we went about finding no occasion to use sticks on the natives. We saw a great number of beggars who, true to their trade, whined forth, with outstretched hands, their plaintive appeals, but they were not so intrusive or bothersome that they necessitated our giving them the cane instead of alms. The majority of these beggars presented such repulsive forms of misery that in place of appealing to my sympathetic nature, as is generally the case, they had a hardening effect on me. They seemed to thrust their deformities in our faces in order to compel us to give money to buy their absence from our sight.

While standing looking after a train of camels that had just come in loaded with firewood I saw some Egyptian women. They were small in stature and shapelessly clad in black. Over their faces, beginning just below the eyes, they wore black veils that fell almost to their knees. As if fearing that the veil alone would not destroy all semblance of features they wear a thing that spans the face between the hair and the veil down the line of their noses. In some cases this appears to be of gold, and in others it is composed of some black material. One Egyptian woman carried a little naked baby with her. She held it on her hips, its little black legs clinging to her waist much after the fashion of a boy climbing a pole.

Down at the beach we came upon a group of naked men clustered about an alligator that they had caught. It was securely fastened in some knotted rope, the end of which was held by some half dozen black fellows. The public water-carriers, with well-filled goat-skins flung across their backs, we met making their way to the town for the last trip that day.

Darkness came on us very suddenly and sent us rushing off for our ship. This time we found the boatmen would not permit us even to enter their boats until we paid them to take us across to the Victoria. Their price now was just double what they had charged to bring us to land. We protested, but they said it was the law to double the price after sunset.

They were just finishing the coaling when we reached the ship, but the sight we caught of the coal barges, lighted by some sputtering, dripping stuff, held in iron cages on the end of long poles, that showed the hurrying naked people rushing with sacks of coal up a steep gangplank, between the barges and the ship, was one long to be remembered. Nor were they working quietly. Judging from the noise, every one of them was yelling something that pleased his own fancy and humor.

The next morning I got up earlier than usual so anxious was

I to see the famous Suez Canal.[29] Rushing up on deck, I saw
we were passing through what looked like an enormous ditch,
enclosed on either side with high sand banks. We seemed to be
hardly moving, which made us feel the heat very intensely.
They tell me, that according to law, a ship must not travel
through the canal at a speed exceeding five knots an hour, because a rapid passage of the ship would make a strong current
that would wash in the sand banks. One gentleman, who had
traveled all his life, helped us to pass some of the tedious, stifling hours in the canal by telling us the history of it.

It was begun in 1859 and took ten years to build. The work
is estimated to have cost nearly £18,250,000, although the
poor blacks that were employed to do the labor commanded
the lowest possible wages.[30] It is claimed that the lives of
100,000 laborers were sacrificed in the building of this canal, which is only 100 English miles, 88 geographical miles, in
length.

When first completed the width of the surface of the canal
was three hundred and twenty-five feet, but the constant washing in of the banks has reduced it to one hundred and ninety-
five feet. The bottom is said to be seventy-two feet wide and
the depth is but twenty-six feet. The trip through the canal
can be made in from twenty to twenty-four hours.

About noon of our first day in the canal we anchored in the
bay fronting Ismailia.[31] Here passengers were taken on, which
gave us time to see the Khedive's palace, which is built a little
way back from the beach in the heart of a beautiful green forest. Continuing the journey through the canal we saw little of
interest. The signal stations were the only green spots that met
the eye, but they were proof of what could be done, even in
this sandy desert by the expenditure of time and energy.

The one thing that enlivened this trip was the appearance of
naked Arabs, who would occasionally run along the banks of
the canal, crying in pitiful tones, "bahkshish."[32] This we understood meant money, which many of the kind hearted passengers would throw to them, but the beggars never seemed to
find it, and would keep on after us, still crying, "bahkshish"
until they were exhausted.

We passed several ships in the canal. Generally the passengers would call to the passengers on the other ships, but the conversation was confined mainly to inquiries as to what kind of a voyage had been theirs. We saw at one place in the canal, a lot of Arabs, both men and women, at work. Among them were a number of camels that were employed in carrying stone with which the laborers were endeavoring to strengthen the banks.

In the night the boat hung an electric light from the front, and by the aid of this light, moving it from side to side, were able to continue on their way. Before the introduction of electric headlights for this purpose, the vessels were always compelled to tie up in the canal over night, because of the great danger of running into the sand banks. In addition to making the trip longer, this stoppage added greatly to the discomfort of the passengers, who found that even the slow motion of the boat, helped, in a measure, to lessen the stifling heat that seemed to come from out the sand banks during the night as well as when the blazing sun was in the cloudless sky.

We saw, when near the end of the canal, several Arab encampments. They were both picturesque and interesting. First we would notice a small dull red fire, and between that fire and us we could see the outlines of people and resting camels. At one encampment we heard music, but at the others we saw the people either working over the fire, as if preparing their evening meal, or in sitting positions crouching about it in company with their camels.

Shortly after this we dropped anchor in the Bay of Suez. Hardly had we done so when the ship was surrounded by a number of small sail boats that, in the semi-darkness, with their white sails before the breeze, reminded me of moths flocking to a light, both from their white, winged-like appearance, and the rapid way in which numbers of them floated down on us. These sail boats were filled with men with native fruits, photographs and odd shells to sell. They all came on board, and among them were a number of jugglers. The passengers took very little interest in the vendors, but all had a desire to see what was to be offered by the jugglers. There was one among them, a black man, who wore little else than a sash, a turban and a baggy pocket, in the lining of which he carried two lizards and a small rabbit. He was very anxious to show us his tricks and to get the money for them. He refused, however, to do anything with the rabbit and lizards until after he had shown us what he could do with a handkerchief and some bangles that he brought along for this purpose. He selected me from among the crowd, to hold the handkerchief, which he had first shaken as if to show us that it contained nothing. He then showed us a small brass bangle, and pretended to put the bangle in the handkerchief; he then placed the handkerchief in my hand, telling me to hold it tightly. I did so, feeling the presence of the bangle very plainly. He blew on it and jerking the handkerchief loose from my grasp, shook it. Much to the amazement of the crowd the bangle was gone. Some of the passengers in the mean time stole the juggler's rabbit, and one of the lizards had quietly taken itself off to some secluded spot. He was very much concerned about the loss of them and refused to perform any more tricks until they were restored to his keeping. At last one young man took the rabbit from his pocket and returned it to the juggler, much to his gratification. The lizard was not to be found, and as it was time for the ship to sail, the juggler was forced to return to his boat. After he had gone, several people came to know if I had any idea how the trick with the handkerchief had been done. I explained to them that it was an old and very uninteresting trick; that the man had one bangle sewn in the handkerchief, and the other bangle, which he showed to the people, he slipped quietly out of sight. Of course, the one who held the handkerchief held the bangle, but when the juggler would jerk the handkerchief from the hand, and shake it, in full view of his audience, the bangle being sewn to the handkerchief, would naturally not fall to the floor, and as he carefully kept the side to which the bangle was attached turned towards himself, he successfully duped his audience into thinking, that by his magic, he had made the bangle disappear. One of the men who listened to this explanation became very indignant, and wanted to know if I knew positively how this trick had been done, and why I had not exposed the man. I merely explained that I wanted to see the juggler get his money, much to the disgust of the Englishman.

Where we anchored at Suez some claim is the historic place where the Israelites crossed the Red Sea. Some people who bother themselves greatly about facts, figures and ancient history, bought views, which showed that at certain stages of the tide, people, in even this day, can wade around there without any risk of life or comfort. The next morning when we arose we were out of sight of land and well out on the Red Sea. The weather now was very hot, but still some of the passengers did their best to make things lively on board. One evening a number of young men gave a minstrel show.[33] They displayed both energy and perseverance in preparing for it as well as in the execution of it. One end of the deck was set aside for the show. A stage was put up and the whole corner was enclosed by awnings, and the customary green curtain hung in place during service, as drop curtain between acts, as well appearing before and after the performance.

The young men filled their different roles in a very commendable manner, but as the night was so dreadfully warm, the passengers feeling the heat more than usual, owing to the deck being enclosed by awnings, it was difficult to awake any enthusiasm on the part of the audience. We had an intermission, when all retired to the dining room for punch and biscuits, and I know that no one appreciated the refreshments more than the actors, who joined us, their blackened faces streaked with perspiration. . . .

The days were spent mainly on deck lounging about in easy chairs. I found that no one enjoyed as much comfort as I did. I had changed my heavy waist for my silk bodice, and I felt cool and comfortable and lazily happy. When dinner hour approached we would see a few rush off to dress for dinner and later they would appear in full dress, low bodice and long train, much to the amusement of that class of passengers who maintained that it was decidedly not the thing to appear in full dress on an ocean steamer.

The evening dress, made of white linen, in which the young men in the East generally made their appearance at dinner, impressed me as being not only comfortable and appropriate, but decidedly becoming and elegant.

It is very seldom that men do not get more enjoyment out of

life than women under like circumstances. Between cricket, to which they were passionately attached, and quoits and the smoking-room, which was the scene of many exciting games for large stakes and, later on, an hour or so spent in a dark corner of the deck pleasing and being pleased by some congenial companion of the opposite sex, the enforced rest was quite an agreeable one to the men. . . .

The nights were so warm while on the Red Sea that the men left their cabins and spent their nights on deck. It is usually customary for the women to sleep on deck, one side of which, at such times, is reserved exclusively for them. During this trip none of the women had the courage to set the example, so the men had the decks to themselves.

Sleeping down below was all the more reason why women arising early would go on the decks before the sun began to boil in search of a refreshing spot where they could get a breath of cool air. At this hour the men were usually to be seen promenading about in their pajamas, but I heard no objections raised until much to the dismay of the women the Captain announced that the decks belonged to the men until after eight o'clock in the morning, and that the women were expected to remain below until after that hour.

Just before we came to Aden we passed in the sea a number of high brown mountains. They are known as the Twelve Apostles. Shortly after this we came in sight of Aden. It looked to us like a large, bare mountain of wonderful height, but even by the aid of glasses we were unable to tell that it was inhabited. Shortly after eleven o'clock in the morning we anchored in the bay. Our boat was soon surrounded by a number of small boats, which brought to us men who had things to sell, and the wonderful divers of the East.

The passengers had been warned by the officers on board not to go ashore at Aden because of the intense heat. So the women spent their time bargaining with the Jews who came to the ship to sell ostrich feathers and feather boas. The men helped them to close with the sellers always to the sellers' advantage, much as they might congratulate themselves to the contrary.

I, in company with a few of the more reckless ones, decided to brave the heat and go ashore and see what Aden had to offer.

CHAPTER VIII

Aden to Colombo

Hiring a large boat, I went ashore with a half dozen acquaintances who felt they could risk the sun. The four oarsmen were black fellows, thin of limb, but possessed of much strength and tireless good humor. They have, as have all the inhabitants of Aden, the finest white teeth of any mortals. This may be due to the care they take of them and the manner of that care. From some place, I am unable to state where, as I failed to see one living thing growing at Aden, they get tree branches of a soft, fibrous wood which they cut into pieces three and four inches in length. With one end of this stick, scraped free of the bark, they rub and polish their teeth until they are perfect in their whiteness. The wood wears into a soft pulp, but as one can buy a dozen sticks for a penny one can well afford to throw the stick away after once using; although, if necessary, a stick can be used many times. I bought several sticks and found them the most efficient as well as pleasant tooth brush I had ever tried. I felt a regret that some enterprising firm had not thought of importing this useful bit of timber to replace the tooth-destroying brush used in America.

The man in charge of the boat that carried us to land was a small black fellow with the thinnest legs I ever saw. Somehow they reminded me of smoked herrings, they were so black, flat and dried looking. He was very gay notwithstanding his lack of weight. Around his neck and over his bare breast were twined strings of beads, black and gold and silver. Around his waist was a highly colored sash, and on his arms and ankles were heavy bracelets, while his fingers and toes seemed to be trying to outdo one another in the way of rings. He spoke English quite well, and to my rather impertinent question as to what number constituted his family told me that he had three wives and eleven children, which number, he added piously, by the grace of the power of his faith, he hoped to increase.

His hair was yellow which, added to his very light dress of jewelry and sash, gave him rather a strange look. The bright yellow hair and the black skin forming a contrast which was more startling than the black eyes and yellow hair that flashed upon the astonished vision of the American public some years ago, but has become since an old and tiresome sight. Some of the boatmen had their black wool pasted down and hidden under a coating of lime. I was very curious about it until the first man explained that they were merely bleaching their hair; that it was always done by covering the head with lime, which, being allowed to remain on for several days, exposed to the hot sun and the water, bleached the hair yellow or red at the expiration of that time. This bleaching craze, he also informed me, was confined to the men of Aden. So far, none of the women had tried to enhance their black beauty in that way, but it was considered very smart among the men.

While we were talking our men were vigorously pulling to the time of a rousing song, one line of which was sung by one man, the others joining in the refrain at the end. Their voices were not unpleasant, and the air had a monotonous rhythm that was very fascinating.

We landed at a well-built pier and walked up the finely-cut, white-stone steps from the boat to the land. Instantly we were surrounded by half-clad black people, all of whom, after the manner of hack-drivers at railway stations, were clamoring for our favor. They were not all drivers, however. Mingling with the drivers were merchants with jewelry, ostrich plumes and boas to sell, runners for hotels, beggars, cripples and guides. This conglomeration besought us to listen to every individual one of them until a native policeman, in the Queen's uniform, came forward and pushed the black fellows back with his hands, sometimes hastening their retreat with his boot.

A large board occupied a prominent position on the pier. On it was marked the prices that should be paid drivers, boatmen, and like people. It was, indeed, a praiseworthy thoughtfulness that caused the erection of that board, for it prevented tourists being robbed. I looked at it, and thought that even in that land there was more precaution taken to protect helpless and igno-rant strangers than in New York city, where the usual custom of night hack-men is to demand exorbitant prices, and if they are not forthcoming, to pull off their coats and fight for it.

Perched on the side of this bleak, bare mountain is a majestic white building, reached by a fine road cut in the stone that forms the mountain. It is a club house, erected for the benefit of the English soldiers who are stationed on this barren spot. In the harbor lay an English man-of-war, and near a point where the land was most level, numbers of white tents were pitched for soldiers.

From the highest peak of the black, rocky mountain, prob-ably 1700 feet above sea level, floated the English flag. As I traveled on and realized more than ever before how the En-glish have stolen almost all, if not all, desirable sea-ports, I felt an increased respect for the level-headedness of the English government, and I cease to marvel at the pride with which Englishmen view their flag floating in so many different climes and over so many different nationalities.

Near the pier were shops run by Parsees. A hotel, post-office and telegraph office are located in the same place. The town of Aden is five miles distant. We hired a carriage and started at a good pace, on a wide, smooth road that took us along the beach for a way, passing low rows of houses, where we saw many mis-erable, dirty-looking natives; passed a large graveyard, liberally filled, which looked like the rest of that stony point, bleak, black and bare, the graves often being shaped by cobblestones.

The roads at Aden are a marvel of beauty. They are wide and as smooth as hardwood, and as they twist and wind in pleasing curves up the mountain, they are made secure by a high, smooth wall against mishap. Otherwise their steepness might result in giving tourists a serious roll down a rough mountainside.

Just before we began to ascend we saw a black man at his devotions. He was kneeling in the centre of a little square formed by rocks. His face was turned heavenward, and he was oblivious to all else except the power before which he was lay-ing bare his inmost soul, with a fervor and devotion that com-manded respect, even from those who thought of him as a heathen. I inferred that he was a sun worshipper from the way in which he constantly had his face turned upward, except when he bent forward to kiss the ground on which he knelt.

On the road we saw black people of many different tribes. A number of women I noticed, who walked proudly along, their brown, bare feet stepping lightly on the smooth road. They had long purple-black hair, which was always adorned with a long, stiff feather, dyed of brilliant red, green, purple, and like striking shades. They wore no other ornament than the colored feather, which lent them an air of pride, when seen beside the much-bejeweled people of that quaint town. Many of the women, who seemed very poor indeed, were lavishly dressed in jewelry. They did not wear much else, it is true, but in a place as hot as Aden, jewelry must be as much as anyone would care to wear.

To me the sight of these perfect, bronze-like women, with a graceful drapery of thin silk wound about the waist, falling to the knees, and a corner taken up the back and brought across the bust, was most bewitching. On their bare, perfectly modeled arms were heavy bracelets, around the wrist and muscle, most times joined by chains. Bracelets were also worn about the ankles, and their fingers and toes were laden with rings. Sometimes large rings were suspended from the nose, and the ears were almost always outlined with hoop rings, that reached from the inmost edge of the lobe to the top of the ear joining the head. So closely were these rings placed that, at a distance, the ear had the appearance of being rimmed in gold. A more pleasing style of nose ornament was a large gold ornament set in the nostril and fastened there as screw rings fasten in the ear. Still, if that nose ornamentation was more pleasing than the other, the ear adornment that accompanied it was disgusting. The lobe of the ear was split from the ear, and pulled down to such length that it usually rested on the shoulder. The enormous loop of flesh was partially filled with large gold knobs.

At the top of the hill we came to a beautiful, majestic, stone double gate, the entrance to the English fort and also spanning the road that leads to the town. Sentinels were pacing to and fro but we drove past them without stopping or being stopped, through a strange, narrow cut in the mountain, that towered at the sides a hundred feet above the roadbed. Both these narrow, perpendicular sides are strongly fortified. It needs but one glance at Aden, which is in itself a natural fort, to strengthen the assertion that Aden is the strongest gate to India.

The moment we emerged from the cut, which, besides being so narrow that two carriages pass with great difficulty, is made on a dangerous steep grade, we got a view of the white town of Aden, nestling in the very heart of what seems to be an extinct volcano. We were driven rapidly down the road, catching glimpses of gaudily attired mounted policemen, water-carriers from the bay, with their well-filled goat-skins flung across their backs, camels loaded with cut stone, and black people of every description.

When we drove into the town, which is composed of low adobe houses, our carriage was surrounded with beggars. We got out and walked through an unpaved street, looking at the dirty, uninviting shops and the dirty, uninviting people in and about them. Very often we were urged to buy, but more frequently the natives stared at us with quiet curiosity. In the heart of the town we found the camel market, but beyond a number of camels standing, lying, and kneeling about, the sight was nothing extraordinary. Near by was a goat market, but business seemed dull in both places.

Without buying anything we started to return to the ship. Little naked children ran after us for miles, touching their foreheads humbly and crying for money. They all knew enough English to be able to ask us for charity.

When we reached the pier, we found our driver had forgotten all the English he knew when we started out. He wanted one price for the carriage and we wanted to pay another. It resulted in our appealing to a native policeman, who took the right change from us, handed it to the driver, and gave him, in addition, a lusty kick for his dishonesty.

Our limited time prevented our going to see the water tanks, which are some miles distant from Aden. When we returned to the ship we found Jews there, selling ostrich eggs and plumes, shells, fruit, spears of swordfish, and such things. In the water, on one side of the boat, were numbers of men, Somali boys, they called them, who were giving an exhibition of wonderful diving and swimming.

They would actually sit in the water looking like bronze statues, as the sun rested on their wet, black skins. They sat in a row, and turning their faces up towards the deck, would yell methodically, one after the other, down the entire line:

"Oh! Yo! Ho!"

It sounded very like a chorus of bull-frogs and was very amusing. After finishing this strange music they would give us a duet, half crying, persuasively, in a sing-song style:

"Have a dive! Have a dive! Have a dive!"

The other half, meanwhile, would put their hands before their widely opened mouths, yelling through their rapidly moving fingers with such energy that we gladly threw over silver to see them dive and stop the din.

The moment the silver flashed over the water all the bronze figures would disappear like flying fish, and looking down we would see a few ripples on the surface of the blue water— nothing more. After a time that seemed dangerously long to us, they would bob up through the water again. We could see them coming before they finally appeared on the surface, and one among the number would have the silver between his teeth, which would be most liberally displayed in a broad smile of satisfaction. Some of these divers were children not more than eight years old, and they ranged from that up to any age. Many of them had their hair bleached. As they were completely naked, excepting a small cloth twisted about the loins, they found it necessary to make a purse out of their cheeks, which they did with as much ease as a cow stows away grass to chew at her leisure.

I have often envied a cow this splendid gift. One wastes so much time eating, especially when traveling, and I could not help picturing the comfort it would be sometimes to dispose of our food wholesale and consume it at our leisure afterwards. I am certain there would be fewer dyspeptics then.

No animal, waterborn and bred, could frisk, more gracefully in the water than do these Somali boys. They swim about, using the legs alone, or the arms alone, on their backs, or sides, and, in most cases, with their faces under water. They never get out of the way of a boat. They merely sink and come up in the same spot when the boat passes. The bay at Aden is filled with sharks, but they never touch these black men, so they tell me, and the safety with which they spend their lives in the water proves the truth of the assertion. They claim that a shark will not attack a black man, and after I had caught the odor of the grease with which these men anoint their bodies, I did not blame the sharks.

After a seven hours' stay at Aden we left for Colombo, being followed a long ways out from land by the divers. One little boy went out with us on the ship, and when he left us he merely took a plunge from the upper deck into the sea and went happily back towards Aden, on his side, waving a farewell to us with his free hand.

The passengers endeavored to make the time pass pleasantly between Aden and Colombo. The young women had some *tableaux vivants*[34] one evening, and they were really very fine. In one they wished to represent the different countries. They asked me to represent America, but I refused, and then they asked me to tell them what the American flag looked like! They wanted to represent one as nearly as possible and to use it to drape the young woman who was to represent America. Another evening we had a lantern slide exhibition that was very enjoyable.

The loyalty of the English to their Queen on all occasions, and at all times, had won my admiration. Though born and bred a staunch American, with the belief that a man is what he makes of himself, not what he was born, still I could not help admiring the undying respect the English have for their royal family. During the lantern slide exhibition, the Queen's picture was thrown on the white sheet, and evoked warmer applause than anything else that evening. We never had an evening's amusement that did not end by everybody rising to their feet and singing "God Save the Queen." I could not help but think how devoted that woman, for she is only a woman after all, should be to the interests of such faithful subjects.

With that thought came to me a shamed feeling that there I was, a free born American girl, the native of the grandest country on earth, forced to be silent because I could not in honesty speak proudly of the rulers of my land, unless I went back to those two kings of manhood, George Washington and Abraham Lincoln.

CHAPTER IX

Delayed Five Days

About nine o'clock in the morning we anchored in the bay at Colombo, Ceylon.³⁵ The island, with its abundance of green trees, was very restful and pleasing to our eyes after the spell of heat we had passed through on the ocean coming from Aden.

Preparations had been made by the passengers before we anchored, to go ashore, and as we came slowly into the small harbor, where a number of vessels were lying, we all stood impatiently on deck waiting for the first opportunity to desert the ship.

With all our impatience we could not fail to be impressed with the beauties of Colombo and the view from the deck of our incoming steamer. As we moved in among the beautiful ships laying at anchor, we could see the green island dotted with low arcaded buildings which looked, in the glare of the sun, like marble palaces. In the rear of us was the blue, blue sea, jumping up into little hills that formed into snowdrifts which softly sank into the blue again. Forming the background to the town was a high mountain, which they told us was known as Adam's Peak.³⁶ The beach, with a forest of tropical trees, looked as if it started in a point away out in the sea, curving around until near the harbor it formed into a blunt point, the line of which was carried out to sea by a magnificent breakwater surmounted by a lighthouse. Then the land curved back again to a point where stood a signal station, and on beyond a wide road ran along the water's edge until it was lost at the base of a high green eminence that stood well out over the sea, crowned with a castle-like building glistening in the sunlight.

Little boats filled with black men, we could see coming out towards us from the shore, but my eyes were fastened on a strangely shaped object, resting on the surface of the water in the bay. It seemed a living, feathered thing of so strange a shape that I watched it with feelings akin to horror. What horrible feathered monster could that lovely island produce, I wondered, noticing with dismay that the ship was heading for it. Just as we were upon it, there was a flutter of wings and a cloud of birds flew across and settled down upon the breakwater, where some fishermen, their feet overhanging the stony sides, were watching their lines. I looked back at what had raised so much consternation in my mind, and saw now that it was relieved of a feathered mass of birds,—a harmless red buoy!

NELLIE BLY DELAYED

The Delay at Colombo

Nellie Bly's admirers and The World's guessers will learn with regret that Miss Bly has been delayed at Colombo. She reached the Singahlese port Sunday morning two days ahead of her itinerary, and expected to get away immediately. She found, however, that circumstances would compel her to devote five days to sight-seeing in Ceylon. The editor of The World has received a cable message from her which simply states the fact of her delay. No explanation can be offered, as none is at hand. She will not now be able to leave Colombo until tomorrow. This changes that part of her itinerary which applies to the 3,500 miles between Colombo and Hong Kong. She will leave Ceylon three days behind time. Instead of arriving at Singapore on Dec. 18, as she expected to, she should now arrive there on Dec. 21. This will give her seven days to make Hong Kong, which she may still reach in time for the Occidental and Oriental steamship Oceanic, scheduled to leave there Dec. 28. If Miss Bly is lucky the three days lost at Colombo will not affect her chances of reaching San Francisco Jan. 22, as was originally arranged. . . .

Guessers must remember that Miss Bly can yet, with fortune favoring her, complete her tour in less than seventy-five days, but it is only fair to everybody to state that the elements are against her in that part of the journey where it is most essential that they should be propitious.

FROM *The New York World*, DEC. 12, 1889

———

Accompanied by a friend, I was the first to step ashore. Some passengers who started in advance of us, took a steam launch. My escort said that he would give me a novel experience, and also show me a small boat that traveled faster than a steam launch. The gentleman who had offered to be my escort during our jaunt on land, was a traveler of vast experience. He has averaged a yearly tour of the world for several years, and knows the eastern countries as he knows his home. Still, when I saw the boat in which he intended to take me ashore, I rather doubted his judgment, but I said nothing.

The boat was a rudely constructed thing. The boat proper was probably five feet in length and two feet in width across the top, narrowing down to the keel, so that it was not wide enough to allow one's feet to rest side by side in the bottom. There were two seats in the middle of the boat facing one another. They are shaded by a bit of coffee sack that must be removed to give room for passengers to get in. The two men sit at either end of this peculiar boat, and with one paddle each. The paddle is a straight pole, with a board the shape and size of a cheese-box head tied to the end of it, and with both those paddles on the same side they row us ashore. The boat is balanced by a log the length of the boat and fastened out by two curved poles, probably three feet from the boat. These boats are called by tourists, outriggers, but are called by the people of Ceylon, catamarans.

With but slight exertion the men sent the boat cutting through the water, and in a few moments we had distanced the steam launch and had accommodations engaged at the hotel before the launch had landed its passengers. It is said at Colombo that catamarans are used by the native fishermen, who go out to sea in them, and that they are so seaworthy and so secure against capsizing that no case of an accident to a catamaran has ever been reported.

A nearer view of the hotel, the Grand Oriental, did not tend to lessen its attractiveness—in fact it increased it. It was a fine, large hotel, with tiled arcades, corridors airy and comfortable, furnished with easy chairs and small marble topped tables which stood close enough to the broad arm-rests, for one to sip the cooling lime squashes or the exquisite native tea, or eat of the delicious fruit while resting in an attitude of ease and laziness. I found no place away from America where smoking was prohibited, and in this lovely promenade the men smoked, consumed gallons of whiskey and soda and perused the newspapers, while the women read their novels or bargained with the pretty little copper-colored women who came to sell dainty hand-made lace, or with the clever, high-turbaned merchants who would snap open little velvet boxes and expose, to the admiring gaze of the charmed tourists, the most bewildering gems. There were deeply-dark emeralds, fire-lit diamonds, exquisite pearls, rubies like pure drops of blood, the lucky cat's-eye with its moving line, and all set in such beautiful shapes that even the men, who would begin by saying, "I have been sold before by some of your kind," would end by laying down their cigars and papers and examining the glittering ornaments that tempt all alike. No woman who lands at Colombo ever leaves until she adds several rings to her jewel box, and these rings are so well known that the moment a traveler sees one, no difference in what part of the globe, he says to the wearer, inquiringly:

"Been to Colombo, eh?"

For the first time since leaving America I saw American money. It is very popular in Colombo and commands a high price—as jewelry! It goes for nothing as money. When I offered it in payment for my bills I was told it would be taken at sixty per cent discount. The Colombo diamond merchants are very glad to get American twenty-dollar gold pieces and pay a high premium on them. The only use they make of the money is to put a ring through it and hang it on their watch chains for ornaments. The wealth of the merchant can be estimated by his watch chain, they tell me; the richer the merchant the more American gold dangles from his chain. I saw some men with as many as twenty pieces on one chain. Most of the jewelry bought and sold in Colombo is sold in the corridor of the Grand Oriental Hotel. Merchants bring their wares with them and tourists find it pleasanter than visiting the shops.

Leading off from this corridor, pleasant in its coolness,

interesting in its peculiarities, is the dining-hall, matching the other parts of the hotel with its picturesque stateliness. The small tables are daintily set and are richly decorated daily with the native flowers of Colombo, rich in color, exquisite in form, but void of perfume. From the ceiling were suspended embroidered punkas,[37] that invention of the East which brings comfort during the hottest part of the day. The punkas are long strips of cloth, fastened to bamboo poles that are suspended within a short distance of the tables. They are kept in motion by a rope pulley, worked by a man or boy. They send a lazy, cooling air through the building, contributing much to the ease and comfort of the guest. Punkas are also used on all the ships that travel in the East.

Very good food was served at the hotel—which was all the more palatable to the passengers from the Victoria after the trials they had had for the past fortnight in eating the same kind of food under daily different names. Singalese waiters were employed, and they were not only an improvement on the English stewards, to whose carelessness and impudence we had been forced to submit, but they were interesting to the Westerner.

They managed to speak English very well and understood everything that was said to them. They are not unpleasing people, being small of stature and fine of feature, some of them having very attractive, clean-cut faces, light bronze in color. They wore white linen apron-like skirts and white jackets. Noiselessly they move over the smooth tile floor, in their bare, brown feet. Their straight black hair is worn long, twisted in a Psyche knot at the back of the head. On the crown of the head, instead of circling it from ear to ear, is always set a tortoise shell comb, like those worn by American school children. It was some time before I could tell a Singalese man from a Singalese woman. It is not difficult to distinguish the different sexes after one knows that the Singalese men wear the comb, which is as distinct a feature of their dress as men's trousers in America. Singalese women would not think of donning this little comb any more than a sensitive American woman would think of wearing men's apparel. . . .

At tiffin[38] I had some real curry, the famous native dish of

India. I had been unable to eat it on the Victoria, but those who knew said it was a most delicious dish when prepared rightly and so I tested it on shore. First a divided dish containing shrimps and boiled rice was placed before me. I put two spoonfuls of rice on my plate, and on it put one spoonful of shrimps; there was also chicken and beef for the meat part of the curry, but I took shrimps only. Then was handed me a much divided plate containing different preserved fruits, chuddah and other things hot with pepper. As instructed, I partook of three of this variety and put it on top of what had been placed first on my plate. Last came little dried pieces of stuff that we heard before we saw, its odor was so loud and unmistakable. They called it Bombay duck. It is nothing more or less than a small fish, which is split open, and after being thoroughly dried, is used with the curry. One can learn to eat it.

After all this is on the plate it is thoroughly mixed, making a mess very unsightly, but very palatable, as I found. I became so given to curry that I only stopped eating it when I found, after a hearty meal, curry threatened to give me palpitation of the heart. A story is told concerning the Bombay duck that is very amusing.

The Shah of Persia was notified that some high official in India intended to send him a lot of very fine Bombay duck. The Shah was very much pleased and, in anticipation of their arrival, had some expensive ponds built to put the Bombay ducks in! Imagine his consternation when he received those ill-smelling, dried fish!

After tiffin we drove to mount Lavania.[39] We went along the smoothest, most perfectly made roads I ever saw. They seemed to be made of red asphalt, and I was afterwards told that they are constructed by convicts. Many of these roads were picturesque bowers, the over-reaching branches of the trees that lined the waysides forming an arch of foliage above our heads, giving us charming telescopic views of people and conveyances along the road. Thatched huts of the natives and glimpses of the dwellers divided our attention with the people we passed on the road.

Mount Lavania we found to be the place we had noticed on entering the harbor. It is a fine hotel situated on an eminence overlooking the sea, and is a favorite resort during the hot seasons. It is surrounded by a smooth green lawn and faces the blue sea, whence it gets a refreshing breeze all the year through.

After dinner, everybody at the Grand Oriental Hotel went out for a drive, the women, and many of the men going bareheaded. Driving through the town, down the wide streets, past beautiful homes set well back in tropical gardens, to the Galle Face drive that runs along the beach just out of reach of the waves that break on the sandy banks with a more musical roar than I ever heard water produce before. The road lies very close to the water's edge, and by the soft rays of the moon its red surface was turned to silver, the deep blue of the sea was black, and the foamy breakers were snow drifts. In the soft, pure light we would see silent couples strolling along arm and arm, apparently so near the breakers that I felt apprehensive lest one, stronger than the others, should catch them unawares and wash them out to that unknown land where we all travel to rest. Lounging on the benches that face the sea were occasional soldiers in the Queen's uniform, whom I looked at anxiously, unable to tell whether their attitude of weariness bespoke a rest from labor or hungry homesickness. One night I saw a native standing waist deep fishing in the roaring breakers. They tell me that many of the fish bite more freely after night, but I thought how easily the fisherman might be washed away, and no one would be the wiser until his absence was noticed by his friends.

Where the Galle Face drive merges into another road, stands the Galle Face Hotel surrounded by a forest of palm trees. Lounging on long-bottomed, easy chairs, on the stone-floored and stone-pillared verandah, one can see through the forest of tall palms where the ocean kisses the sandy beach, and while listening to the music of the wave, the deep, mellow roar, can drift—drift out on dreams that bring what life has failed to give; soothing pictures of the imagination that blot out for a moment the stern disappointment of reality. Or, when the dreams fade away, one can drown the sigh with the cooling lime squash which the noiseless, bare-footed, living bronze has placed on the white arm-rest, at the same time lazily watching the jinrickshas[40] come silently in through the gas-lit gate, the naked black runners coming to a sudden stop, letting the shafts drop so the passenger can step out.

Lazily I sat there one sweet, dusky night, only half hearing my escort's words that came to me mingled with the sound of the ocean. A couple stood close together, face bending over a face up-turned, hand clasped in hand and held closely against a manly heart, standing, two dark figures, beneath an arch of the verandah, outlined against the gate lamp. I felt a little sympathy for them as wrapped in that delusion that makes life heaven or hell, that forms the foundation for every novel, play or story, they stood, until a noisy new arrival wakened her from blissful oblivion, and she rushed, scarcely waiting for him to kiss the hand he held, away into the darkness. I sighed again, and taking another sip of my lime squash, turned to answer my companion.

Early next morning I was awakened by a Singalese waiter placing coffee and toast on a small table which he drew up close to my curtained bed, after which he went out. I knew from the dim light that crept in through the open glass door which led to the balcony, that it was still early, and I soon went off to sleep. I was awakened shortly by a rattling of the dishes on the table, and opening my eyes I saw, standing on the table, quietly enjoying my toast, a crow!

I was not then used to having toast and tea before arising, as is the custom in Ceylon, so I let the crow satisfy his appetite and leisurely take his departure without a protest. I arose earlier than was my habit, because I had a desire to see what there might be to see while I had the opportunity.

After a cool, refreshing bath, I dressed hastily and went down below. I found almost all of my friends up, some having already started out to enjoy the early morning. I regretted my generosity to the crow when I learned that breakfast was never served until nine o'clock, and as everybody endeavored to have the benefit of the cool, sweet morning, toast and tea was very sustaining.

In a light wagon we again drove down Galle Face road, and out past a lake in which men, women, children, oxen, horses, buffalo and dogs were sporting. It was a strange sight. Off on a little green island we saw the laundry folk at work, beating, sousing and wringing the clothes, which they afterwards spread upon the grass to dry. Almost all of the roads through which we drove were perfect with their picturesque curves, and often bordered and arched with magnificent trees, many of which were burdened with beautiful brilliant blossoms.

Everybody seemed to be out. The white people were driving, riding, riding bicycles, or walking. The breakwater, which is a good half-mile in length, is a favorite promenade for the citizens of Colombo. Morning and evening gaily dressed people can be seen walking back and forth between the lighthouse and the shore. When the stormy season comes the sea dashes full forty feet above this promenade, which must be cleansed of a green slime, after the storms are over, before it can be traveled with safety. The Prince of Wales laid the first stone of this beautiful breakwater in 1875, and ten years later it was finished. It is considered one of the finest in existence.

Colombo reminded me of Newport, R. I. Possibly—in my eyes, at least—Colombo is more beautiful. The homes may not be as expensive, but they are more artistic and picturesque. The roads are wide and perfect; the view of the sea is grand, and while unlike in its tropical aspect, still there is something about Colombo that recalls Newport.

After breakfast, which usually leaves nothing to be desired, guests rest in the corridor of the hotel; the men who have business matters to attend to look after them and return to the hotel not later than eleven. About the hour of noon everybody takes a rest, and after luncheon they take a nap. While they sleep the hottest part of the day passes, and at four they are again ready for a drive or a walk, from which they return after sunset in time to dress for dinner. After dinner there are pleasant little rides in jinrickshas or visits to the native theaters. . . .

Among the natives that haunt the hotel are the snake charmers. They are almost naked fellows, sometimes with ragged jackets on and sometimes turbans on their heads, but more often the head is bare. They execute a number of tricks in a very skillful manner. The most wonderful of these tricks, to me, was that of growing a tree. They would show a seed, then they would place the seed on the ground, cover it with a handful of earth, and cover this little mound with a handkerchief, which they first passed around to be examined, that we might be positive there was nothing wrong with it. Over this they would chant, and after a time the handkerchief is taken off and then up through the ground is a green sprout. We look at it incredulously, while the man says:

"Tree no good; tree too small," and covering it up again he renews his chanting. Once more he lifts the handkerchief and we see the sprout is larger, but still it does not please the trickster, for he repeats: "Tree no good; tree too small," and covers it up again. This is repeated until he has a tree from three to five feet in height. Then he pulls it up, shows us the seed and roots.

Although these men always asked us to "See the snake dance?" we always saw every other trick but the one that had caught us. One morning, when a man urged me to "See the snake dance?" I said that I would, but that I would pay to see the snake dance and for nothing else. Quite unwillingly the men lifted the lid of the basket, and the cobra crawled slowly out, curling itself up on the ground. The "charmer" began to play on a little fife, meanwhile waving a red cloth which attracted the cobra's attention. It rose up steadily, darting angrily at the red cloth, and rose higher at every motion until it seemed to stand on the tip end of its tail. Then it saw the charmer and it darted for him, but he cunningly caught it by the head and with such a grip that I saw the blood gush from the snake's mouth. He worked for some time, still firmly holding the snake by the head before he could get it into the basket, the reptile meanwhile lashing the ground furiously with its tail. When at last it was covered from sight, I drew a long breath, and the charmer said to me sadly:

"Cobra no dance, cobra too young, cobra too fresh!"

I thought quite right; the cobra was too fresh!

At Colombo I saw the jinricksha for the first time. The jinricksha is a small two-wheel wagon, much in shape like a sulky,[41] except that it has a top which can be raised in rainy weather. It has long shafts joined at the end with a crossbar. The jinricksha men are black and wear little else than a sash. When the sun is hot they wear large hats that look like enormous mushrooms, but most of the time these hats are hanging to the back of the 'ricksha. There are stands at different places for these men as well as carriage stands. While waiting for patrons they let their 'rickshas rest on the shafts and they sit in the bottom, their feet on the ground. Besides dressing in a sash these men dress in an oil or grease, and when the day is hot and they run, one wishes they wore more clothing and less oil! The grease has an original odor that is entirely its own.

One day I was going out in a 'ricksha and an acquaintance was going with me. The man put his foot on the shaft when I got in, and as he raised it, ready to start, I saw my friend step into her 'ricksha. She sat down and instantly went out—the other way! The man did not have his foot on the shaft and she overbalanced.

I had a shamed feeling about going around the town drawn by a man, but after I had gone a short way, I decided it was a great improvement on modern means of travel; it was so comforting to have a horse that was able to take care of itself! When we went into the shops it was so agreeable not to have the worry of fearing the horses were not blanketed, and when we made them run we did not have to fear we might urge them into a damaging speed. It is a great relief to have a horse whose tongue can protest.

I have spoken about the perfect roads in Ceylon. I found the roads in the same state of perfection in almost all the Eastern ports at which I stopped. I could not decide, to my own satisfaction, whether the smoothness of the road was due to the entire and blessed absence of beer wagons, or to the absence of the New York street commissioners.

I visited at the temples in Colombo, finding little of interest, and always having to pay liberally for the privilege of looking about. One day I went to the Buddhist college, and while there I met the famous high priest of Ceylon. He was sitting on a verandah, that surrounded his low bungalow, writing on a table placed before him. His gown consisted of a straight piece of old gold silk wrapped deftly around the body and over the waist. The silk had fallen to his waist, but after he greeted us he pulled it up around his shoulders. He was a copper-colored old fellow, with gray hair that was shaved very close to the head. He spoke English quite well, and among other things told me he received hundreds of letters from the United States every year, and that they found more converts to the Buddhist religion in America than in any other land. . . .

Arriving at Kandy[42] at last, we hired a carriage and went to see the lake, the public library and the temples. In one old temple, surrounded by a moat, we saw several altars, of little consequence, and a bit of ivory which they told us was the tooth of Buddha. Kandy is pretty, but far from what it is claimed to be. They said it was cool, but we found it so hot that we thought with regret of Colombo. Disgusted with all we found worth seeing we drove to Parathenia to see the great botanical garden. It well repaid us for the visit. That evening we returned to Colombo. I was tired and hungry and the extreme heat had given me a sick headache. On the way down, the Spanish gentleman endeavored to keep our falling spirits up, but every word he said only helped to increase my bad temper, much to the amusement of the Irish boy. He was very polite and kind, the Spaniard, I mean, but he had an unhappy way of flatly contradicting one, that, to say the least, was very exasperating. It was to me, but it only made the Irish boy laugh. When we were going down the mountainside the Spaniard got up, and standing, put his head through the open window in the door to get a view of the country.

"We are going over," he said, with positive conviction, turning around to us. I was leaning up in a corner trying to sleep and the Irish boy, with his feet braced against the end of the compartment, was trying to do the same.

"We won't go over," I managed to say, while the Irish boy smiled.

"Yes, we will," the Spaniard shouted back, "Make your prayers!"

The Irish boy screamed with laughter, and I forgot my sickness as I held my sides and laughed. It was a little thing, but it is often little things that raise the loudest laughs. After that all I needed to say to upset the dignity of the Irish boy was: "Make your prayers!"

I went to bed that night too ill to eat my dinner. The next morning I had intended to go to the pearl market, but felt unequal to it, and when my acquaintances returned and told me that at the very end of the sale a man bought some left over oysters for one rupee and found in them five hundred dollars worth of pearls, I felt sorry that I had not gone, although there was great danger of getting cholera.

One day I heard a man ask another if he knew the meaning of the word "jinricksha." The first replied the word meant "Draw man power," and the second said, with innocent surprise, "I thought it was 'Pull man car!'" I heard a passenger who came ashore from an Australian boat ask Andrew, a clever native who stands at the hotel door, to get him one of those carts to take a ride. Andrew did not know just what the man wanted as there were many different kinds of carts about.

"I don't recall the name of them," the passenger said, in a hesitating manner, "but I believe you call them Jim-Jams!"

He got a jinricksha.

CHAPTER X

In the Pirate Seas

One night, after I had been five days in Colombo, the blackboard in the hotel corridor bore the information that the Oriental would sail for China the following morning, at eight o'clock. I was called at five o'clock and some time afterwards left for the ship. The "Spanish minister," as we called the Spaniard, wanted me to go to some of the shops with him until he should buy some jewelry, but I was so nervous and anxious to be on my way that I could not wait a moment longer than was necessary to reach the boat that was to carry me to China.

When farewells had been said, and I was on the Oriental, I found my patience had given way under the long delay. The ship seemed to be deserted when I went on deck, with the exception of a handsome, elderly man, accompanied by a young blonde man in a natty white linen suit, who slowly promenaded the deck, watching out to sea while they talked. I was trying to untie my steamer chair so as to have some place to sit, when the elderly man came up and politely offered to assist me.

"When will we sail," I asked shortly.

"As soon as the Nepaul comes in," the man replied. "She was to have been here at daybreak, but she hasn't been sighted yet. Waiting for the Nepaul has given us this five days' delay. She's a slow old boat."

"May she go to the bottom of the bay when she does get in!" I said savagely. "The old tub! I think it an outrage to be kept waiting five days for a tub like that."

"Colombo is a pleasant place to stay," the elderly man said with a twinkle in his eye.

"It may be, if staying there does not mean more than life to one. Really, it would afford me the most intense delight to see the Nepaul go to the bottom of the sea."

Evidently my ill humor surprised them, and their surprise amused me, for I thought how little anyone could realize what this delay meant to me, and the mental picture of a forlorn little self creeping back to New York ten days behind time, with a shamed look on her face and afraid to hear her name spoken, made me laugh outright. They gazed at me in astonishment, while I laughed immoderately at my own unenviable position. My better nature surged up with the laugh, and I was able to say, once again: "Everything happens for the best."

"There is the Nepaul," I said, pointing out a line of smoke just visible above the horizon. They doubted it, but a few moments proved that I was correct. "I am very ill-natured," I said, glancing from the kindly blue eyes of the elderly man to the laughing blue eyes of the younger man; "but I could not help it. After being delayed for five days I was called at five o'clock because they said the ship was to sail at eight, and here it is nine o'clock and there's no sign of the ship sailing and—I am simply famished."

As they laughed at my woes the gong sounded for breakfast and they took me down. The Irish lad, with his sparkling eyes and jolly laugh, was there, as was a young Englishman who had also traveled on the ship Victoria to Colombo. I knew him by sight, but as he was a sworn woman-hater I did not dare to speak to him. There were no women on board. I was the only woman that morning, and a right jolly breakfast we had.

The captain, a most handsome man, and as polite and courteous as he was good looking, sat at the head of the table.

Officers, that any ship might boast of, were gathered about him. Handsome, good natured, intelligent, polite, they were, every single one of them. I found the elderly man I had been talking to was the chief engineer, and the young man was the ship's doctor.

The dining-hall was very artistic and pleasant, and the food was good. The ship, although much smaller than the Victoria, was very much better in every way. The cabins were more comfortable, the ship was better ventilated, the food was vastly superior, the officers were polite and good natured, the captain was a gentleman in looks and manners, and everything was just as agreeable as it could be. For several days I let things go on and said nothing about myself, nor did I give them the letter which the London agent had kindly sent. It had brought me no attention or courtesy on the Victoria, and I decided to take my chances on the Oriental. When I saw that uniform kindness and politeness was the rule on this ship, I then gave them the letter, and though the captain was pleased to receive it, still, it could not have made his treatment of me any kinder than it was at first.

It was well on to one o'clock before the passengers were transferred from the Nepaul to the Oriental. In the meantime the ship was amply peopled with merchants from the shore, who were selling jewels and lace. How they did cheat the passengers! They would ask, and sometimes get, fabulous prices for things, and when the ship was ready to sail, they offered to sell at any price. They were quite saucy chaps, too. I heard a vendor reply to a man who offered him a small price for some so-called precious stones:

"I am not charging you for looking at these."

In fact they grew so impudent and bold, that I am surprised that the steamship lines do not issue orders prohibiting their presence on board.

At one o'clock we sailed. The first day and the two days following were passed lazily on deck. I found it a great relief to be again on the sweet, blue sea, out of sight of land, and free from the tussle and worry and bustle for life which we are daily, hourly even, forced to gaze upon on land. Although the East is, in a very great measure, free from the dreadful crowding for life, still one is bound to see signs of it even among the most indolent of people. Only on the bounding blue, the grand, great sea, is one rocked into a peaceful rest at noon of day, at dusk of night, feeling that one is drifting, drifting, not seeing, or knowing, or caring, about fool mortals striving for life. True, the sailors do this and that, but it has an air far from that of elbowing each other for a living. To the lazy passengers it seems that they merely hoist a sail or pull it down, that they may drift—dream—sleep—talk—live for happiness and not for gain.

The fourth day out was Sunday. The afternoon was spent on deck looking at the most beautiful green islands which we slowly passed. Sometimes we would lazily conjecture as to whether they were inhabited or not.

The next day we anchored at Penang, or Prince of Wales Island, one of the Straits Settlements.[43] As the ship had such a long delay at Colombo, it was said that we would have but six hours to spend on shore. With an acquaintance as escort, I made my preparations and was ready to go to land the moment we anchored. We went ashore in a Sampan, an oddly shaped flat boat with the oars, or rather paddles, fastened near the stern.[44] The Malay oarsman rowed hand over hand, standing upright in the stern, his back turned towards us as well as the way we were going. Frequently he turned his head to see if the way was clear, plying his oars industriously all the while. Once landed he chased us to the end of the pier demanding more money, although we had paid him thirty cents, just twenty cents over and above the legal fare.

Hiring a carriage we drove to where a waterfall comes bounding down the side of a naturally verdant mountain which has been transformed, half way up, into a pleasing tropical garden. The picturesque waterfall is nothing marvelous. It only made me wonder from whence it procured its water supply, but after walking until I was much heated, and finding myself apparently just as far from the fount, I concluded the waterfall's secret was not worth the fatigue it would cost.

On the way to the town we visited a Hindoo[45] temple. Scarcely had we entered when a number of half-clad, barefooted priests rushed frantically upon us, demanding that we

remove our shoes. The temple being built open, its curved roof
and rafters had long been utilized by birds and pigeons as a
bedroom. Doubtless ages had passed over the stone floor, but I
could swear nothing else had, so I refused emphatically and
unconditionally to un-boot myself. I saw enough of their idols
to satisfy me. One was a black god in a gay dress, the other
was a shapeless black stone hung with garlands of flowers, the
filthy stone at its base being buried 'neath a profusion of rich
blossoms.

English is spoken less in Penang than in any port I visited. A
native photographer, when I questioned him about it, said:

"The Malays are proud, Miss. They have a language of their
own and they are too proud to speak any other."

That photographer knew how to use his English to advantage. He showed me cabinet-sized proofs for which he asked
one dollar each.

"One dollar!" I exclaimed in astonishment, "That is very
high for a proof."

"If Miss thinks it is too much she does not need to buy. She
is the best judge of how much she can afford to spend," he replied with cool impudence.

"Why are they so expensive?" I asked, nothing daunted by
his impertinence.

"I presume because Penang is so far from England," he re-
joined, carelessly.

I was told afterwards that a passenger from the Oriental
pulled the photographer's long, thin, black nose for his impudence, and I was pleased to hear it.

A Chinese joss-house,[46] the first I had seen, was very interesting. The pink and white roof, curved like a canoe, was
ornamented with animals of the dragon tribe, with their
mouths open and their tails in the air. The straggling worship-
pers could be plainly seen from the streets through the arcade
sides of the temple. Chinese lanterns and gilt ornaments made
gay the dark interior. Little josses,[47] with usual rations of rice,
roast pig and smouldering joss-sticks[48] disbursing a strangely
sweet perfume, were no more interesting than a dark corner in
which the superstitious were trying their luck, a larger crowd
of dusky people than were about the altars. In fact, the only

devotee was a waxed-haired Chinese woman, with a slit-eyed brown babe tied on her back, bowing meekly and lowly before a painted, be-bangled joss.

Some priests with shaven heads and old-gold silk garments, who were in a summer-house in the garden, saw us when we were looking at the gold-fish ponds. One came forth, and, taking me by the hand, gracefully led me to where they were gathered. They indicated their wish that we should sit with them and drink tea with them, milkless and sugarless, from child-like China cups, which they re-filled so often that I had reasons for feeling thankful the cups were so like unto play-dishes. We were unable to exchange words, but we smiled liberal smiles, at one another.

Mexican silver is used almost exclusively in Penang. American silver will be accepted at the same value, but American gold is refused and paper money is looked on with contempt. The Chinese jinricksha men in Penang, compared with those in Colombo, are like over-fed pet horses besides racers in trim. They were the plumpest Chinamen I ever saw; such round fat legs and arms!

When we started back to the ship the bay was very rough. Huge waves angrily tossed our small boat about in a way that blotted the red from my escort's cheeks and caused him to hang his head in a care-for-nothing way over the boat's side. I could not help liking the sea to a coquette, so indifferent and heedless is it to the strange emotions it raises in the breast of man. It was a reckless spring that landed us on the ship's ladder, the rolling of the coal barge helping to increase the swell which had threatened to engulf us. Hardly had we reached deck when the barge was ordered to cut loose; even as this was being done the ship hoisted anchor and started on its way. Almost immediately there was a great commotion on board. About fifty ragged black men rushed frantically on deck to find that while depositing their last sacks of coal in the regions below, their barge and companions had cast off and were rapidly nearing the shore. Then followed dire chattering, wringing of hands, pulling of locks and crying after the receding barge, all to no avail. The tide was coming in, a very strong tide it was, too, and despite the efforts of those on it the barge was steadily swept inland.

The captain appeased the coolies'[49] fears by stating that they should go off in the pilot's boat. We all gathered to see the sight and a funny one it was! The tug being lashed to the ship they first tried to take the men off without slowing down but after one man got a dangerous plunge bath and the sea threatened to bury the tug then the ship was forced to slow down. Some coolies slid down a cable, their comrades grabbing and pulling them wet and frightened white on to the tug. Others went down the ladder which lacked five feet of touching the pilot boat. Those already on board would clutch the hanging man's bare legs, he meanwhile clinging despairingly to the ladder, fearing to loosen his grasp and only doing so when the ship officers would threaten to knock him off.

The pilot, a native, was the last to go down. Then the cable was cast off and we sailed away seeing the tug, so overloaded that the men were afraid to move even to bail it out, swept back by the tide towards the place where we had last seen the land. . . .

It was so damply warm in the Straits of Malacca that for the first time during my trip I confessed myself uncomfortably hot. It was sultry and foggy and so damp that everything rusted, even the keys in one's pockets, and the mirrors were so sweaty that they ceased to reflect. The second day out from Penang we passed beautiful green islands. There were many stories told about the straits being once infested with pirates, and I regretted to hear that they had ceased to exist, I so longed for some new experience.

We expected to reach Singapore that night. I was anxious that we should, for the sooner we got in the sooner we should leave, and every hour lost meant so much to me. The pilot came on at six o'clock. I waited tremblingly for his verdict. A wave of despair swept over me when I heard that we should anchor outside until morning, because it was too dangerous to try to make the port after dark. And this was the result of slowing down to leave off the coolies at Penang. The mail contract made it compulsory for the ship to stay in port twenty-four hours, and while we might have been consuming our stay and so helping me on in my race against time I was wasting precious hours lying outside the gates of hope, as it were, merely because some black men had been too slow. Those few hours might mean the loss of my ship at Hong Kong; they might mean days added to my record. What agony of suspense and impatience I suffered that night!

When I came on deck the next morning the ship lay along side the wharf, and naked Chinese coolies carrying, two by two, baskets of coal suspended between them on a pole, were constantly traversing the gang-plank between the ship and shore, while in little boats about were peddlers with silks, photographs, fruits, laces and monkeys to sell.

The doctor, a young Welshman, and I hired a gharry, a light wagon with latticed windows and comfortable seating room for four with the driver's seat on the same level outside. They are drawn by a pretty spotted Malay pony whose speed is marvelous compared with its diminutive size, and whose endurance is of such quality that the law confines their working hours to a certain limit.

Driving along a road as smooth as a ball-room floor, shaded by large trees, made picturesque by native houses built on pins in marshy land on either side, which tended to dampen our surprise at the great number of graveyards and the generous way in which they were filled, we drove to the town. The graves were odd, being round mounds with walls shaped like horse-shoes. A flat stone where the mound ends and the wall begins bears the inscriptions done in colored letters.

There are no sidewalks in Singapore, and blue and white in the painting of the houses largely predominate over other colors. Families seem to occupy the second story, the lower being generally devoted to business purposes. Through latticed windows we got occasional glimpses of peeping Chinese women in gay gowns, Chinese babies bundled in shapeless, wadded garments, while down below through widely opened fronts we could see people pursuing their trades. Barbering is the principal trade. A chair, a comb, a basin and a knife are all the tools a man needs to open shop, and he finds as many patrons if he sets up shop in the open street as he would under shelter. Sitting doubled over, Chinamen have their heads shaven back almost to the crown, when a spot about the size of a tiny saucer is left to bear the crop of hair which forms the pig-tail. When braided and finished with a silk tassel the Chinaman's hair is "done" for the next fortnight.

The people here, as at other ports where I stopped, constantly chew betel nut, and when they laugh one would suppose they had been drinking blood. The betel nut stains their teeth and mouths blood-red. Many of the natives also fancy tinting their finger-nails with it.

Nothing is patronized more than the 'rickshas in Singapore, and while they are to be had for ten cents an hour it is no unusual sight to see four persons piled in one jinricksha and drawn by one man. We visited a most interesting museum, and saw along the suburban roads the beautiful bungalows of the European citizens. People in dog-carts and wheelmen on bicycles crowded the splendid drives.

We found the monkey-cage, of course. There was besides a number of small monkeys one enormous orang-outang. It was as large as a man and was covered with long red hair. While seeming to be very clever he had a way of gazing off in the distance with wide, unseeing eyes, meanwhile pulling his long red hair up over his head in an aimless, insane way that was very fetching. The doctor wanted to give him a nut, but feared to put his hand through the bars. The grating was too small for the old fellow to get his hand through, but he did not intend to be cheated of his rights, so he merely stuck his lips through the gratings until they extended fully four inches. I burst into laughter at the comical sight. I had heard of mouths, but that beat anything I ever saw, and I laughed until the old fellow actually smiled in sympathy. He got the nut!

The doctor offered him a cigar. He did not take it, but touched it with the back of his hand, afterwards smelling his hand, and then subsided into that dreamy state, aimlessly pulling his hair up over the back of his head.

At the cable office, in the second story of a building, I found the agents conversant with the English language. They would accept American silver at par, but they did not care to handle our other money. The bank and post-office are open places on the ground floor with about as much comfort and style as is found in ordinary wharf warehouses. Chinese and English are employed in both places.

We had dinner at the Hotel de l'Europe, a long, low, white building set back in a wide, green lawn, with a beautiful esplanade, faced by the sea, fronting it. Upon the verandah were long white tables where a fine dinner was served by Chinamen.

On our return from the Governor's House, I heard a strange, weird din as of many instruments in dire confusion and discord, very like in sound to a political procession the night after the presidential election.

"That's a funeral," my Malay driver announced.

"Indeed! If that is the way you have funerals here, I'll see one," I said. So he pulled the gharry to one side where we waited eagerly for a funeral that was heralded by a blast of trumpets. First came a number of Chinamen with black and white satin flags which, being flourished energetically, resulted in clearing the road of vehicles and pedestrians. They were followed by musicians on Malay ponies, blowing fifes, striking cymbals, beating tom-toms, hammering gongs, and pounding long pieces of iron, with all their might and main. Men followed carrying on long poles roast pigs and Chinese lanterns, great and small, while in their rear came banner-bearers. The men on foot wore white trousers and sandals, with blue top dress, while the pall-bearers wore black garments bound with blue braid. There were probably forty pall-bearers. The casket, which rested on long poles suspended on the shoulders of the men, was hidden beneath a white-spotted scarlet cloth with decorations of Chinese lanterns or inflated bladders on arches above it. The mourners followed in a long string of gharries. They were dressed in white satin from head to toe and were the happiest looking people at the funeral. We watched until the din died away in the distance when we returned to town as delighted as if we had seen a circus parade.

"I would not have missed that for anything," Doctor Brown said to me.

"You could not," I replied laughingly, "I know they got it up for our special benefit."

And so laughing and jesting about what had to us no suggestion of death, we drove back to see the temples. None of us were permitted to pass beneath the gate of the Mahommedan temple, so we went on to a Hindoo temple. It was a low stone building, enclosed by a high wall. At the gateway leading to it were a superfluity of beggars, large and small, lame and blind, who asked for alms, touching their foreheads respectfully. The temple was closed but some priests rushed forth to warn us not to step on the sacred old dirty stone-passage leading to it with our shoes on. Its filth would have made it sacred to me with my shoes off! My comrades were told that removing their shoes would give them admission but I should be denied that privilege because I was a woman.

"Why?" I demanded, curious to know why my sex in heathen lands should exclude me from a temple, as in America it confines me to the side entrances of hotels and other strange and incommodious things.

"No, Señora, no mudder," the priest said with a positive shake of the head.

"I'm not a mother!" I cried so indignantly that my companions burst into laughter, which I joined after a while, but my denials had no effect on the priest. He would not allow me to enter. . . .

The people in Singapore have ranks as have people in other lands. There they do not wait for one neighbor to tell another or for the newspapers to inform the public as to their standing but every man, woman, and child carries his mark in gray powder on the forehead so that all the world may look and read and know his caste.

We stopped at the driver's humble home on our way to the ship and I saw there on the ground floor, his pretty little Malay wife dressed in one wrapping of linen, and several little brown naked babies. The wife had a large gold ring in her nose, rings on her toes and several around the rim of her ears, and gold ornaments on her ankles. At the door of their home was a monkey. I did resist the temptation to buy a boy at Port Said and also smothered the desire to buy a Singalese girl at Colombo, but when I saw the monkey my willpower melted and I began straightway to bargain for it. I got it.

"Will the monkey bite?" I asked the driver, and he took it by the throat, holding it up for me to admire as he replied:

"Monkey no bite." But he could not under the circumstances.

CHAPTER XI

Against the Monsoon

That evening we sailed for Hong Kong. The next day the sea was rough and head winds made the run slower than we had hoped for. Towards noon almost all the passengers disappeared. The roughness increased and the cook enjoyed a holiday. There was some chaffing among the passengers who remained on deck. During dinner the chief officer began to relate the woes of people he had seen suffering from the dire disease that threatened now to even overpower the captain. I listened for quite a while, merely because I could not help hearing; and if there was anything the chief could do well it was relating anecdotes. At last one made me get up and run, it was so vivid, and the moment the doctor, who sat opposite, saw me go he got up and followed. I managed to overcome my faintness without really being sick, but the doctor gave way entirely. I went back to dinner to find the cause of our misery had disappeared. When I saw him later, his face was pale and he confessed contritely that his realistic joke had made even him seasick.

During the roughness that followed the doctor would always say to me pleadingly:

"Don't make a start, for if you do I will have to follow."

The terrible swell of the sea during the Monsoon was the most beautiful thing I ever saw. I would sit breathless on deck watching the bow of the ship standing upright on a wave then dash headlong down as if intending to carry us to the bottom. Some of the men made no secret of being seasick and were stretched out in their chairs on deck where they might hope to catch the first breath of air. Although there was a dreadful swell, still the atmosphere was heavy and close. Sometimes I felt as if I would smother. One man who had been quite attentive to me became seasick. I was relieved when I heard it, still I felt very cruel when I would see his pale face and hear him plead for sympathy. As heartless as I thought it was I could not sympathize with a seasick man. There was an effort on the part of others to tease the poor fellow. When I sat down on deck they would carefully take away all the chairs excepting those occupied by themselves, but it mattered little to the sea-sick man. He would quietly curl up on his rugs at my feet and there lie, in all his misery, gazing at me.

"You would not think that I am enjoying a vacation, but I am," he said plaintively to me one day.

"You don't know how nice I can look," he said pathetically at another time. "If you would only stay over at Hong Kong for a week you would see how pretty I can look."

"Indeed, such a phenomenon might induce me to remain there six weeks," I said coldly.

At last some one told him I was engaged to the chief officer, who did not approve of my talking to other men, thinking this would make him cease following me about, but it only served to increase his devotion. Finding me alone on deck one stormy evening he sat down at my feet and holding to the arms of my chair began to talk in a wild way.

"Do you think life is worth living?" he asked.

"Yes, life is very sweet. The thought of death is the only thing that causes me unhappiness," I answered truthfully.

"You cannot understand it or you would feel different. I could take you in my arms and jump overboard, and before they would know it we would be at rest," he said passionately.

"You can't tell. It might not be rest—" I began and he broke in hotly.

"I know, I know. I can show you. I will prove it to you. Death by drowning is a peaceful slumber, a quiet drifting away."

"Is it?" I said, with a pretense of eagerness. I feared to get up for I felt the first move might result in my burial beneath the angry sea.

"You know, tell me about it. Explain it to me," I gasped, a feeling of coldness creeping over me as I realized that I was alone with what for the time was a mad man. Just as he began to speak I saw the chief officer come on deck and slowly advance towards me. I dared not call. I dared not smile, lest he should notice. I feared the chief would go away, but no, he saw me, and with a desire to tease the man who had been so devoted he came up on tip-toe, then, clapping the poor fellow on the back, he said: "What a very pretty love scene!"

"Come," I shouted, breaking away before the startled man could understand. The chief, still in a spirit of fun, took my hand and we rushed down below. I told him and the captain what had occurred and the captain wanted to put the man in irons but I begged that he be left free. I was careful afterwards not to spend one moment alone and unprotected on deck. . . .

NELLIE BLY ON TIME

She Reached Singapore Yesterday and Is Off for Hong Kong

HALF WAY ROUND THE WORLD IN 34 DAYS

A Message Received from the Globe-Trotter Yesterday— She Sends Word That She Will Be in Hong Kong on Christmas Eve, Four Days Ahead of Sailing Time.

Nellie Bly was yesterday in Singapore. Today she is in the China Sea, en route for Hong Kong, where she is due Dec. 24. So far all is well. She can safely lose four days in traveling the 1,150 miles between Singapore and the Chinese port, which will give her ten days to make the distance in, and which calls for the slow rate of progress of about one hundred and fifteen miles per day. There is rough weather in the China Sea at this time of year and she may need this leeway. News of delayed vessels and of disasters come from the waters in which Miss Bly is now riding, but the unswerving good luck of the plucky little woman will no doubt prevail against the dreadful monsoons and terrible typhoons that have so often and so deferentially been mentioned in connection with this part of her trip.

FROM *The New York World*, DEC. 19, 1889

———

One night during the monsoon the sea washed over the ship in a frightful manner. I found my cabin filled with water, which, however, did not touch my berth. Escape to the lower deck was impossible, as I could not tell the deck from the angry, pitching sea. As I crawled back into my bunk a feeling of awe crept over me and with it a conscious feeling of satisfaction. I thought it very possible that I had spoken my last word to any mortal, that the ship would doubtless sink, and with it all I thought, if the ship did go down, no one would be able to tell whether I could have gone around the world in seventy-five days or not. The thought was very comforting at that time, for I felt then I might not get around in one hundred days.

I could have worried myself over my impending fate had I not been a great believer in letting unchangeable affairs go their way. "If the ship does go down," I thought, "there is time enough to worry when it's going. All the worry in the world cannot change it one way or the other, and if the ship does not go down, I only waste so much time." So I went to sleep and slumbered soundly until the breakfast hour.

The ship was making its way laboriously through a very frisky sea when I looked out, but the deck was drained, even if it was not dry.

When I went out, the jolly Irish lad, for whom I had a great fondness, was stretched out languidly in a willow chair with a bottle of champagne on one armrest and a glass on the other. Every little motion of the ship made him vow that when he reached Hong Kong he would stay there until he could return to England overland!

"You should have seen my cabin-mate last night," he said with a laugh when I sat down beside him. The man he spoke of, a very clever Englishman, was the man who posed as a woman-hater, and naturally we enjoyed any joke at his expense.

"Finding our cabin filling with water, he got out of bed, put on a life preserver and bailed out the cabin with a cigarette box!"

I laughed until my sides ached at the mental picture presented to me of the little chunky Englishman in an enormous life preserver, bailing out his cabin with a tiny cigarette box!

Even the box of the deadly cigarette seems to have its Christian mission to perform. While I was wiping away the tears brought there by the strength of my laughter, the Englishman came up, and hearing what had amused us, said:

"While I was bailing out the cabin, 'the boy,'" as we fondly called him, "clung to the upper berth all the time groaning and praying! He was certain the ship would sink, and I could not persuade him to get out of the top berth to help bail. He would do nothing but groan and pray."

The boy answered with a laugh, "I did not want to sleep the rest of the night in wet pajamas," which caused the woman-hater to flee!

Later in the day the rolling was frightful. I was sitting on deck when all at once the ship went down at one side like a wagon in a deep rut. I was thrown in my chair clear across the deck. A young man endeavored to come to my assistance just as the ship went the other way in a still deeper sea-rut. It flung me back again, and only by catching hold of an iron bar did I save my neck at least, for in another moment I would have been dashed through the skylight into the dining hall on the deck below.

As I caught the bar, I saw the man who had rushed to my assistance turned upside down and land on his face. I began to laugh, his position was so ludicrous. When I saw he made no move to get up, I ran to his side, still convulsed with laughter. I found his nose was bleeding profusely, but I was such an idiot that the sight of the blood only served to make the scene to me the more ridiculous. Helping him to a chair, I ran for the doctor and from laughing could hardly tell him what I wanted. The man's nose was broken, and the doctor said he would be scarred for life. Even the others laughed when I described the accident, and, although I felt a great pity for the poor fellow, hurt as he was in my behalf, still an irresistible impulse to laugh would sweep over me every time I endeavored to express my appreciation of his attempt to assist me.

Our passengers were rather queer. I always enjoy the queerness of people. One day, when speaking about the boat, I said:

"Everything is such an improvement on the Victoria. The food is good, the passengers are refined, the officers are polite and the ship is comfortable and pleasant."

When I finished my complimentary remarks about the ship, a little bride who had been a source of interest to us looked up and said:

"Yes, everything is very nice; but the life preservers are not quite comfortable to sleep in."

Shocked amazement spread over the countenances of all the passengers, and then in one grand shout that dining-room resounded with laughter. The bride said that ever since they left home on their bridal tour they had been sleeping in the life preservers. They thought it was the thing to do on board a ship.

But I never knew how queer our passengers were until we reached Hong Kong, which we did two days ahead of time, although we had the monsoon against us. When we landed, a man sued the company for getting him in ahead of time. He said he bought his tickets to cover a certain length of time, and if the company got him in before it expired they were responsible for his expenses, and they had to pay his hotel bill.

The captain asked a minister who was on board to read the service one Sunday. He did so, and when he reached Hong Kong he put in a bill for two pounds! He said he was enjoying a vacation and did not propose to work during that time unless he was paid for it! The company paid, but warned the officers not to let ministers read the service thereafter until they knew their price.

The evening of December 22 we all sat on deck in a dark corner. The men were singing and telling stories. The only other woman who was able to be up and I were the interested and appreciative audience. We all felt an eagerness for morning and yet the eagerness was mingled with much that was sad. Knowing that early in the day we would reach Hong Kong, and while it would bring us new scenes and new acquaintances, it would take us from old friends.

CHAPTER XII

British China

We first saw the city of Hong Kong in the early morning. Gleaming white were the castle-like homes on the tall mountainside.

We fired a cannon as we entered the bay, the captain saying that this was the custom of mail ships. A beautiful bay was this magnificent basin, walled on every side by high mountains. Once within this natural fortified harbor we could discern, in different directions, only small outlets between the mountains, but so small, indeed, they appeared that one could hardly believe a ship would find space large enough for passage. In fact, these outlets are said to be dangerously narrow, the most vigilant care being necessary until the ship is safely beyond on the ocean blue. Mirror-like was the bay in the bright sun, dotted with strange craft from many countries. Heavy iron-clads, torpedo boats, mail steamers, Portuguese lorchas,[50] Chinese junks[51] and sampans. Even as we looked, a Chinese ship wended its way slowly out to sea. Its queer, broad stern hoisted high out of the water and the enormous eye gracing its bow, were to us most interesting. A graceful thing I thought it, but I heard an officer call it most ungraceful and unshapely.

Hong Kong is strangely picturesque. It is a terraced city, the terraces being formed by the castle-like, arcaded buildings perched tier after tier up the mountain's verdant side. The regularity with which the houses are built in rows made me wildly fancy them a gigantic staircase, each stair made in imitation of castles.

The doctor, another gentleman, and I left the boat, and walking to the pier's end selected sedan chairs, in which we were carried to the town. The carriers were as urgent as our hackmen around railway stations in America. There is a knack of getting into a chair properly. It is placed upon the ground, the carrier tilts the shafts down, and the patron steps inside, back towards the chair, and goes into it backward. Once seated, the carriers hoist the chair to their shoulders and start off with a monotonous trot, which gives the chair a motion not unlike that of a pacing saddle horse.

We followed the road along the shore, passing warehouses of many kinds and tall balconied buildings filled with hundreds of Chinese families, on the flat-house plan. The balconies would have lent a pleasing appearance to the houses had the inhabitants not seemed to be enjoying a washing jubilee, using the balconies for clotheslines. Garments were stretched on poles, after the manner of hanging coats so they will not wrinkle, and those poles were fastened to the balconies until it looked as if every family in the street had placed their old clothing on exhibition.

The town seemed in a state of untidiness, the road was dirty, the mobs of natives we met were filthy, the houses were dirty, the numberless boats lying along the wharf, which invariably were crowded with dirty people, were dirty, our carriers were dirty fellows, their untidy pigtails twisted around their half-shaven heads. They trotted steadily ahead, snorting at the crowds of natives we met to clear the way. A series of snorts or grunts would cause a scattering of natives more frightened than a tie-walker would be at the tooting of an engine's whistle.

Turning off the shore road our carriers started up one of the roads which wind about from tier to tier up the mountain.

My only wish and desire was to get as speedily as possible to the office of the Oriental and Occidental Steamship Company to learn the earliest possible time I could leave for Japan, to continue my race against time around the world. I had just marked off my thirty-ninth day. Only thirty-nine days since leaving New York and I was in China. I was leaving particularly elated, because the good ship Oriental not only made up the five days I had lost in Colombo, but reached Hong Kong two days before I was due, according to my schedule. And that with the northeast monsoon against her. It was the Oriental's maiden trip to China, and from Colombo to Hong Kong she had broken all previous records.

I went to the O. and O. office feeling very much elated over my good fortune, with never a doubt but that it would continue.

"Will you tell me the date of the first sailing for Japan?" I asked a man in the office.

"In one moment," he said, and going into an inner office he brought out a man who looked at me inquiringly, and when I repeated my question, said:

"What is your name?"

"Nellie Bly," I replied in some surprise.

"Come in, come in," he said nervously. We followed him in, and after we were seated he said:

"You are going to be beaten."

"What? I think not. I have made up my delay," I said, still surprised, wondering if the Pacific had sunk since my departure from New York, or if all the ships on that line had been destroyed.

"You are going to lose it," he said with an air of conviction.

"Lose it? I don't understand. What do you mean?" I demanded, beginning to think he was mad.

"Aren't you having a race around the world?" he asked, as if he thought I was not Nellie Bly.

"Yes; quite right. I am running a race with Time," I replied.

"Time? I don't think that's her name."

"Her! Her!!" I repeated, thinking, "Poor fellow, he is quite unbalanced," and wondering if I dared wink at the doctor to suggest to him the advisability of our making good our escape.

"Yes, the other woman; she is going to win. She left here three days ago."

I stared at him; I turned to the doctor; I wondered if I was awake; I concluded the man was quite mad, so I forced myself to laugh in an unconcerned manner, but I was only able to say stupidly:

"The other woman?"

"Yes," he continued briskly; "Did you not know? The day you left New York another woman started out to beat your time, and she's going to do it. She left here three days ago. You probably met somewhere near the Straits of Malacca. She says she has authority to pay any amount to get ships to leave in advance of their time. Her editor offered one or two thousand dollars to the O. and O. if they would have the Oceanic leave San Francisco two days ahead of time. They would not do it, but they did do their best to get her here in time to catch the English mail for Ceylon. If they had not arrived long before they were due, she would have missed that boat, and so have been delayed ten days. But she caught the boat and left three days ago, and you will be delayed here five days."

"That is rather hard, isn't it?" I said quietly, forcing a smile that was on the lips, but came from nowhere near the heart.

"I'm astonished you did not know anything about it," he said. "She led us to suppose that it was an arranged race."

"I do not believe my editor would arrange a race without advising me," I said stoutly. "Have you no cables or messages for me from New York?"

"Nothing," was his reply.

"Probably they do not know about her," I said more cheerfully.

"Yes they do. She worked for the same newspaper you do until the day she started."

"I do not understand it," I said quietly, too proud to show my ignorance on a subject of vital importance to my well-doing. "You say I cannot leave here for five days?"

"No, and I don't think you can get to New York in eighty days. She intends to do it in seventy. She has letters to steamship officials at every point requesting them to do all they can to get her on. Have you any letters?"

"Only one, from the agent of the P. and O., requesting the captains of their boats to be good to me because I am traveling alone. That is all," I said with a little smile.

"Well, it's too bad; but I think you have lost it. There is no chance for you. You will lose five days here and five in Yokohama, and you are sure to have a slow trip across at this season."

Just then a young man, with the softest black eyes and a clear pale complexion, came into the office. The agent, Mr. Harmon, introduced him to me as Mr. Fuhrmann, the purser of the Oceanic, the ship on which I would eventually travel to Japan and America. The young man took my hand in a firm, strong clasp, and his soft black eyes gave me such a look of sympathy that it only needed his kind tone to cheer me into a happier state.

"I went down to the Oriental to meet you; Mr. Harmon thought it was better. We want to take good care of you now that you are in our charge, but, unfortunately, I missed you. I returned to the hotel, and as they knew nothing about you there I came here, fearing that you were lost."

"I have found kind friends everywhere," I said, with a slight motion towards the doctor, who was speechless over the ill-luck that had befallen me. "I am sorry to have been so much trouble to you."

"Trouble! You are with your own people now, and we are only too happy if we can be of service," he said kindly. "You must not mind about the possibility of some one getting around the world in less time than you may do it. You have had the worst connections it is possible to make, and everybody knows the idea originated with you, and that others are merely trying to steal the work of your brain, so, whether you get in before or later, people will give you the credit of having originated the idea."

"I promised my editor that I would go around the world in seventy-five days, and if I accomplish that I shall be satisfied," I stiffly explained. "I am not racing with anyone. I would not race. If someone else wants to do the trip in less time, that is their concern. If they take it upon themselves to race *against* me, it is their lookout that they succeed. I am not racing. I promised to do the trip in seventy-five days, and I will do it; although had I been permitted to make the trip when I first proposed it over a year ago, I should then have done it in sixty days."

We returned to the hotel, where a room had been secured for me, after arranging the transfer of my luggage and the monkey from the Oriental to the Oceanic. I met a number of people after tiffin, who were interested in my trip, and were ready and anxious to do anything they could to contribute to my pleasure during my enforced stay.

Having but the one dress I refused to attend any dinners or receptions that were proposed in my honor. During the afternoon the wife of a prominent Hong Kong gentleman waited upon me to place herself and her home at my disposal. She was anxious that I should make her home mine during my stay, but I told her I could not think of accepting her kindness, because I would wish to be out most of the time, and could not make my hours conform to the hours of the house, and still feel free to go, come and stay, as I pleased. Despite her pleadings I assured her I was not on pleasure bent, but business, and I considered it my duty to refrain from social pleasures, devoting myself to things that lay more in the line of work.

I had dinner on the Oriental. As I bade the captain and his officers farewell, remembering their kindness to me, I had a wild desire to cling to them, knowing that with the morning light the Oriental would sail, and I would be once again alone in strange lands with strange people.

That evening the purser of the Oceanic, another acquaintance and I were carried in chairs up a winding road, arched with green trees, on which the leaves hung motionless and still in the silent night.

Our lazy voices, as occasionally we spoke softly to each other, and the steady, monotonous slap-slap-slap of the barefeet of our carriers made the only break in the slumbering stillness. All earth seemed to have gone to rest. Silently we went along, now getting, by dim gas lamps at garden gates, glimpses of comfortable homes in all their Eastern splendor, and then, for a moment emerging from beneath the over-lapping arch of verdant trees, we would get a faint glimmer of the quivering stars and cloudless heavens. The ascent was made at last. We were above the city, lying dark and quiet, but no nearer the glorious starlit sky. A little rush through a wide gate in a high wall, a sudden blindness in a road banked and roofed by foliage, a quick lowering to the ground at the foot of wide steps that led to an open door through which a welcoming light shed its soft, warm rays upon us and we had reached our journey's end.

Inside, where a cordial welcome awaited us, was a bright wood fire before which I longed to curl up on a rug and be left alone to dream—dream. But there were friends instead of dreams, and realities in the shape of a splendid dinner. A table, graced with a profusion of tropical blossoms—a man, handsomer than an ideal hero, at its head—a fine menu, guests, handsome, witty and just enough in number to suit my ideas, were the items of what made up an ideal evening.

It is said people do not grow old in Hong Kong. Their youthful looks bear ample testimony to the statement. I asked the reason why, and they said it is because they are compelled to invent amusements for themselves, and by inventing they find, not time to grow *blasé*, but youth and happiness.

The theatre in Hong Kong knows few professional troupes, but the amateur actors in the English colony leave little to be desired in the way of splendid entertainments. The very best people in the town take part, and I believe they all furnish their own stage costumes. The regiments stationed there turn out very creditable actors in the persons of the young officers.

I went one night to see "Ali Baba and the Forty Thieves"[52] as given by the Amateur Dramatic Club of Hong Kong. . . .

Afterwards, the sight of handsomely dressed women stepping into their chairs, the daintily-colored Chinese lanterns, hanging fore and aft, marking the course the carriers took in the darkness, was very oriental and affective. It is a luxury to have a carriage, of course, but there is something even more luxurious in the thought of owning a chair and carriers. A fine chair with silver mounted poles and silk hangings can be bought, I should judge, for a little more than twenty dollars. Some women keep four and eight carriers; they are so cheap that one can afford to retain a number. Every member of a well established household in Hong Kong has his or her own private chair. Many men prefer a coverless willow chair with swinging step, while many women have chairs that close entirely, so they can be carried along the streets secure against the gaze of the public. Convenient pockets, umbrella stands and places for parcels are found in all well-appointed chairs.

At every port I touched I found so many bachelors, men of position, means and good appearance, that I naturally began to wonder why women do not flock that way. It was all very well some years ago to say, "Go West, young man;" but I would say, "Girls, go East!" There are bachelors enough and to spare! And a most happy time do these bachelors have in the East. They are handsome, jolly and good-natured. They have their own fine homes with no one but the servants to look after them. Think of it, and let me whisper, "Girls, go East!"

The second day after my arrival, Captain Smith, of the Oceanic,[53] called upon me. I expected to see a hard-faced old man; so, when I went into the drawing-room and a youthful, good-looking man, with the softest blue eyes that seemed to have caught a tinge of the ocean's blue on a bright day, smiled down at me, I imagine I must have looked very stupid indeed. I looked at the smooth, youthful face, with its light-brown moustache, and I felt inclined to laugh at the long iron-gray beard my imagination had put upon the Captain of the Oceanic. I caught a laughing gleam of the bluest of blue eyes, and I thought of imaginary stern ones, and had to smother another insane desire to laugh. I looked at the tall, slender, shapely body, and recalled the imaginary short legs, holding upright a wide circumference under an ample waistcoat, and I laughed audibly.

"You were so different to what I imagined you would be," I said afterwards, when we talked over our first meeting.

"And I could not believe you were the right girl, you were so unlike what I had been led to believe," he said, with a laugh, in a burst of confidence. "I was told that you were an old maid with a dreadful temper. Such horrible things were said about you that I was hoping you would miss our ship. I said if you did come I supposed you would expect to sit at my table, but I would arrange so you should be placed elsewhere."

The Captain took me out to see "Happy Valley" that day before we separated. In jinrickshas we rode by the parade and cricket grounds where some lively games are played, the city hall, and the solid, unornamented barracks; along smooth, tree-lined roads, out to where the mountains make a nest of one level, green space. This level has been converted into a racecourse. The judges' stand was an ordinary, commonplace racecourse stand, but the stands erected by and for private families, were built of palms and were more pleasing because they were out of the usual.

During the month of February races are held here annually. They last three days, and during that period everybody stops work, rich and poor alike flocking to the racecourse. They race with native-bred Mongolian ponies, having no horses, and the racing is pronounced most exciting and interesting.

"Happy Valley" lines the hillside. There are congregated the graveyards of all the different sects and nationalities in Hong Kong. The Fire Worshipers lie in ground joining the Presbyterians, the Episcopalians, the Methodists and the Catholics, and Mahommedans are just as close by. That those of different faiths should consent to place their dead together in this lovely tropical valley is enough to give it the name of Happy Valley, if its beauty did not do as much. In my estimation it rivals in beauty the public gardens, and visitors use it as a park. One wanders along the walks looking at the beautiful shrubs and flowers, never heeding that they are in the valley of death, so thoroughly is it robbed of all that is horrible about graveyards.

We rode back to town through the crowded districts, where the natives huddle together in all their filth. It is said that over 100,000 people live within a certain district in Hong Kong not exceeding one-half square mile, and they furthermore positively affirm, that sixteen hundred people live in the space of an acre. This is a sample of the manner in which the Chinese huddle together. They remind me of a crowd of ants on a lump of sugar. An effort is being made in Hong Kong to compel owners to build differently, so as to make the huddling and packing impossible, for the filth that goes with it invariably breeds disease.

Queen's road is interesting to all visitors. In it is the Hong Kong Club, where the bachelors are to be found, the post office, and greater than all, the Chinese shops. The shops are not large, but the walls are lined with black-wood cabinets, and one feels a little thrill of pleasure at the sight of the gold, the silver, ivory carvings, exquisite fans, painted scrolls and the odor of the lovely sandal-wood boxes, coming faintly to the visitor, creates a feeling of greed. One wants them all—everything.

The Chinese merchants cordially show their goods, or follow as one strolls around, never urging one to buy, but cunningly bringing to the front the most beautiful and expensive part of their stock. . . .

While strolling about the Chinese localities, seeing shops more worthy a visit, being more truly Chinese, I came upon an eating-house, from which a conglomeration of strange odors strolled out and down the road. Built around a table in the middle of the room, was a circular bench. The diners perched on this bench like chickens on a fence, not letting their feet touch the floor, or hang over, nor "hunkering" down, nor squatting crossed-legged like a Turk or tailor, but sitting down with their knees drawn up until knees and chin met; they held large bowls against their chins, pushing the rice energetically with their chop-sticks into their mouths. Cup after cup of tea is consumed, not only at meals, but at all hours during the day. The cup is quite small and saucerless, and the tea is always drunk minus sugar and cream.

Professional writers, found in nooks and recesses of prominent thoroughfares, are interesting personalities. Besides writing letters for people they tell fortunes, and their patrons never go away without having their fates foretold. I noticed when paying for articles, merchants invariably weigh the money. It is also customary for merchants to put their private stamp upon silver dollars as an assurance of its legality and worth. Much silver is beaten into such strange shapes by this queer practice that at first I was afraid to accept it in change.

I saw a marriage procession in Hong Kong. A large band of musicians, who succeeded in making themselves heard, were followed by coolies carrying curious looking objects in blue and gilt, which, I was told, represent mythical and historical scenes. A number of very elegant Chinese lanterns and gorgeous looking banners were also carried along. I was told that in such processions they carry roast pig to the temples of the josses, but it is afterwards very sensibly carried off by the participants.

It would be a hopeless thing for a man to go to Hong Kong in search of employment. The banking and shipping houses, controlled by Europeans, certainly employ numbers of men, but they are brought from England under three and five years' contracts. When a vacancy occurs from a death, or a transfer, the business house immediately consults its representatives in London, where another man signs an agreement, and comes out to Hong Kong to work.

One day I went up to Victoria Peak, named in honor of the Queen. It is said to be 1,800 feet high, the highest point on the island. An elevated tramway is built from the town to Victoria Gap, 1,100 feet above the sea. It was opened in 1887. Before that time people were carried up in sedans.

The first year after its completion 148,344 passengers were carried up the mountain side. The fare is thirty cents up and fifteen cents down. During the summer months Hong Kong is so hot that those who are in a position to do so seek the mountaintop, where a breeze lives all the year round. Level places for buildings are obtained by blasting, and every brick, stone, and bit of household furniture is carried by coolies from the town up to the height of 1,600 feet.

At the Gap we secured sedan chairs, and were carried to the Hotel Craigiburn, which is managed by a colored man. The hotel—Oriental in style—is very liberally patronized by the citizens of Hong Kong, as well as visitors. After the proprietor had shown us over the hotel and given us a dinner that could not be surpassed we were carried to Victoria Peak. It required three men to a chair ascending the peak. At the Umbrella Seat, merely a bench with a peaked roof, everybody stops long enough to allow the coolies to rest, then we continue on our way, passing sight-seers and nurses with children. After a while they stop again, and we travel on foot to the signal station.

The view is superb. The bay, in a breastwork of mountains, lies calm and serene, dotted with hundreds of ships that seem like tiny toys. The palatial white houses come half way up the mountain side, beginning at the edge of the glassy bay. Every house we notice has a tennis-court blasted out of the mountain side. They say that after night the view from the peak is unsurpassed. One seems to be suspended between two heavens. Every one of the several thousand boats and sampans carries a light after dark. This, with the lights on the roads and in the houses, seems to be a sky more filled with stars than the one above.

Early one morning a gentleman, who was the proud possessor of a team of ponies, the finest in Hong Kong, called at the hotel to take me for a drive. In a low, easy phaeton behind the spirited ponies that seem like playthings in their smallness but giants in their strength, we whirled along through the town and were soon on the road edging the bay. We had a good view of the beautiful dry dock on the other side, which is constructed entirely of granite and is said to be of such size that it can take in the largest vessels afloat. I thought there were other things more interesting, so I refused to go over to it.

During our drive we visited two quaint and dirty temples. One was a plain little affair with a gaudy altar. The stone steps leading to it were filled with beggars of all sizes, shapes, diseases and conditions of filth. They were so repulsive that instead of appealing to one's sympathy they only succeed in arousing one's disgust.

At another temple, near by a public laundry where the washers stood in a shallow stream slapping the clothes on flat stones, was a quaint temple hewed, cave-like, in the side of an enormous rock. A selvage of rock formed the altar, and to that humble but picturesque temple Chinese women flock to pray for sons to be born unto them that they may have some one to support them in their old age.

After seeing everything of interest in Hong Kong I decided to go to a real Simon-pure Chinese city. I knew we were trying to keep the Chinamen out of America,[54] so I decided to see all of them I could while in their land. Pay them a farewell visit, as it were! So, on Christmas eve, I started for the city of Canton.[55]

CHAPTER XIII

Christmas in Canton

The O. and O. agent escorted me to the ship Powan, on which I was to travel to Canton. He gave me in charge of Captain Grogan, the Powan's commander, an American, who has lived for years in China. A very bashful man he was, but a most kindly, pleasant one. I never saw a fatter man, or a man so comically fattened. A wild inclination to laugh crept over me every time I caught a glimpse of his roly-poly body, his round red face embedded, as it were, in the fat of his shoulders and breast. The thoughts of how sensitive I am concerning remarks about my personal appearance, in a measure subdued my impulse to laugh. I have always said to critics, who mercilessly write about the shape of my chin, or the cut of my nose, or the size of my mouth, and such personal attributes that can no more be changed than death can be escaped:

"Criticise the style of my hat or my gown, I can change them, but spare my nose, it was born on me."

Remembering this, and how nonsensical it is to blame or criticise people for what they are powerless to change, I pocketed my merriment, letting a kindly feeling of sympathy take its place.

Soon after we left, night descended. I went on deck where everything was buried in darkness. Softly and steadily the boat swam on, the only sound—and the most refreshing and restful sound in the world—was the lapping of the water.

To sit on a quiet deck, to have a star-lit sky the only light above or about, to hear the water kissing the prow of the ship, is, to me, paradise. They can talk of the companionship of men, the splendor of the sun, the softness of moonlight, the beauty of music, but give me a willow chair on a quiet deck, the world with its worries and noise and prejudices lost in distance, the glare of the sun, the cold light of the moon blotted out by the dense blackness of night. Let me rest rocked gently by the rolling sea, in a nest of velvety darkness, my only light the soft twinkling of the myriads of stars in the quiet sky above; my music, the sound of the kissing waters, cooling the brain and easing the pulse; my companionship, dreaming my own dreams. Give me that and I have happiness in its perfection.

But away with dreams. This is a work-a-day world and I am racing Time around it. After dinner, when the boat anchored, waiting for the tide which was to carry us safely over the bar, I went below to see the Chinese passengers. They were gambling, smoking opium, sleeping, cooking, eating, reading and talking, all huddled together on one deck, which was in one large room, not divided into cabins. They carry their own beds, a bit of matting, and their own food, little else than rice and tea.

Before daybreak we anchored at Canton. The Chinamen went ashore the moment we landed, but the other passengers remained for breakfast.

While we were having breakfast, the guide whom the captain had secured for us, came on board and quietly supervised the luncheon we were to take with us. A very clever fellow was that guide, Ah Cum. The first thing he said to us was "A Merry Christmas!" and as it had even slipped our minds, I know we all appreciated the polite thoughtfulness of our Chinese guide. Ah Cum told me later that he had been educated in an American mission located in Canton, but he assured me, with great earnestness, that English was all he learned. He would have none of the Christian religion. Ah Cum's son was also educated in an American mission, and, like his father, has put his learning to good account. Besides being paid as guide, Ah Cum collects a percentage from merchants for all the goods bought by tourists. Of course the tourists pay higher prices than they would otherwise, and Ah Cum sees they visit no shops where he is not paid his little fee.

Ah Cum is more comely in features than most Mongolians,

his nose being more shapely and his eyes less slit-like than those of most of his race. He had on his feet beaded black shoes with white soles. His navy-blue trousers, or tights, more properly speaking, were tied around the ankle and fitted very tight over most of the leg. Over this he wore a blue, stiffly starched shirt-shaped garment, which reached his heels, while over this he wore a short padded and quilted silk jacket, somewhat similar to a smoking jacket. His long, coal-black queue, finished with a tassel of black silk, touched his heels, and on the spot where the queue began rested a round black turban.

Ah Cum had chairs ready for us. His chair was a neat arrangement in black, black silk hangings, tassels, fringe and black wood-poles finished with brass knobs. Once in it, he closed it, and was hidden from the gaze of the public. Our plain willow chairs had ordinary covers, which, to my mind, rather interfered with sightseeing. We had three coolies to each chair. Those with us were barefooted, with tousled pig-tail and navy-blue shirts and trousers, much the worse for wear both in cleanliness and quality. Ah Cum's coolies wore white linen garments, gaily trimmed with broad bands of red cloth, looking very much like a circus clown's costume.

Ah Cum led the way, our coolies following. For a time I was only conscious of a confused mass of black faces and long pig-tails, though shortly I became accustomed to it, and was able to distinguish different objects along the crowded thorough-fare; could note the different stands and the curious looks of the people. We were carried along dark and dirty narrow ways, in and about fish stands, whence odors drifted, filling me with disgust, until we crossed a bridge which spanned a dark and sluggish stream.

This little island, guarded at every entrance, is Shameen, or Sandy Face, the land set aside for the habitation of Europeans. An unchangeable law prohibits Celestials from crossing into this sacred precinct, because of the hatred they cherish for Europeans. Shameen is green and picturesque, with handsome houses of Oriental design, and grand shade trees, and wide, velvety green roads, broken only by a single path, made by the bare feet of the chair-carriers.

Here, for the first time since leaving New York, I saw the

stars and stripes. It was floating over the gateway to the American Consulate. It is a strange fact that the further one goes from home the more loyal one becomes. I felt I was a long ways off from my own dear land; it was Christmas day, and I had seen many different flags since last I gazed upon our own. The moment I saw it floating there in the soft, lazy breeze I took off my cap and said: "That is the most beautiful flag in the world, and I am ready to whip anyone who says it isn't."

No one said a word. Everybody was afraid! I saw an Englishman in the party glance furtively towards the Union Jack, which was floating over the English Consulate, but in a hesitating manner, as if he feared to let me see.

Consul Seymour received our little party with a cheery welcome. He was anxious that we should partake of his hospitality, but we assured him our limited time only gave us a moment to pay our respects, and then we must be off again.

Mr. Seymour was an editor before he went to China with his wife and only daughter, to be consul. Since then he has conceived a hobby for embroideries and carved ivories, which he is able to ride to the top of his bent in Canton. When tourists go there he always knows some place where he can guide them to bargains. Mr. Seymour is a most pleasant, agreeable man, and a general favorite. It is to be hoped that he will long have a residence in Shameen, where he reflects credit upon the American Consulate.

What a different picture Canton presents to Shameen. They say there are millions of people in Canton. The streets, many of which are roughly paved with stone, seem little over a yard in width. The shops, with their gaily colored and handsomely carved signs, are all open, as if the whole end facing the street had been blown out. In the rear of every shop is an altar, gay in color and often expensive in adornment. As we were carried along the roads we could see not only the usually rich and enticing wares, but the sellers and buyers. Every shop has a bookkeeper's desk near the entrance. The bookkeepers all wear tortoise-shell rimmed glasses of an enormous size, which lend them a look of tremendous wisdom. I was inclined to think the glasses were a mark of office, for I never saw a man employed in clerical work without them.

I was warned not to be surprised if the Chinamen should stone me while I was in Canton. I was told that Chinese women usually spat in the faces of female tourists when the opportunity offered. However, I had no trouble. The Chinese are not pleasant appearing people; they usually look as if life had given them nothing but trouble; but as we were carried along the men in the stores would rush out to look at me. They did not take any interest in the men with me, but gazed at me as if I was something new. They showed no sign of animosity, but the few women I met looked as curiously at me, and less kindly.

The thing that seemed to interest the people most about me were my gloves. Sometimes they would make bold enough to touch them, and they would always gaze upon them with looks of wonder.

The streets are so narrow that I thought at first I was being carried through the aisles of some great market. It is impossible to see the sky, owing to the signs and other decorations, and the compactness of the buildings; and with the open shops, just like stands in a market, except that they are not even cut off from the passing crowd by a counter, the delusion is a very natural one. When Ah Cum told me that I was not in a market-house, but in the streets of the city of Canton, my astonishment knew no limit. Sometimes our little train would meet another train of chairs, and then we would stop for a moment and there would be great yelling and fussing until we had safely passed, the way being too narrow for both trains to move at once in safety.

Coolie number two of my chair was a source of great discomfort to me all the day. He had a strap spanning the poles by which he upheld his share of the chair. This band, or strap, crossed his shoulders, touching the neck just where the prominent bone is. The skin was worn white and hard-looking from the rubbing of the band; but still it worried me, and I watched all the day expecting to see it blister. His long pigtail was twisted around his head, so I had an unobstructed view of the spot. He was not an easy traveler, this coolie, there being as much difference in the gait of carriers as there is in the gait of horses. Many times he shifted the strap, much to my misery, and then he would turn and, by motions, convey to me that I was sitting more to one side than to the other.

As a result, I made such an effort to sit straight and not to move that when we alighted at the shops I would be cramped almost into a paralytic state. Before the day was over I had a sick headache, all from thinking too much about the comfort of the Chinamen.

A disagreeable thing about the coolies is that they grunt like pigs when carrying one. I can't say whether the grunt has any special significance to them or not, but they will grunt one after the other along the train, and it is anything but pleasant.

I was very anxious to see the execution ground, so we were carried there. We went in through a gate where a stand erected for gambling was surrounded by a crowd of filthy people. Some few idle ones left it to saunter lazily after us. The place is very unlike what one would naturally suppose it to be. At first sight it looked like a crooked back alley in a country town. There were several rows of half dried pottery. A woman, who was mould-ing in a shed at one side, stopped her work to gossip about us with another female who had been arranging the pottery in rows. The place is probably seventy-five feet long by twenty-five wide at the front, and narrowing down at the other end. I noticed the ground in one place was very red, and when I asked Ah Cum about it he said indifferently, as he kicked the red-colored earth with his white-soled shoe:

"It's blood. Eleven men were beheaded here yesterday."

He added that it was an ordinary thing for ten to twenty criminals to be executed at one time. The average number per annum is something like 400. The guide also told us that in one year, 1855, over 50,000 rebels were beheaded in this nar-row alley.[56]

While he was talking I noticed some roughly fashioned wooden crosses leaned up against the high stone wall, and supposing they were used in some manner for religious pur-poses before and during the executions, I asked Ah Cum about them. A shiver waggled down my spinal cord when he an-swered:

"When women are condemned to death in China they are bound to wooden crosses and cut to pieces.

"Men are beheaded with one stroke unless they are the worst kind of criminals," the guide added, "then they are given the death of a woman to make it the more discreditable. They tie them to the crosses and strangle or cut them to pieces. When they are cut to bits, it is done so deftly that they are entirely dismembered and disemboweled before they are dead. Would you like to see some heads?"

I thought that Chinese guide could tell as large stories as any other guides; and who can equal a guide for highly-colored and exaggerated tales? So I said coldly:

"Certainly; bring on your heads!"

I tipped a man, as he told me, who, with the clay of the pottery on his hands, went to some barrels which stood near to the wooden crosses, put in his hand and pulled out a head!

Those barrels are filled with lime, and as the criminals are beheaded their heads are thrown into the barrels, and when the barrels become full they empty them out and get a fresh supply. If a man of wealth is condemned to death in China he can, with little effort, buy a substitute. Chinamen are very indifferent about death; it seems to have no terror for them.

I went to the jail and was surprised to see all the doors open. The doors were rather narrow, and when I got inside and saw all the prisoners with thick, heavy boards fastened about their necks, I no longer felt surprised at the doors being unbarred. There was no need of locking them.

I went to the court, a large, square, stone-paved building. In a small room off one side I was presented to some judges who were lounging about smoking opium! In still another room I met others playing fan tan![57] At the entrance I found a large gambling establishment! They took me into a room to see the instruments of punishment. Split bamboo to whip with, thumb screws, pulleys on which people are hanged by their thumbs, and such pleasant things. While I was there they brought in two men who had been caught stealing. The thieves were chained with their knees meeting their chins, and in that distressing position were carried in baskets suspended on a pole between two coolies. The judges explained to me that as these offenders had been caught in the very act of taking what belonged not to them, their hands would be spread upon flat stones and with smaller stones every bone in their hands would be broken. Afterwards they would be sent to the hospital to be cured. Prisoners dying in jail are always beheaded before burial. . . .

Canton is noted for its many curious and interesting temples. There are over eight hundred temples in the city. The most interesting one I saw during my flying trip was the Temple of the Five Hundred Gods. While there the guide asked me if I was superstitious, and upon my answering in the affirmative, he said he would show me how to try my luck. Placing some joss sticks in a copper jar before the luck-god, he took from the table two pieces of wood, worn smooth and dirty from frequent use, which, placed together, were not unlike a pear in shape. With this wood—he called it the "luck pigeon"— held with the flat sides together, he made circling motions over the smoldering joss sticks, once, twice, thrice, and dropped the luck pigeon to the floor. He explained if one side of the luck pigeon turned up and the other turned down it meant good luck, while if they both fell in the same position it meant bad luck. When he dropped it they both turned the one way, and he knew he would have bad luck.

I took the luck pigeon then, and I was so superstitious that my arm trembled and my heart beat in little palpitating jumps as I made the motions over the burning joss sticks. I dropped the wood to the floor, and one piece turned one way and one the other, and I was perfectly happy. I knew I was going to have good luck.

I saw the Examination Hall, where there are accommodations for the simultaneous examination of 11,616 celestial students, all male. We went to the entrance-gate through a dirty park-like space where a few stunted trees grew feebly and a number of thin, black pigs rooted energetically. Dirty children in large numbers followed us, demanding alms in boisterous tones, and a few women who, by the aid of canes, were hobbling about on their cramped small feet, stopped to look after us with grins of curiosity and amusement. The open space is the principal entrance, then we go through a small gate called the gate of Equity, and later still another called the Dragon gate, which leads into the great avenue. A most strange and curious sight this avenue gives. An open space with a tower on the end known as the watchtower, has a god of literature in the second story. On each side of the open green space are rows of whitewashed buildings, not unlike railway cattle yards in appearance. In these ranges of cells, cells that measure 5-1/2 by 3-2/3 feet, 11,616 pig-tailed students undergo their written examination. On the sides facing the avenue are Chinese inscriptions showing what study is examined in that range. In each cell is a board to sit on, and one a little higher for a desk. This roughly improvised desk must be slid out to allow the student to enter or depart unless he crawls under or jumps over. The same texts are given to all at daylight, and very often when essays are not finished at night the students are kept over night in their cells. The Hall is about 1,380 feet long by 650 feet wide, and is really a strangely interesting place well worth a visit. It is said the examinations are very severe, and from the large number of candidates examined, sometimes only one hundred and fifty will be passed. The place in which the essays are examined is called the Hall of Auspicious Stars, and the Chinese inscription over the avenue translated reads, "The opening heavens circulate literature."

I had a great curiosity to see the leper village, which is commonly supposed to contain hundreds of Chinese lepers. The village consists of numbers of bamboo huts, and the lepers present a sight appalling in its squalor and filth. Ah Cum told us to smoke cigarettes while in the village so that the frightful odors would be less perceptible. He set the example by lighting one, and we all followed his lead. The lepers were simply ghastly in their misery. There are men, women and children of all ages and conditions. The few filthy rags with which they endeavored to hide their nakedness presented no shape of any garment or any color, so dirty and ragged were they. On the ground floors of the bamboo huts were little else than a few old rags, dried grass and things of that kind. Furniture there was none. It is useless to attempt a description of the loathsome appearance of the lepers. Many were featureless, some were blind, some had lost fingers, others a foot, some a leg, but all were equally dirty, disgusting and miserable. Those able to work cultivate a really prosperous-looking garden, which is near their village. Ah Cum assured me they sold their vegetables in the city market! I felt glad to know we had brought our luncheon from the ship. Those lepers able to walk spend the day in Canton begging, but are always compelled to sleep in their village, still I could not help wondering what was the benefit of a leper village if the lepers are allowed to mingle with the other people. On my return to the city I met several lepers begging in the market. The sight of them among the food was enough to make me vow never to eat anything in Canton. The lepers are also permitted to marry, and a surprising number of diseased children are brought into a cursed and unhappy existence.

As we left the leper city I was conscious of an inward feeling of emptiness. It was Christmas day, and I thought with regret of dinner at home, although one of the men in the party said it was about midnight in New York. The guide said there was a building near by which he wanted to show us and then we would eat our luncheon. Once within a high wall we came upon a pretty scene. There was a mournful sheet of water undisturbed by a breath of wind. In the background the branches of low, overhanging trees kissed the still water just where stood some long-legged storks, made so familiar to us by pictures on Chinese fans.

Ah Cum led us to a room which was shut off from the court by a large carved gate. Inside were hard wood chairs and tables. While eating I heard chanting to the weird, plaintive sound of a tom-tom and a shrill pipe. When I had less appetite and more curiosity, I asked Ah Cum where we were, and he replied: "in the Temple of the Dead."

And in the Temple of the Dead I was eating my Christmas luncheon. But that did not interfere with the luncheon. Before we had finished a number of Chinamen crowded around the gate and looked curiously at me. They held up several children, well-clad, cleanly children, to see me. Thinking to be agreeable, I went forward to shake hands with them, but they kicked and screamed, and getting down, rushed back in great fright, which amused us intensely. Their companions succeeded after awhile in quieting them and they were persuaded to take my hand. The ice once broken, they became so interested in me, my gloves, my bracelets and my dress, that I soon regretted my friendliness in the outset. . . .

On our return to the Powan I found some beautiful presents from Consul Seymour and the cards of a number of Europeans who had called to see me. Suffering from a sick-headache, I went to my cabin and shortly we were on our way to Hong Kong, my visit to Canton on Christmas day being of the past.

CHAPTER XIV

To the Land of the Mikado

Shortly after my return to Hong Kong I sailed for Japan on the Oceanic. A number of friends, who had contributed so much towards my pleasure and comfort during my stay in British China, came to the ship to say farewell, and most regretfully did I take leave of them. Captain Smith took us into his cabin, where we all touched glasses and wished one another success, happiness and the other good things of this earth. The last moment having come, the final good-bye being said, we parted, and I was started on my way to the land of the Mikado.

The Oceanic, on which I traveled from Hong Kong to San Francisco, has quite a history. When it was designed and launched twenty years ago by Mr. Harland, of Belfast, it startled the shipping world. The designer was the first to introduce improvements for the comfort of passengers, such as the saloon amidships, avoiding the noise of the engines and especially the racing of the screw in rough weather. Before that time ships were gloomy and somber in appearance and constructed without a thought of the happiness of passengers. Mr. Harland, in the Oceanic, was the first to provide a promenade deck and to give the saloon and staterooms a light and cheerful appearance. In fact, the Oceanic was such a new departure that it aroused the jealousy of other ship companies, and was actually condemned by them as unseaworthy. It is said that so great was the outcry against the ship that sailors and firemen were given extra prices to induce them to make the first trip.

Instead of being the predicted failure, the Oceanic proved a great success. She became the greyhound of the Atlantic, afterwards being transferred to the Pacific in 1875. She is the favorite ship of the O. and O. line, making her voyages with speed and regularity. She retains a look of positive newness and seems to grow younger with years. In November, 1889, she made the fastest trip on record between Yokohama and San Francisco. No expense is spared to make this ship comfortable for the passengers. The catering would be hard to excel by even a first-class hotel. Passengers are accorded every liberty, and the officers do their utmost to make their guests feel at home, so that in the Orient the Oceanic is the favorite ship, and people wait for months so as to travel on her.

When I first went to the ship the monkey had been transferred from the Oriental. Meeting the stewardess I asked how the monkey was, to which she replied dryly:

"We have met."

She had her arm bandaged from the wrist to the shoulder!

"What did you do?" I asked in consternation.

"I did nothing but scream; the monkey did the rest!" she replied.

I spent New Year's eve between Hong Kong and Yokohama. The day had been so warm that we wore no wraps. In the fore-part of the evening the passengers sat together in Social Hall talking, telling stories and laughing at them. The captain owned an organette which he brought into the hall, and he and the doctor took turns at grinding out the music. Later in the evening we went to the dining-hall where the purser had punch and champagne and oysters for us, a rare treat which he had prepared in America just for this occasion. . . .

When eight bells rang we rose and sang Auld Lang Syne with glasses in hand, and on the last echo of the good old song toasted the death of the old year and the birth of the new. We shook hands around, each wishing the other a happy New Year. 1889 was ended, and 1890 with its pleasures and pains began. Shortly after, the women passengers retired. I went to sleep lulled by the sounds of familiar Negro melodies sung by the men in the smoking-room beneath my cabin.

CHAPTER XV

One Hundred and Twenty Hours in Japan

After seeing Hong Kong with its wharfs crowded with dirty boats manned by still dirtier people, and its streets packed with a filthy crowd, Yokohama has a cleaned-up Sunday appearance. Travelers are taken from the ships, which anchor some distance out in the bay, to the land in small steam launches. The first-class hotels in the different ports have their individual launches, but like American hotel omnibuses, while being run by the hotel to assist in procuring patrons, the traveler pays for them just the same.

An import as well as an export duty is charged in Japan, but we passed the custom inspectors unmolested. I found the Japanese jinricksha men a gratifying improvement upon those I had seen from Ceylon to China. They presented no sight of filthy rags, nor naked bodies, nor smell of grease. Clad in neat navy-blue garments, their little pudgy legs encased in unwrinkled tights, the upper half of their bodies in short jackets with wide flowing sleeves; their clean, good-natured faces, peeping from beneath comical mushroom-shaped hats; their blue-black, wiry locks cropped just above the nape of the neck, they offered a striking contrast to the jinricksha men of other countries. Their crests were embroidered upon the back and sleeves of their top garment as are the crests of every man, woman and child in Japan. . . .

I stayed at the Grand Hotel while in Japan. It is a large building, with long verandas, wide halls and airy rooms, commanding an exquisite view of the lake in front. Barring an enormous and monotonous collection of rats, the Grand would be considered a good hotel even in America. The food is splendid and the service excellent. The "Japs," noiseless, swift, anxious to please, stand at the head of all the servants I encountered from New York to New York; and then they look so neat in their blue tights and white linen jackets.

I always have an inclination to laugh when I look at the Japanese men in their native dress. Their legs are small and their trousers are skintight. The upper garment, with its great wide sleeves, is as loose as the lower is tight. When they finish their "get up" by placing their dishpan-shaped hat upon their heads, the wonder grows how such small legs can carry it all! Stick two straws in one end of a potato, a mushroom in the other, set it up on the straws and you have a Japanese in outline. Talk about French heels! The Japanese sandal is a small board elevated on two pieces of thin wood fully five inches in height. They make the people look exactly as if they were on stilts. These queer shoes are fastened to the foot by a single strap running between toes number one and two, the wearer when walking necessarily maintaining a sliding instead of an up and down movement, in order to keep the shoe on.

On a cold day one would imagine the Japanese were a nation of armless people. They fold their arms up in their long, loose sleeves. A Japanese woman's sleeves are to her what a boy's pockets are to him. Her cards, money, combs, hair pins, ornaments and rice paper are carried in her sleeves. Her rice paper is her handkerchief, and she notes with horror and disgust that after using we return our handkerchiefs to our pockets. I think the Japanese women carry everything in their sleeves, even their hearts. Not that they are fickle—none are more true, more devoted, more loyal, more constant, than Japanese women—but they are so guileless and artless that almost any one, if opportunity offers, can pick at their trusting hearts.

If I loved and married, I would say to my mate: "Come, I know where Eden is," and like Edwin Arnold,[58] desert the land of my birth for Japan, the land of love—beauty—poetry—cleanliness. I somehow always connected Japan and its people with China and its people, believing the one no improvement on the other. I could not have made a greater mistake. Japan is beautiful. Its women are charmingly sweet. I know little about the men except that they do not go far as we judge manly beauty, being undersized, dark, and far from prepossessing. They have the reputation of being extremely clever, so I do not speak of them as a whole, only of those I came in contact with. I saw one, a giant in frame, a god in features; but he was a public wrestler. . . .

They have two very pretty customs in Japan. The one is decorating their houses in honor of the new year, and the other celebrating the blossoming of the cherry trees. Bamboo saplings covered with light airy foliage and pinioned so as to incline towards the middle of the street, where meeting they form an arch, make very effective decorations. Rice trimmings mixed with sea-weed, orange, lobster and ferns are hung over every door to insure a plentiful year, while as sentinels on either side are large tubs, in which are three thick bamboo stalks, with small evergreen trees for background.

In the cool of the evening we went to a house that had been specially engaged to see the dancing, or *geisha*, girls.[59] At the door we saw all the wooden shoes of the household, and we were asked to take off our shoes before entering, a proceeding rather disliked by some of the party, who refused absolutely to do as requested. We effected a compromise, however, by putting cloth slippers over our shoes. The second floor had been converted into one room, with nothing in it except the matting covering the floor and a Japanese screen here and there. We sat upon the floor, for chairs there are none in Japan, but the exquisite matting is padded until it is as soft as velvet. It was laughable to see us trying to sit down, and yet more so to see us endeavor to find a posture of ease for our limbs. We were about as graceful as an elephant dancing. A smiling woman in a black kimono set several round and square charcoal boxes containing burning charcoal before us. These are the only Japanese stoves. Afterwards she brought a tray containing a number of long-stemmed pipes—Japanese women smoke constantly—a pot of tea and several small cups.

Impatiently I awaited the *geisha* girls. In the tiny maidens glided at last, clad in exquisite trailing, angel-sleeved kimonos. The girls bow gracefully, bending down until their heads touch their knees, then kneeling before us murmur gently a greeting which sounds like *"Kombanwa!"* drawing in their breath with a long, hissing suction, which is a token of great honor. The musicians sat down on the floor and began an alarming din upon *samisens*,[60] drums and gongs, singing meanwhile through their pretty noses. If the noses were not so pretty I am sure the music would be unbearable to one who has ever heard a chest note. The *geisha* girls stand posed with open fan in hand above their heads, ready to begin the dance. They are very short with the slenderest of slender waists. Their soft and tender eyes are made blacker by painted lashes and brows; their midnight hair, stiffened with a gummy wash, is most wonderfully dressed in large coils and ornamented with gold and silver flowers and gilt paper pompoms. The younger the girl the more gay is her hair. Their kimonos, of the most exquisite material, trail all around them, and are loosely held together at the waist with an obi-sash; their long flowing sleeves fall back, showing their dimpled arms and baby hands. Upon their tiny feet they wear cunning white linen socks cut with a place for the great toe. When they go out they wear wooden sandals. The Japanese are the only women I ever saw who could rouge and powder and be not repulsive, but the more charming because of it. They powder their faces and have a way of reddening their under lip just at the tip that gives them a most tempting look. The lips look like two luxurious cherries. The musicians begin a long chanting strain, and these bits of beauty begin the dance. With a grace, simply enchanting, they twirl their little fans, sway their dainty bodies in a hundred different poses, each one more intoxicating than the other, all the while looking so childish and shy, with an innocent smile lurking about their lips, dimpling their soft cheeks, and their black eyes twinkling with the pleasure of the dance. After the dance the *geisha* girls made friends with me, examining, with surprised delight, my dress, my bracelets, my rings, my boots—to them the most wonderful and extraordinary things,—my hair, my gloves, indeed they missed very little, and they approved of all. They said I was very sweet, and urged me to come again, and in honor of the custom of my land—the Japanese never kiss—they pressed their soft, pouting lips to mine in parting.

Japanese women know nothing whatever of bonnets, and may they never! On rainy days they tie white scarfs over their wonderful hairdressing, but at other times they waddle bareheaded, with fan and umbrella, along the streets on their wooden clogs. They have absolutely no furniture. Their bed is a piece of matting, their pillows, narrow blocks of wood, probably six inches in length, two wide and six high. They rest the back of the neck on the velvet covered top, so their wonderful hair remains dressed for weeks at a time. Their tea and pipe always stand beside them, so they can partake of their comforts the last thing before sleep and the first thing after.

A Japanese reporter from Tokyo came to interview me, his newspaper having translated and published the story of my visit to Jules Verne. Carefully he read the questions which he wished to ask me. They were written at intervals on long rolls of foolscap,[61] the space to be filled in as I answered. I thought it ridiculous until I returned and became an interviewee. Then I concluded it would be humane for us to adopt the Japanese system of interviewing.

I went to Kamakura to see the great bronze god, the image of Buddha, familiarly called Diabutsu.[62] It stands in a verdant valley at the foot of two mountains. It was built in 1250 by Ono Goroyemon, a famous bronze caster, and is fifty feet in height; it is sitting Japanese style, ninety-eight feet being its waist circumference; the face is eight feet long, the eye is four feet, the ear six feet six and one-half inches, the nose three feet eight and one-half inches, the mouth is three feet two and one-half inches, the diameter of the lap is thirty-six feet, and the circumference of the thumb is over three feet. I had my photograph taken sitting on its thumb with two friends, one of whom offered $50,000 for the god. Years ago at the feast of the god sacrifices were made to Diabutsu. Quite frequently the hollow interior would be heated to a white heat, and hundreds of victims were cast into the seething furnace in honor of the god. It is different now, sacrifices being not the custom, and the hollow interior is harmlessly fitted up with tiny altars and a ladder stairway by which visitors can climb up into Diabutsu's eye, and from that height view the surrounding lovely country. We also visited a very pretty temple near by, saw a famous fan tree and a lotus-pond, and spent some time at a most delightful tea-house, where two little "Jap" girls served us with tea and sweets. I also spent one day at Tokyo, where I saw the Mikado's[63] Japanese and European castles, which are enclosed by a fifty foot stone wall and three wide moats. The people in Tokyo are trying to ape the style of the Europeans. I saw several men in native costume riding bicycles. Their roads are superb. There is a street car line in Tokyo, a novelty in the East, and carriages of all descriptions. The European clothing sent to Japan is at least ready-made, if not second hand. . . .

The Japanese are very progressive people. They cling to their religion and their modes of life, which in many ways are superior to ours, but they readily adopt any trade or habit that is an improvement upon their own. Finding the European male attire more serviceable than their native dress for some trades they promptly adopted it. The women tested the European dress, and finding it barbarously uncomfortable and inartistic went back to their exquisite kimonos, retaining the use of European underwear, which they found more healthful and comfortable than the utter absence of it, to which they had been accustomed. The best proof of the comfort of kimonos lies in the fact that the European residents have adopted them entirely for indoor wear. Only their long subjection to fashion prevents their wearing them in public. Japanese patriotism should serve as a model for us careless Americans. No foreigner can go to Japan and monopolize a trade. It is true that a little while ago they were totally ignorant of modern conveniences. They knew nothing of railroads, or street cars, or engines, or electric lighting. They were too clever though to waste their wits in efforts to rediscover inventions known to other nations, but they had to have them. Straightway they sent to other countries for men who understood the secret of such things, and at fabulous prices and under contracts of three, five and occasionally ten years duration, brought them to their land. They were set to work, the work they had been hired to do, and with them toiled steadily and watchfully the cleverest of Japanese. When the contract is up it is no longer necessary to fill the coffers of a foreigner. The employé was released, and their own man, fully qualified for the work, stepped into the position. And so in this way they command all business in their country.

Kimonos are made in three parts, each part an inch or so longer than the other. I saw a kimono a Japanese woman bought for the holidays. It was a suit, gray silk crepe, with pink peach blossoms dotting it here and there. The whole was lined with the softest pink silk, and the hem, which trails, was thickly padded with a delicate perfume sachet. The under-clothing was of the flimsiest white silk. The whole thing cost sixty dollars, a dollar and a half of which paid for the making. Japanese clothing is sewed with what we call a basting stitch, but it is as durable as it could be if sewed with the smallest of stitches. Japanese women have mirrors in which they view their numerous charms. Their mirrors are round, highly pol-ished steel plates, and they know nothing whatever of glass mirrors. All the women carry silk card cases in their long sleeves, in which are their own diminutive cards.

English is taught in the Japan schools and so is gracefulness. The girls are taught graceful movements, how to receive, en-tertain and part with visitors, how to serve tea and sweets gracefully, and the proper and graceful way to use chopsticks. It is a pretty sight to see a lovely woman use chopsticks. At a tea-house or at an ordinary dinner a long paper laid at one's place contains a pair of chopsticks, probably twelve inches in length, but no thicker than the thinner size of lead pencils. The sticks are usually whittled in one piece and split only half apart to prove that they have never been used. Every one breaks the sticks apart before eating, and after the meal they are destroyed. . . .

The prettiest sight in Japan, I think, is the native streets in the afternoons. Men, women and children turn out to play shuttlecock and fly kites. Can you imagine what an enchanting sight it is to see pretty women with cherry lips, black bright eyes, ornamented, glistening hair, exquisitely graceful gowns, tidy white-stockinged feet thrust into wooden sandals, dimpled cheeks, dimpled arms, dimpled baby hands, lovely, innocent, artless, happy, playing shuttlecock in the streets of Yokohama?

Japanese children are unlike any other children I ever saw at play. They always look happy and never seem to quarrel or cry. Little Japanese girls, elevated on wooden sandals and with babies almost as large as themselves tied on their backs, play shuttle-cock with an abandon that is terrifying until one grows confident of the fact that they move with as much agility as they could if their little backs were free from nursemaid bur-dens. Japanese babies are such comical little fellows. They wear such wonderfully padded clothing that they are as shapeless as a feather pillow. Others may think, as I did, that the funny little shaven spots on their heads was a queer style of ornamentation, but it is not. I am assured the spots are shaven to keep their baby heads cool. . . .

In Yokohama, I went to the Hundred Steps, at the top of which lives a Japanese belle, Oyuchisan, who is the theme for artist and poet, and the admiration of tourists. One of the pleasant events of my stay was the luncheon given for me on the Omaha, the American war vessel lying at Yokohama. I took several drives, enjoying the novelty of having a Japanese running by the horses' heads all the while. I ate rice and eel. I visited the curio shops, one of which is built in imitation of a Japanese house, and was charmed with the exquisite art I saw there; in short, I found nothing but what delighted the finer senses while in Japan.

CHAPTER XVI

Across the Pacific

It was a bright sunny morning when I left Yokohama. A number of new friends in launches escorted me to the Oceanic, and when we hoisted anchor the steam launches blew loud blasts upon their whistles in farewell to me, and the band upon the Omaha played "Home, Sweet Home," "Hail Columbia," and "The Girl I Left Behind Me," in my honor; and I waved my handkerchief so long after they were out of sight that my arms were sore for days. My feverish eagerness to be off again on my race around the world was strongly mingled with regret at leaving such charming friends and such a lovely land.

Everything promised well for a pleasant and rapid voyage. Anticipating this, Chief-engineer Allen caused to be written over the engines and throughout the engine room, this date and couplet:

> "For Nellie Bly,
> We'll win or die.
> January 20, 1890."

It was their motto and was all very sweet to me. The runs were marvelous until the third day out, and then a storm came upon us. They tried to cheer me, saying it would only last that day, but the next day found it worse, and it continued, never abating a moment; head winds, head sea, wild rolling, frightful pitching, until I fretfully waited for noon when I would slip off to the dining-room to see the run, hoping that it would have gained a few miles on the day before, and always being disappointed. And they were all so good to me! Bless them for it! If possible, they suffered more over the prospect of my failure than I did.

"If I fail, I will never return to New York," I would say despondently; "I would rather go in dead and successful than alive and behind time."

"Don't talk that way, child," Chief Allen would plead, "I would do anything for you in my power. I have worked the engines as they never were worked before; I have sworn at this storm until I have no words left; I have even prayed—I haven't prayed before for years—but I prayed that this storm may pass over and that we may get you in on time."

"I know that I am not a sinner," I laughed hysterically. "Day and night my plea has been, 'Be merciful to me a sinner,' and as the mercy has not been forthcoming, the natural conclusion is that I'm not a sinner. It's hopeless, it's hopeless!"

"Don't think so," the purser would beg; "don't be so disheartened; why, child, if by jumping overboard I could bring you happiness and success, I should do so in a moment."

"Never mind, little girl, you're all right," the jolly, happy-hearted captain would laugh. "I've bet every cent I have in the bank that you'll get in before you are due. Just take my word for it, you'll be in New York at least three days ahead of time."

"Why do you try to cheat me? You know we are way behind time now," I urged, longing to be still farther cheated into fresh hope, to which the doctor would say, dryly:

"Look here, Nellie Bly, if you don't stop talking so I'll make you take some pills for your liver."

"You mean wretch, you know I can't help being blue. It's head sea, and head winds, and low runs—not liver!"

And then I would laugh, and so would they; and Mr. Allen, who had been pleading for me to "smile just once, give them but one glimpse of my old, jolly smile," would go away content. This is but a repetition of the way in which I was coaxed out of my unhappiness every day, by those great-hearted, strong, tender men.

Now for Dear Old Home

NELLIE BLY IS STEAMING OVER THE PACIFIC, BOUND FOR 'FRISCO

Nellie Bly is homeward bound.

She is on the bosom of the broad Pacific—the largest extent of water in the universe, and withal the smoothest and the most benign, unrippled as it is by storms and not made terrorizing by wave-roughing hurricanes. If the fates are kind, Miss Bly should reach the western metropolis of the western boundary of the United States by Jan. 20, or at the very latest the 21st.

Miss Bly sailed from Yokohama yesterday on the steamship Oceanic of the Oriental and Occidental Steamship line, armed with the same wonderful little gripsack that she started with from New York City on Nov. 14, when she bade her friends goodbye from the deck of the Augusta Victoria. Her grit has been more than masculine.

FROM *The New York World*, JAN. 8, 1890

At last a rumor became current that there was a Jonah on board the ship. It was thought over and talked over and, much to my dismay, I was told that the sailors said monkeys were Jonahs. Monkeys brought bad weather to ships, and as long as the monkey was on board we would have storms. Some one asked if I would consent to the monkey being thrown overboard. A little struggle between superstition and a feeling of justice for the monkey followed. Chief Allen, when I spoke to him on the subject, told me not to do it. He said the monkey had just gotten outside of a hundred weight of cement, and had washed it down with a quart of lamp oil, and he, for one, did not want to interfere with the monkey's happiness and digestion! Just then some one told me that ministers were Jonahs; they always brought bad weather to ships. We had two ministers on board! So I said quietly, if the ministers were thrown overboard I'd say nothing about the monkey. Thus the monkey's life was saved. . . .

Nearing Home

NELLIE BLY WILL SOON BE IN SIGHT OF THE GOLDEN GATE

Fifty-six hours more ought to bring Nellie Bly within sight of the shores of her native land. She has been away from home just sixty-five days this morning at 9.40.30 o'clock, and if the captain of the steamship Oceanic maintains the record he will land the traveler at San Francisco on the evening of the 20th or the morning of the 21st. Then for the flying trip across the continent!

Within the last twenty-four hours the interest in Miss Bly's undertaking has increased more than fourfold. Queries from all parts of the United States began pouring in Thursday night and continued all day yesterday. A Dakota rancher telegraphed that he had made a bet of $500 that the plucky little circumnavigator would beat seventy-three days. Two young men in Newark want to deposit $250 with The World, to be given to the successful guesser in a pool of seventeen; Mary M. Holmes, of Philadelphia, offers to pay her own expenses to California for the privilege of accompanying the globe-girdler on her homeward journey; the editor of the Burlington *Hawkeye* proposes to board the train at the first stopping-place west of Burlington and secure a flying interview, and from every principal point on the presumed route come notices that preparations are in progress for receptions and welcome. Every boy who writes to The World gallantly offers his services as an escort from any point that the editor of The World may designate, and every little girl ends her letter with "My dearest love to darling Nellie Bly."

These childish expressions are all sincere and heartfelt, and if Miss Bly can find time to read half of them her eyes will be moist for a week.

FROM The New York World, JAN. 18, 1890

But even with low runs our trip was bound to come to an end. One night it was announced that the next day we would be in San Francisco. I felt a feverish excitement, and many were the speculations as to whether there would be a snow blockade to hinder my trip across the Continent. A hopefulness that had not known me for many days came back, when in rushed the purser, his face a snow-white, crying:

"My God, the bill of health was left behind in Yokohama."

"Well—well—what does that mean?" I demanded, fearing some misfortune, I knew not what.

"It means," he said, dropping nerveless into a chair, "that no one will be permitted to land until the next ship arrives from Japan. That will be two weeks."

The thought of being held two weeks in sight of San Francisco, in sight of New York almost, and the goal for which I had been striving and powerless to move, was maddening.

"I would cut my throat, for I could not live and endure it," I said quietly, and that spurred him on to make another search, which resulted in finding the report safely lodged in the doctor's desk.

Later came a scare about a smallpox case on board, but it proved to be only a rumor, and early in the morning the revenue officers came aboard bringing the newspapers. I read of the impassable snow blockade which for a week had put a stop to all railroad traffic, and my despair knew no bounds.[64] While the Oceanic was waiting for the quarantine doctor, some men came out on a tug to take me ashore. There was no time for farewells. The monkey was taken on the tug with me, and my baggage, which had increased by gifts from friends, was thrown after me. Just as the tug steamed off the quarantine doctor called to me that he had forgotten to examine my tongue, and I could not land until he did. I stuck it out, he called out "all right;" the others laugh, I wave farewell, and in another moment I was parted from my good friends on the Oceanic.

A White Welcome

NELLIE BLY WILL SEE MORE SNOW THAN SHE EVER SAW BEFORE

Nellie Bly may land in San Francisco tonight or tomorrow morning.

As stated in the Sunday World, the heavy snow-storms in the Sierras may necessitate a change in the overland route. It would not be the part of wisdom to attempt to push over the Central Pacific, as a despatch in another column of The World will indicate. The drifts have become so solidly packed and the fall of snow has been so unprecedentedly heavy, that it may be a week before the road is clear. No eastbound trains can get through for at least three days, and not even then if the snowfall continues. There has not been a storm in the last dozen years that has so completely defied the efforts of the powerful rotary snow-plows as this one.

Guessers who felt quite sure that all elements of uncertainty would be practically eliminated after Miss Bly reached San Francisco, will see that there is more uncertainty now than at any time during the journey. No matter what route is selected, it is impossible to foresee the many obstacles that may suddenly arise, just as the great storm upset all calculations.

FROM *The New York World*, JAN. 20, 1890

CHAPTER XVII

Across the Continent

I only remember my trip across the continent as one maze of happy greetings, happy wishes, congratulating telegrams, fruit, flowers, loud cheers, wild hurrahs, rapid hand-shaking and a beautiful car filled with fragrant flowers attached to a swift engine that was tearing like mad through flower-dotted valley and over snow-tipped mountain, on—on—on! It was glorious! A ride worthy a queen. They say no man or woman in America ever received ovations like those given me during my flying trip across the continent. The Americans turned out to do honor to an American girl who had been the first to make a record of a flying trip around the world, and I rejoiced with them that it was an American girl who had done it. It seemed as if my greatest success was the personal interest of every one who greeted me. They were all so kind and as anxious that I should finish the trip in time as if their personal reputations were at stake. The special train had been waiting for my arrival in readiness to start the moment I boarded it. The Deputy Collector of the port of San Francisco, the Inspector of Customs, the Quarantine Officer and the Superintendent of the O. and O. steamers sat up all the night preceding my arrival, so there should be no delay in my transfer from the Oceanic to the special train. Nor were they the only ones to wait for me. One poor little newspaperwoman did not see bed that night so anxious was she for an interview which she did not get. I was so entirely ignorant about what was to be done with me on landing, that I thought I was someone's guest until I was many miles away from San Francisco. Had I known in advance the special train was mine, every newspaperman and woman who cared to should have been my guest.

My train consisted of one handsome sleeping-car, the San Lorenzo, and the engine, The Queen, was one of the fastest on the Southern Pacific.

"What time do you want to reach New York, Miss Bly?" Mr. Bissell, General Passenger Agent of the Atlantic and Pacific system, asked me.

"Not later than Saturday evening," I said, never thinking they could get me there in that time.

"Very well, we will put you there on time," he said quietly, and I rested satisfied that he would keep his word.

It did not seem long after we left Oakland Mole until we reached the great San Joaquin valley, a level green plain through which the railroad track ran for probably three hundred miles as straight as a sunbeam. The roadbed was so perfect that though we were traveling a mile a minute the car was as easy as if it were traveling over a bed of velvet.

At Merced, our second stop, I saw a great crowd of people dressed in their best Sunday clothes gathered about the station. I supposed they were having a picnic and made some such remark, to be told in reply that the people had come there to see me. Amazed at this information I got up, in answer to calls for me, and went out on the back platform. A loud cheer, which almost frightened me to death, greeted my appearance and the band began to play "By Nellie's Blue Eyes." A large tray of fruit and candy and nuts, the tribute of a dear little newsboy, was passed to me, for which I was more grateful than had it been the gift of a king.

We started on again, and the three of us on the train had nothing to do but admire the beautiful country through which we were passing as swiftly as a cloud along the sky, to read, or count telegraph poles, or pamper and pet the monkey. I felt little inclination to do anything but to sit quietly and rest, bodily and mentally. There was nothing left for me to do now. I could hurry nothing, I could change nothing; I could only sit and wait until the train landed me at the end of my journey. I enjoyed the rapid motion of the train so much that I dreaded to think of the end. At Fresno, the next station, the town turned out to do me honor, and I was the happy recipient of exquisite fruits, wines and flowers, all the product of Fresno County, California.

The men who spoke to me were interested in my sunburnt nose, the delays I had experienced, the number of miles I had traveled. The women wanted to examine my one dress in which I had traveled around, the cloak and cap I had worn, were anxious to know what was in the bag, and all about the monkey.

FLYING HOME

"The World's" Earth-Circler Is Nearly Half Way Across the Continent

---

SHE ACTS AS AN ENGINEER

A Wild Ride in the Cab of the Big Locomotive

A TERRIBLE DEATH ESCAPED

The following special despatch was received at 2 o'clock this morning:

"GALLUP, N.M., Jan. 22.—Nellie Bly will only know how narrowly she escaped death today when she reads this:

"She passed here on a special train running at the rate of over fifty miles an hour. Three miles east of this place the track repairers were replacing the stringers[65] on the bridge over a deep canyon.

"The rails were in place, but only held up by jackscrews. The workmen heard the special coming and tried to flag it, but they were too late.

"The engine and car went thundering over the ravine and passed over safely.

"The escape is a miraculous one, and section-men who witnessed the train flash past on its straw-like structure regard the escape as one of the most marvelous in railway history."

If the same good fortune attends Nellie Bly in the latter part of her trip across the continent that has attended her in the 23,000 miles already travelled she ought to reach Chicago tomorrow in time to make regular connection with the Pennsylvania Railroad.

FROM *The New York World*, JAN. 23, 1890

While we were doing some fine running the first day, I heard the whistle blow wildly, and then I felt the train strike something.

Brakes were put on, and we went out to see what had occurred. It was hailing just then, and we saw two men coming up the track. The conductor came back to tell us that we had struck a hand-car, and pointed to a piece of twisted iron and a bit of splintered board—all that remained of it—laying alongside. When the men came up, one remarked, with a mingled expression of wonder and disgust upon his face:

"Well, you ARE running like h—!"

"Thank you; I am glad to hear it," I said, and then we all laughed. I inquired if they had been hurt; they assured me not, and good humor being restored all around, we said good-bye, the engineer pulled the lever, and we were off again. At one station where we stopped there was a large crowd, and when I appeared on the platform, one yell went up from them. There was one man on the outskirts of the crowd who shouted:

"Nellie Bly, I must get up close to you!"

The crowd evidently felt as much curiosity as I did about the man's object, for they made a way and he came up to the platform.

"Nellie Bly, you must touch my hand," he said, excitedly. Anything to please the man. I reached over and touched his hand, and then he shouted:

"Now you will be successful. I have in my hand the left hind foot of a rabbit!"

Well, I don't know anything about the left hind foot of a rabbit, but when I knew that my train had run safely across a bridge which was held in place only by jack-screws, and which fell the moment we were across;[66] and when I heard that in another place the engine had just switched off from us when it lost a wheel, then I thought of the left hind foot of a rabbit, and wondered if there was anything in it.

One place, where a large crowd greeted me, a man on the limits of it yelled:

"Did you ride on an elephant, Nellie?" and when I said I had not, he dropped his head and went away. At another place the policemen fought to keep the crowd back; everybody was wanting to shake hands with me, but at last one officer was shoved aside, and the other seeing the fate of his comrade, turned to me, saying: "I guess I'll give up and take a shake," and while reaching for my hand was swept on with the crowd. I leaned over the platform and shook hands with both hands at every station, and when the train pulled out crowds would run after, grabbing for my hands as long as they could. My arms ached for almost a month afterwards, but I did not mind the ache if by such little acts I could give pleasure to my own people, whom I was so glad to be among once more.

"Come out here and we'll elect you governor," a Kansas man said, and I believe they would have done it, if the splendid welcomes they gave me are any criterion. Telegrams addressed merely to "Nellie Bly, Nellie Bly's Train," came from all parts of the country filled with words of cheer and praise at all hours of the day and night. I could not mention one place that was kinder than another. Over ten thousand people greeted me at Topeka. The mayor of Dodge City presented me, in behalf of the citizens, with resolutions of praise. I was very anxious to go to Kansas City, but we only went to the station outside of the limits, in order to save thirty minutes. At Hutchinson a large crowd and the Ringgold Cornet Band greeted me, and at another place the mayor assured me that the band had been brought down, but they forgot to play. They merely shouted like the rest, forgetting in the excitement all about their music.

GUESS EARLY AND OFTEN

The guessing coupon in the Nellie Bly contest appears today for the last time, because the circumnavigator will, if nothing happens, reach Chicago tomorrow, and after that all guessing ceases. Due allowance will be made for the distance between the post-office address of the sender and The World office. Miss Bly's tour around the world will be considered at an end when she steps from the train at Jersey City. As both feet touch the platform three stop watches in the hands of three timers will record the exact time to the fifth of a second that the great race against time has taken.

FROM *The New York World*, JAN. 23, 1890

———

I was up until four o'clock, talking first with a little newspaper girl from Kearney, Nebraska, who had traveled six hundred miles to meet and interview me, and later dictating an account of my trip to a stenographer, who was sea-sick from the motion of the train. I had probably slept two hours when the porter called me, saying we would soon be in Chicago. I dressed myself leisurely and drank the last drop of coffee there was left on our train, for we had been liberally entertaining everybody who cared to travel any distance with us. I was surprised, on opening the door of my stateroom, to see the car quite filled with good-looking men. They were newspapermen, members of the Chicago Press Club, I found a moment later, who had come out to Joliet to meet me and to escort me to their city. Mr. Cornelius Gardener, the vice-president of the club, in the absence of the president, took charge of our little party. Before we were in I had answered all their questions, and we joked about my sunburnt nose and discussed the merits of my one dress, the cleverness of the monkey, and I was feeling happy and at home and wishing I could stay all day in Chicago.

Carriages were waiting to take us to the rooms of the Press Club. I went there in a coupe with Vice-President Gardener who said, in a published narration of my visit afterwards, that he was strongly tempted to steal me, which clever idea so amused me that had the case been reversed, I know I should have acted on it, much to the confusion of a waiting public in New York. In the beautiful rooms of the Press Club I met the president, Stanley Waterloo, and a number of clever newspapermen. I had not been expected in Chicago until noon, and the club had arranged an informal reception for me, and when they were notified of my speedy trip and consequently earlier arrival, it was too late to notify the members. After a most delightfully informal reception I was escorted to Kinsley's, where the club had a breakfast prepared. And then I learned that, owing to some misunderstanding, none of the men had had anything to eat since the night before.

After breakfast the members of the Press Club, acting as my escort, took me to visit the Chicago Board of Trade. When we went in, the pandemonium which seems to reign during business hours was at its height. My escorts took me to the gallery, and just as we got there a man raised his arm to yell something to the roaring crowd, when he saw me, and yelled instead:

"There's Nellie Bly!"

In one instant the crowd that had been yelling like mad became so silent that a pin could have been heard fall to the floor. Every face, bright and eager, was turned up towards us, instantly every hat came off, and then a burst of applause resounded through the immense hall. People can say what they please about Chicago, but I do not believe that anywhere else in the United States a woman can get a greeting which will equal that given by the Chicago Board of Trade. The applause was followed by cheer after cheer and cries of "Speech!" but I took off my little cap and shook my head at them, which only served to increase their cheers.

Shortly afterwards the Press Club escorted me to the Pennsylvania Station, where I reluctantly bade them good-bye, unable to thank them heartily enough for the royal manner in which they had treated a little sunburnt stranger.

Now I was on a regular train which seemed to creep, so noticeable was the difference in the speed of traveling. Instead of a fine sleeping-car at my disposal, I had but a state-room, and my space was so limited that floral and fruit offerings had to be left behind. In Chicago, a cable which afforded me much pleasure reached me, having missed me at San Francisco.

"Mr. Verne wishes the following message to be handed to Nellie Bly the moment she touches American soil: M. and Mme. Jules Verne address their sincere felicitations to Miss Nellie Bly at the moment when that intrepid young lady sets foot on the soil of America."

The train was rather poorly appointed, and it was necessary for us to get off for our meals. When we stopped at Logansport for dinner, I being the last in the car, was the last to get off. When I reached the platform a young man, whom I never saw before or since, sprang upon the other platform, and waving his hat, shouted:

"Hurrah for Nellie Bly!"

The crowd clapped hands and cheered, and after making

way for me to pass to the dining-room, pressed forward and cheered again, crowding to the windows at last to watch me eat. When I sat down, several dishes were put before me bearing the inscription, "Success, Nellie Bly."

It was after dark when we reached Columbus, where the depot was packed with men and women waiting for me. A delegation of railroad men waited upon me and presented me with beautiful flowers and candy, as did a number of private people. I did not go to bed until after we had passed Pittsburgh, and only got up in the morning in time to greet the thousands of good people who welcomed me at Harrisburg, where the Harrisburg Wheelman's Club sent a floral offering in remembrance of my being a wheelman. A number of Philadelphia newspapermen joined me there, and at Lancaster I received an enthusiastic reception.

HOME AGAIN

Nellie Bly Will Roll Into the Jersey City Railroad Depot This Afternoon

GUNS WILL WELCOME HER

A Salute to be Fired in New York and in Brooklyn

THE FLYING RECORD OF A DAY

Nellie Bly will have completed her flying trip around the world at 3.52 o'clock this afternoon, if the Pennsylvania Railroad Train on which she is a passenger is on time. The moment her feet touch the depot platform in Jersey City all New York will know it. Ten guns will boom a thunderous welcome from Battery Park and at the same instant ten guns will roar a salute from Fort Greene Park, Brooklyn. The timers will stop their watches, and for the first time in the history of the world there will be recorded the circumnavigation of the earth by a woman without guide, escort or attendant.

FROM *The New York World*, JAN. 25, 1890

———

Almost before I knew it I was at Philadelphia, and all too soon to please me, for my trip was so pleasant I dreaded the finish of it. A number of newspapermen and a few friends joined me at Philadelphia to escort me to New York. Speechmaking was the order from Philadelphia on to Jersey City. I was told when we were almost home to jump to the platform the moment the train stopped at Jersey City, for that made my time around the world. The station was packed with thousands of people, and the moment I landed on the platform, one yell went up from them, and the cannons at the Battery and Fort Greene boomed out the news of my arrival. I took off my cap and wanted to yell with the crowd, not because I had gone around the world in seventy-two days, but because I was home again.

VI.

ON THE FIRING LINE

In August 1914, four days after World War I broke out, Bly left the United States for Europe. She wasn't planning on writing war correspondence, however. She had just been indicted for obstruction of justice, in the latest twist in the long-running and complex legal fight over the manufacturing business she had inherited upon her husband's death in 1904. By fleeing the indictment, she hoped to buy some time to appeal to a wealthy Viennese friend to finance her own new manufacturing venture. Once she made it to Austria, however, Bly's priorities quickly shifted away from her personal finances and toward battlefield journalism: she wanted to get to the front. She prevailed upon her friends and contacts—which included the U.S. ambassador to Austria and an assortment of wealthy Americans and Austrians—to get permission to visit the war zone. After two months of trying, she succeeded. The *Journal* used Bly's name in the headline of every report: NELLIE BLY ON THE FIRING LINE, NELLIE BLY AT FRONT, NELLIE BLY AT SCENE OF SLAUGHTER, and so on. To make the most of these rare firsthand accounts from the eastern front, the editors divided Bly's reports, spreading them out over several days.[1] Timeliness was not a major priority; as the war raged on throughout Europe, Bly's articles did not see print for weeks, sometimes even months, after their original datelines. In her month-long battlefield tour, she visited both the Russian and Serbian fronts, with a rest at Budapest in between. Her first stop was Przemysl, a city on today's Polish-Czech border that, at the outbreak of World War I, was a heavily fortified part of the Austrian empire bordering Russia. The terrain and weather were forbidding; the nearby mountains were steep, and the few roads and passes were often blocked by snow or mud. Thousands of troops on both sides died of exposure that winter. The fortress of Przemysl was a crucial outpost for both Austrians and their German allies, and ultimately the site of a crushing defeat of the Austro-Hungarian forces. After a brutal six-month siege—one of the war's longest—the city surrendered to the Russians in March 1915. Bly's visit to Przemysl in late October and early November 1914 coincided with a relatively peaceful period between the Russian army's brief first siege and its much longer second one. Still, Bly witnessed much suffering and, at one point, had to dive into a trench during a Russian shelling attack. Later, when she walked away from her group during a stop in a small village on the way to Budapest, Hungarian officers detained her on suspicion of being a British spy. A crowd began to gather, but she was saved when a doctor recognized her name. "My God! Nellie Bly!" he cried. "I have told them every child seven years old in America knows Nellie Bly."[2]

NELLIE BLY ON THE BATTLEFIELD

Hides in Trenches as Russ Shells Rain About Her

SOLDIERS FIVE DAYS WITHOUT FOOD

*Following is a continuation of the article by Miss Nellie Bly,
special correspondent for the Evening Journal at Przemysl, in
Austria:*

Przemysl, Oct. 30.—We left the battery and proceeded
along the muddy road. There was Colonel John,[3] Baron Mednyanszky, a painter of renown;[4] Cesare Santoro, a writer, editor and owner of a newspaper in Rome, Italy;[5] Alexander
Exax, photographer,[6] and myself. In Herr Hollitzer's cape![7]
That meant labor.

Along the road were deep, muddy trenches, and into these
we were ordered to go and follow our leader in single file,
thirty feet apart.

We were on ground plainly visible to the Russians, who fire
as soon as they see anything move or that looks like a human
being.

The trench was muddy and filthy. I slipped and slid and held
my breath—all I had. The weight of Herr Hollitzer's cape,
which I had to carry in folds over my arms to keep from soil-
ing it, had left me little breath to hold.

I almost despaired of getting out of the trench. At that particular spot it was fully eight feet high and as slippery as a
greased pole. I had no nails in my shoes, and as I made a step I
slid back.

Baron Mednyanszky had missed me and turned back. His
head and walking stick were visible above the edge of the trench.
He held out the curved end to me. I grasped it and was quickly
pulled up the slippery bank.

We darted across the road, expecting a Russian bullet to
greet the two of us in the worst exposed spot.

NOWHERE TO HIDE AND
AS SLIPPERY AS ICE!

But none came. And now we were on a bare, muddy hill. Not a blade of grass, not a tree or shrub, nothing but shiny, smooth-worn mud, more slippery than ice.

It seemed to be laid out in terraces, and each terrace was but a series of half-dug graves. Just the size of a grave, and the shape, and possibly three feet deep.

I looked at them in horror. Were they filled graves which had sunk? Were they graves half-prepared, waiting for the next battle?

Down where the slope ended in the valley were long lines of rude crosses made from tree branches. They marked plainly visible graves.

In some of these open graves was straw. In some were empty cartridges. In others bullets not yet taken from their paste-board boxes. Here were bloody bandages, a lost shoe, a piece of a coat, an abandoned cooking pan, another with a bullet hole through it, a buckle from a belt. Then I realized where I was. I was on a battlefield. These were not half-dug or sunken graves. They were the trenches in which the soldiers had lain for three weeks fighting constantly.

Each of these hundreds of grave-like holes had been the tent, the home, the retreat of a soldier. Here they ate when food could reach them. Here they starved when food could not be had. Here they killed and were killed.

I have spoken to soldiers who were in trenches for five days without food. That does not mean supplies were exhausted. Food may have been in sight, yet could not be brought to them for the constant rain of the enemy's bullets.

UNDER FIRE FOR WEEKS IN THE
RAIN AND COLD

In rain, in cold, in wind—hungry, wet, weary, under constant fire for weeks! Is it surprising that cholera, dysentery and all other ills, including insanity, seize them?

And what is here in the Austrian army is as bad, perhaps worse, in the Russian front. The wild, primitive country in which these two nations fight make conditions most terrible and suffering unspeakable to man and beast.

I could only view the bloody bandages with the most helpless horror. It is as if the last day had come and one could not change or better the inevitable torture. Imagine a man with a bullet in his lungs or head or arm, or a bit of shrapnel in his chest or abdomen, or his arms or feet torn off, lying in the trench for days without one soul to help tie up his gaping wounds or hand him a bite to eat.

Dr. Kling told me of a soldier whose shoulder blade was torn out by shrapnel, leaving a gaping wound bigger than two fists, and that man lay in a trench for six days in that condition without aid.

PICKED OUT BULLETS WITH POCKETKNIFE

He told me of others who had been for days with bullets buried in them and when they reached him they let him dig the bullets out with a pocketknife. No ether or cocaine to ease the pain, yet never cry or moan.

I saw one man whose jaws were broken in thirty-two pieces by a shrapnel. It hung shapeless on his chest.

That man lay in a trench six days after he was injured. No food, no aid and rain all the while. His jaw has been mended by silver wire, is growing together and he is walking around the hospital.

It was growing dark. We retraced our steps. I was saddened and heartsick by what I had seen. I felt indifferent to the constant bellowing of cannon and whizzing of shells through the air. Campfires were glowing and the smell of smoke made the land more wholesome. The shapeless, huddled mass of men by the cholera hovels lay still, silently motionless in the straw. I turned my eyes away.

The air was chilled. The last glimmer of sun tinted the black clouds with a golden edge. Two officers on horseback met on the brow of the hill and were outlined against the sky like statues. Hundreds of cattle and horses were standing in vast groups in the valley, eating. Wagons were unhitched and in line. Men were eating in groups or standing around small fires. To the south-west a long balloon, cigar-shaped, hung motionless in the sky.

AND SUDDENLY WAR LET LOOSE ITS FURIES

It was a scene of peaceful nightfall. Then suddenly the most terrific explosion of the day bellowed out just back of us. We turned. We saw a cloud of black smoke rise in the air, appar-ently from the place we had just left—the trenches where, three weeks ago, the Russians left and retreated before the fire of the Austrians.

We heard a Russian shell come singing through the air. Then—it fell on our left, less than 200 feet away! We could not see it; like the men who shoot, it is not visible to the eye. But the shower of black mud showed where it struck. It missed a stable and the edge of a camp by 50 feet only.

The spraying mud had hardly returned to earth until the whole scene had changed from stillness to the utmost anima-tion. The cattle were driven westward on a run—campfires were deserted, horses were hitched to wagons and whipped into the fastest speed. From the stables horses were led run-ning in groups. Everything seemed moving with the greatest rapidity and at an instant's notice.

Colonel John yelled for us to fly to the trenches. But like the famous lady who turned to salt, I turned to look![8]

Another frightful explosion in the east, another cloud of black smoke and one after the other six shells fell and buried themselves in the same soft earth.

Then I got into the trench. Two hundred feet was near enough for me. I was not afraid, I would not run. Yet my mind was busy. I thought another shot would follow. It will doubt-less be better aimed. If it does, we shall die.

And, if so, what then?

New York Evening Journal, DEC. 8, 1914

NELLIE BLY DESCRIBES WAR HORRORS

Tells How Troops Suffer in the Trenches

Following is a continuation of the article by Miss Nellie Bly, special correspondent for the Evening Journal, now on the firing line in Austria:

Przemysl, Sunday, Nov. 1, 1914.—I was called at 4 A.M. to-day, having received orders to meet our party at the Bahnhof square at 5. It was crow-dark and cold—not the brisk, fresh cold that stings and braces, but the dead damp cold that eats in until every nerve shivers. I had no light to dress by. I had no water. I had no bell, the hotel has no servants.

With cotton waste I rubbed my face and teeth. I put an inch-square chocolate and five soldier's biscuits in my pocket. The biscuits are the size of a two-cent stamp and one-quarter of an inch thick.

I lingered, shivering in bed, after I was called. So I rushed with my dressing and ran down stairs. Halfway I found one servant cleaning boots on the stairs. In the cubbyhole supposed to be the office I stepped over a sleeping form, wrapped completely in a gray blanket. All over the floor were similar sleeping men.

I hung my key on a peg marked 33. I walked out the unlocked door on which a card, written in six languages, invited everybody to please close it.

STREETS DARK AND DESOLATE AS THE START WAS MADE

I looked up and down the narrow curved street. There was no one, not even a policeman. I looked at the station clock. It was ten minutes to five. I walked to the square. It was deserted. I walked the short block to the Coffee House Stieber. It was dark and desolate. Still my desire for coffee made me knock and rattle with vigor.

Useless; there was no response. There was nowhere else to go. Everywhere it was dark. I walked back to the Bahnhof square. Our quaint wagons were arriving, six in all. They formed in line.

My former driver recognized me and took off his black-lambskin fez. He smiled kindly with his one blue eye and the corner of his mouth, and motioned for me to get in.

But that was not military. I stood still waiting. A form ran around the corner. It was Mr. Exax with his kodak hanging around his neck, his linen bag on his back.

"Oh, Miss Bly! The first?" he asked.

From out the dark appeared Mr. Santoro, the beautifully complete. A gray aviator's cap covered his head complete but for his eyes. Over his arm was a handsome lap-shawl. Around his neck was a thermos bottle.

COMMANDER OF PARTY
WAS 30 MINUTES LATE

"Good morning, Miss Bly," he said. "Here is your coffee; it is warm."

He unscrewed the top, and, filling it with coffee, handed it to me. I drank with delight. The Kino᷊ man, Mr. Findels, arrived, followed by his servant bearing his camera. He complained he had no coffee, but he distributed delicious chocolate wafers to us. Mr. Exax said he had made coffee in his room, which was around the corner, and they went off together.

One by one the others came—all but the Baron. Minute by minute the station clock crept past five. Our commander, Captain Miakich (that is, he was to be promoted to-day), had not appeared. It was twenty minutes past. Twenty minutes at this hour of the morning is terribly long after one's out of bed. Terribly short if one is called and must get up.

A consultation resulted in our gendarme being sent to get Miakich. At five-thirty they appeared—he and the gendarme— mounted on a white and a bay pony. We piled into our wagons. Santoro sat beside me and shared his lap-shawl. I had the high end of the stuffed seat again. Exax crawled in the hay at the back end of the wagon and called to me to envy his comfort. The drivers yelled something that sounds like pistachio ice cream without the p and the ice cream, and the little, willing beasts, in their rope harness, started—Miakich and the gendarme leading.

ELECTRIC LAMP AND A MAP
TO GUIDE THEM

Miakich has an electric lamp tied to his breast and a map in his hand. Within three blocks we stop at the crossroads. Two policemen and an officer come out of the darkness to consult with Miakich, his map and his light. Another man, a rare sight, a civilian, appears. He seems to know what no one else knows—which way we should travel. He climbs up on the straw-filled sack beside my driver. He directs the way.

Daylight begins to come. With it appear soldiers at doors and the quaint walls. First a few early ones, and the farther up we go the more their number increases, like a rising tide. Sometimes we pass great lines of soldiers marching silently. Their dark blue attire and their silence make them appear like a long low black fog.

INTENSE COLD CHILLS TO THE
LAST DROP OF BLOOD

In heavy fur-lined coat, sweater, flannel waist, cap, gloves, mitts, I am chilled to the last drop of blood. I think with fainting heart of the thousands of weary, sick, hungry men lying in mud trenches. Not here alone in bleak but lovely Galiscze,[2] not only these kind childlike Austrians, but those of other nations. The Russians just back of these wonderful hills, the Germans and the French gentlemen and peasants lying in their terrible mud trenches. Not thousands but millions of them. I try to realize all it means—the untold, indescribable suffering of millions of the world's best men, and when I say millions of men I must multiply those millions by ten to count the wives, children, parents and sweethearts and relatives who are suffering untold mental agony.

New York Evening Journal, DEC. 9, 1914

AT SCENE OF SLAUGHTER
DEAD FILL PITS

---

*Following is a continuation of the story of Miss Nellie Bly,
special correspondent for the Evening Journal, on the firing
line at Przemysl, Austria:*

Pryzemysl, Nov. 1.—After the hospitable feast all the officers and the Prince[1] posed for photographs. Colonel John was
very anxious that no journalists should be in the group. The
Prince then bade us good-bye and disappeared over the hill,
followed by two officers.

We returned to our wagons. Our drivers were roasting potatoes among burning branches. They grabbed the hot potatoes
and put them in the pockets of their sheepskin coats.

Lieutenant Pichl and Acting Captain Arthur Nichl—the
only black eyed man among the thousands—asked me to stop
at the Red Cross hospital. They both belong to the Tyrol and
have been stationed here since the beginning of the war. They
mounted their really fine horses and rode along, one on each
side of my wagon.

Dr. Johann Hand, the commander of the second Red Cross
station, was delighted to see us. He proudly led me around to
see all points of interest.

HOW RED CROSS CARES
FOR WOUNDED SOLDIERS

His "palace," as he called his cave, was just being finished. It
was constructed just like all others except that a pane of glass,
from a destroyed house, furnished him with one window. He
insisted on my having a cup of tea—with rum—and drank a
toast to America as I drank one to Austria.

Dr. Hand has forty ambulances. They carry four men lying,

or two lying and four sitting, or eight sitting. He has eighty well-fed, good-looking strong horses. Splendid covered shelters have been built for them. Well-made, strong tents warmly lined with straw are provided for all the soldiers, and larger ones, with good-looking bunks, are ready for patients.

Splendid kitchens are under shelter, and small kitchens, which can be carried by a man, set down anywhere and used, are kept for emergency.

The man who made the tea had a broad smile all the while. Finally, when we were inspecting the different places, he touched me on the elbow.

NEW YORK BARBER ANXIOUS
TO RETURN

"Please put in the Journal," he said, "that I am Henry Cross. I come from Lemberg. I had a barber shop on Fourth avenue for many years. I came home to visit friends, and here I am. I want to go back to America. I will be an American citizen and stay there."

Dr. Hand insisted on having me pose with him for a photograph. Beside us stood his assistant surgeon; his chaplain, George Kiener, of Salzburg, and others of his staff. The doctor held a bottle of medicine. It was iodine, the one remedy here for cholera.

Between us and the Russians is a distance only of 1,500 feet. In the valley between us and the Russians is a village. The name I must not tell you. A fierce battle was fought there, and firing is kept on the village constantly. The land is covered with dead soldiers and officers of both armies. Perhaps the living are among them. They have been there for ten days. The dead cannot be buried, the living cannot be aided until the rain of hellish fire ceases. Meanwhile the air is putrid.

RUSS SOLDIERS DYING OF CHOLERA
IN TRENCHES

There can be no doubt but that at this point the Russian condition must be frightful. Dead and dying of cholera, the Russian soldiers are found along the line of battle or left behind in the trenches, where they are found by the advancing Austrians.

Several times at night Russians have returned to the trenches to recover straw, and abandoned arms and knapsacks show with what desperation they seized the remnants of straw. At one point a river or stream divides the two enemies. In the morning the soldiers of Francis Joseph and the Czar[2] have met on the banks, each in quest of water. They take their water, and even barter with each other for cigarettes. Then they return to their different positions to open deadly fire upon each other.

The day is done. We enter our wagons for our return. I glance sadly at the dark, cold trenches. I say farewell to those I know. And the terrible booming and slaughter keep on ceaselessly.

New York Evening Journal, DEC. 12, 1914

NELLIE BLY AT FRONT

Visits Wounded in Budapest

SEES HORRORS OF WAR

While in Budapest Miss Nellie Bly, Special Correspondent for the Evening Journal in the Austrian fighting zone, paid a visit to some of the hospitals. The following relates some of what she experienced and saw:

Budapest, Nov. 10.—Ten languages are spoken in the hospital, and nurses, German, Austrian, Gulitzin, Hungarian and Servian are employed, so that patients will always have nurses who speak their language.

They have also a series of chapels, Catholic, Protestant and Hebrew. Off each ward are small soundproof rooms called "Death Chambers."

Patients at the point of death are removed to these rooms to spare the feelings of their fellow comrades. Smoking rooms, glass partitioned, are also an adjunct to each ward.

This hospital accommodates 2,000 wounded. The kitchen is superb and needs a column to properly describe it. They showed with pride a large American refrigerator. The doctors and nurses each have their sleeping, eating and rest departments. One large hall, gaily decorated with the national colors, is used for the amusement of the convalescent. Even kino shows[1] are given and concerts.

Men were being received from a train, so we went down to see them. We talked to them, as detachments of twenty were taken at a time to the bath.

I cannot praise too highly the wonderful executive ability of those who conceived and established the astounding perfection of those two hospitals. Nothing is wanting to aid and assist nature to save and heal what man is so inhumanely torturing and destroying.

We had scarcely reached the Astoria when I had a telephone call from Dr. MacDonald.[2]

CALLED TO HOSPITAL

"I want you to get in a taxi and come here, Miss Bly," he said. "I have received just now the worst cases I have ever seen in my entire life. They may interest you."

I rushed to the American Red Cross Hospital. It is located in Mexico street in a large building, formerly used as a home for the blind. I flew in the door and up the stairs over which floats a fifty-foot American flag.

Dr. MacDonald, grave and sad, met us at the head of the stairs.

"Come into the operating room," he said, taking my hand. "I have the most frightful case I ever saw."

Mr. Schriner,[3] who had enough misery for one day, had

tried to induce me not to come. Failing he had come along. Silently he kept at my side.

The operating room was in confusion. On the floor was blood. Filling pails and in piles were bloody bandages. I tried not to see. I began to wish I had not come.

Four American Red Cross nurses stood gravely around an operating table. Dr. MacDonald pointed to two bandaged stumps. I could see one foot was gone at the ankle, the other apparently half way to the knee.

"This is a Russian," said the doctor. "He was wounded by a shot through his body. For eight days he lay in the trench unattended. His feet froze. He was put on a freight train and when we received him an hour ago his feet had dropped off, doubtless in the car, for we never saw them, and the last blood the poor fellow had was pouring from his open veins. We carried him here and bandaged him up, but he cannot live many minutes longer. He has no pulse now. Come, look at him."

A DREADFUL SIGHT

Come, look, reader, with me! My whole soul shrank from the sight. The doctor took me by the hand. I kept my eyes away from the face I was afraid to look upon.

"Look at this body," said the doctor. I looked—I shuddered. The clay pallor of death. The ribs cutting the skin. Bones, bones, no flesh anywhere.

The head turned. Great, hollow black eyes looked into mine. Transfixed I stood, heartsick, soul-sad. Those great hollow eyes searched mine. They tried to question me. They spoke soul language to soul. The lips parted, a moan, a groan of more than physical agony. He spoke. I could not understand. His words were a sound my ears shall never forget. The appeal, the longing, the knowledge!

"What does he say?" I cried, unable to stand it. "Can no one understand? Can't you find someone to speak to him?"

A nurse smoothed his forehead. An attendant held fast the pale, pale hands.

"The attendant understands," the doctor said; and to him, "What does he say?"

ASKED FOR CHILDREN

"He is asking for his children," was the low reply.

The hollow, black eyes turned again to search mine. I could not endure their question. I had no answer to give.

"Let me go!" I said to the doctor.

The low moans seemed to call me back, but I walked steadfastly toward the door and down the corridor.

"Could Emperors and Czars and Kings look on this torturing slaughter and ever sleep again?" I asked the doctor.

"They do not look," he said gently. "Only by witnessing such horrors can one realize them."

"Miss Bly," cried von Leidenfrost,[4] running down the hall, "that poor fellow just died!"

This is only one case. Travel the roads from the scene of battle; search the trains; wounded, frozen, starved thousands are dying by agonizing torture—not hundreds, but thousands. And as they die thousands are being rushed into their pest-filled trenches to be slaughtered in the same way.

Oh, we Christians!

New York Evening Journal, JAN. 19, 1915

VII.

DEAR NELLIE

For her final act as a newspaperwoman, Bly became an advice columnist. From 1919 until her death in January 1922, she published a column of advice, opinions, and letters from readers in *The New York Evening Journal*. She became so well known for finding homes for abandoned children that in December 1919 a baby boy was abandoned at Grand Central Station with a note pinned to his clothes: "To Somebody—For the love of Mike, take this kid. He is too much for the family. Give him to Nellie Bly of the New York *Journal*. He is seven months old and as healthy as they make them. Can't afford him at the price they are charging for milk today. There are others I am trying to support."[1] Bly, of course, stepped in, made arrangements, and wrote about the case.[2] The two columns reprinted below show Bly trumpeting a success and then, in a rare move, documenting a failure. The first is the opening installment of a startling three-part series in which Bly intervenes to help a struggling foster mother find an adoptive parent for her little boy. Illustrated with a large photograph of the sweet-faced boy and crafted like a melodramatic narrative, it ends with a cliffhanger. In the second column, Bly takes a far less triumphant tone, as she shares two letters from a reader who sought her help but did not get it.

NELLIE BLY FINDS A HOME AND FATHER FOR LITTLE WAIF

Noted Woman Writer Tells How Childless Man Is Made Happy

It is a fairy tale come true.

The night was dark and dreary. While a clock somewhere slowly tolled the hour of nine the heavy wood doors slammed shut, the turning of the locks resounded through the empty halls and the lights were extinguished.

A straight-lipped woman stole stealthily from door to door, peering through keyholes for evidence of infringement of rules.

But the occupants of the small cots, standing in close rows, lay silent, closed-eyed, keenly aware of the inspection.

In this grim house the innocent as well as the guilty found shelter.

From under one door came a long, pale streak of light. The woman paused, listened, and passed on into the darkness.

Within a babe had come into the world unwanted, unloved—a scarlet letter child.

The girl who bore him turned her pale face toward the wall and sobbed intermittently. She was bitter and resentful. He who shared her guilt did not share her shame—a light-hearted member of the circle which would banish her if her plight were known.

HANDS OF PITY EXTENDED

A crippled girl with big blue eyes and soft brown hair crept noiselessly to the cot. She turned down the corners of the covers and looked at the little mite lying alone, as far distant from the girl as the size of the bed permitted.

Divine pity swelled the crippled girl's heart. With a rush of tenderness she gathered the unwanted babe to her breast.

A few days later the doors of the mission opened and closed

behind two girls. They stood there for a moment. Then the one hailed a passing taxi and, without a word of farewell, stepped in and the taxi vanished down the street. The other, clasping to her breast a bundle wrapped in a shawl, limped painfully toward the subway.

The one who had sinned had gone back to her world. The one without sin had assumed the self-imposed task of mothering the nameless, abandoned babe.

Four years have passed. The crippled girl, without home or means, has slaved to support herself and the boy. Only the hardest work and poorest pay could she obtain because she would not part with the boy.

Finally she became a worker in a day nursery in the slums. For her work she could have a room for herself and the child and $3 a week.

GRATEFUL IN HER DISTRESS

She was grateful. The work was heavy, but she had shelter for her baby and herself. She needed but little and her old clothes she utilized for the child.

Then the terrible day arrived when she saw with alarm that her boy Richard needed that which with all love and devotion she could not give—an education.

Then she thought and prayed and cried a bit, too. Then, in holy unselfishness, she went to the boy's mother.

That young woman had married, lived in her own beautiful home and had borne two children to her husband. Time had only intensified her fear of detection. She could do nothing for the abandoned boy; she could not see him nor contribute anything toward his education.

The little cripple sought the father, a professional man of means and position. But he, too, repudiated his nameless son and declined to assist in giving the boy an education.

Then the crippled girl came to me. She bared her tender, devoted heart. She felt she would die to part with the child, but for his sake since she could give him no chances in the world— she must give him up. Would I find someone to adopt him?

CHILD A PRECIOUS TREASURE

To see Richard is to love him. With eyes big and blue as forget-me-nots, a complexion of roses and cream, teeth of unsurpassable whiteness and beauty, hair light brown and hands dainty and exquisite and a smile which wins all hearts, he is a precious treasure.

I felt I could not break that noble gentlewoman's heart. I told her so. She begged me only to consider the boy and what was good for him.

I delayed. I hoped to find some better solution than separation. I finally told her I should give her charge of my nursery if ever I got my "Mothers' Club" launched. Keep them together I would if she could only wait. Then the blow fell!

Monday evening a gentleman telephoned and requested a few minutes' interview.

"You don't know me," he said. "I have been stopping here in the same hotel.³ I must see you."

He came up. Tall and large and ruddy, clean-shaven with wide blue eyes and frank smile. A typical man of affairs.

"I hear that you have been finding homes for fatherless children and children for childless homes?" he began. "I am a widower and a grandfather. My children have their own homes. Mine is empty and lonely. I want a boy. Can you get me one?"

Of course I said I could. When? Tomorrow!

I THOUGHT OF RICHARD

He told me of himself and showed credentials. He had enough for himself and a regiment: So why should he be lonely?

I thought of Richard and his devoted foster mother's desire to have him educated. I put the thought aside. I loved the boy, but I could not break that girl's tender heart, even at her bidding.

So I talked of another boy—a black-eyed little tot of three-and-a-half years, a dear child, pathetic and nameless. A letter from the mother came while I spoke. She had gone away to the country for a few days. That excluded adopting the boy until her return.

My heart sank. I knew, much to my sorrow, I must do my duty and offer Richard.

We arranged to meet at ten in the morning and go to the day nursery in the slums where Richard lived.

Squalor, poverty, crowds. The taxi forced its way slowly. Push-cart vendors squeezed from side to side to let us pass. Hatless women and dirty, ragged children crowded sidewalks with overfilled ash cans.

Pushing our way through curious collecting throngs we entered the shelter where the children of the poor stay the long day while their parents work.

NURSERY A BEDLAM

A bedlam was loose within. Children were crying, children were singing, children were reciting, children were yelling, but none was visible, violating the old dictum that children should be seen and not heard. However, the matron soon made visible the source of their noise. She showed us the little babies in their cribs, even then growing quieter as the nurses arranged the milk bottles upon their pillows. Then the older children who were placed two by two in cribs to have an eleven o'clock nap; the still older ones who had gathered thick around low tables for their midday meal.

Boys and girls and girls and boys! I noticed a shade of apprehension over the face of Mr. O. None had touched the father-love in his heart. They were children and he liked them, but none appealed to him like his own.

"Which one is he?" he asked, anxiously. I told him none of them.

A PATHETIC MEETING

The matron said Richard was in the kindergarten. So downstairs we went. The kindergarten children had been dispersed and we stood in the empty schoolroom, marveling at a specimen of a huge wasps' nest, when in rushed Richard.

His blue eyes laughed as merrily as his pretty lips and dimples.

"I have brought some one to see you, Richard," I said as he clung to my hand.

Mr. O. sat down upon one of the low kindergarten benches. He held out his hands.

"Do you know me, Richard?" he asked.

"No," Richard responded promptly.

"You are my little boy! I sent you away when you were a little baby. Now you have grown big and I have come to take you home," Mr. O. explained.

"Why did you send me away?" Richard demanded, curiously.

"Because I had no woman at home to care for you. I am your father. Come to me!"

Richard dropped my hand and flung himself joyously into Mr. O.'s arms. His little hands folded closely around the big man's neck, and the soft, rosy cheek was pressed lovingly against the bronzed one.

"He is my boy!" Mr. O. said, brokenly to me. Tears filled his eyes. I made believe I had something in the other end of the room I particularly wanted to see. To tell the truth, I could not see anything. My own tears blinded me.

When I came back Mr. O. was again sitting on the bench. Richard was lying contentedly in his arms, gazing at him with adoring eyes.

"He's my daddy! He's my daddy!" Richard declared joyously to me.

"Call the girl," Mr. O. said huskily. "I must have this boy!"

(To Be Continued Monday)[4]

FROM *The New York Evening Journal*,
NOV. 29, 1919

NELLIE BLY TELLS OF DISAPPOINTMENTS

Most Bitter Regrets Caused by Inability to Bring Joy to Lonely Hearts Who Appeal to Her for Help

Naturally I am often disappointed.

But disappointment is only a form of selfishness.

Disappointment is the state of being balked, defeated, hindered of result, tantalized. In plain words, deprived of something one wanted.

To grieve over something one wanted and did not get is a special species of selfishness.

So I answer the questions so many correspondents ask me by saying, Yes! Yes!! Yes!!! Again and again I am disappointed, but it does not make me throw up my hands and sink in a sea of hopelessness. Perhaps, after all, the disappointment brings ultimate good. We cannot always see so clearly what is for the best. . . .

One day I had this letter. It was quite simple, but its lonely pathos sank deep into that silly, soft heart of mine and would not be stilled:

GIRL'S PATHETIC APPEAL

"Dear Miss Bly,

"It's selfish of me, I know, to take up your time with my letter, when there are so many who are surely in need of your advice; but I do want so to confide in someone.

"I am, in all probability, illegitimate, brought up in an institution many miles from here. At rather an early age I was hired out for light housework, where lived a farmer, his wife and their one son, a man of about forty years. He became somewhat interested in me and corrected my grammatical errors, for which I was grateful. His mother, though, looked on disapprovingly.

"I tried so hard to please her because I did not want to go back to the institution, but she disliked me, and on one occasion humiliated me so that I ran away. With absolutely no money I didn't get very far, and after two days of wandering and suffering, I was glad when I was found, nearly unconscious, and returned to the institution. I was too sick to be punished.

NEVER HAD GIRL FRIEND

"I soon recovered, though, and a year later got a better opportunity to run away. Finally I drifted to New York. Here I became a music hall dancer (being hired by a proprietor) and later a cabaret dancer. I am not unhappy because I love to dance and how I do love music. Not the kind, though, I dance to. That's only jazz. In my leisure hours I read, write letters, and dream.

"Would you care to know what I dream about? It's just a woman friend. I am sixteen years old and in all my life have never been kissed by a woman. Please accept my sincerest good wishes for your happiness and forgive me for making you the victim of my confidence."

"Nameless"

I did not want "Nameless" to be alone in the world. I wanted her to have real good friends, and so I advertised for her address. Weeks went by and no reply, although I kept hoping, hoping each day would bring some sign.

Finally it did. Two months later came this letter addressed in care of my hotel:

GIRL'S SECOND LETTER

"Dear Miss Bly:

"I wonder why you asked for my name and address. Had you known how much a letter from you surely meant to me, I know you would not have disappointed me so. I had a wild hope that you might even come to see me.

"I did not get out of bed the next day, as I thought I would, because my grip developed into pneumonia, but I was not taken to a hospital.

"Tonight or tomorrow night I am going to Philadelphia with a woman who says she has an excellent position for me there. I never liked her, but I have no choice. It would be at least another week before I could dance again, and she has been very kind to me during my illness, even paying bills that I was unable to meet. I shall return that money when I can.

"Please do not think that because I am a cabaret dancer, I must also be immoral. I have never had any difficulty getting positions, but sometimes I did not hold them long. If I have annoyed you by writing again, please forgive me and do not be angry with me. I shall not write again.

"Nameless"

TELEPATHY ONLY HOPE

So my poor girl was gone without name or address to trace her by. Evidently, she had written to me and her letter had been lost. Reproachfully she drifted out again in the wide, wide world alone and embittered by the belief that her one appeal had been denied.

Upon such accidents life is built. Perhaps my friendship might not have meant much, and again it might have added something to her existence. Not finding her, and knowing she had sent me a letter which never came and had expected my sympathetic understanding only to believe I failed her, made me melancholy. It is one of the disappointments which do not heal. I am hoping, hoping that some mental telegraphy will make her write me or come to me.

For to whom shall I be a friend except those who need friends? For whom shall I smile and speak words of cheer except those who need smiles and cheers?

from "NELLIE BLY TELLS OF DISAPPOINTMENTS," *The New York Evening Journal,* DEC. 5, 1919

Notes

INTRODUCTION

1. My account of Bly's life is indebted throughout to the only full-length biography of Bly, Brooke Kroeger's *Nellie Bly: Daredevil, Reporter, Feminist* (New York: Random House, 1994).
2. See, among others, Sue Macy's *Bylines: A Photobiography of Nellie Bly* (Washington, D.C.: National Geographic Society, 2009); Bonnie Christensen's *The Daring Nellie Bly: America's Star Reporter* (New York: Dragonfly Books, 2003); Nancy Butcher's *It Can't Be Done, Nellie Bly!: A Reporter's Race Around the World* (Atlanta, GA: Peachtree Jr., 2003); Stephen Krensky's *Nellie Bly: A Name to Be Reckoned With* (New York: Aladdin, 2003); Charles Freeden's *Nellie Bly: Daredevil Reporter* (Minneapolis, MN: Lerner, 2000); Joan W. Blos's *Nellie Bly's Monkey* (New York: HarperCollins, 1996); and Martha E. Kendall's *Nellie Bly: Reporter for the World* (Brookfield, Conn.: Millbrook Press, 1992).
3. Kroeger, *Nellie Bly*.
4. After its initial publication in New York and London in 1890, *Nellie Bly's Book: Around the World in Seventy-Two Days* was published in 1991 by Omnigraphics in Detroit; in 1998 by Twenty-First Century Books in Brookfield, Conn.; in 2003 by Indialog Publications in New Delhi; in 2009 by Wildside Press in Rockville, Md.; and in 2009 by Dodo Press in Gloucester, England. *Ten Days in a Mad-House*, after its initial publication in New York in 1887, was published in 2008 by Dodo Press in England; in 2009 by Feather Trail Press in Cedar Lake, Mich.; in 2009 by Wildside Press in Rockville, Md.; and in 2013 by Empire Books in Lexington, Ky.
5. In 2010 a Spanish edition of *Around the World in 72 Days* appeared as *La Vuelta al Mundo en 72 Días, Narrativa Norteamericana 3* by Buck Press in Barcelona, and in 2013 a German edition was issued as *Around the World in 72 Days: Die Schnellst Frau Des 19 Jahrhunderts* by Aviva in Berlin. In 2009 a Spanish edition of *Ten Days in a Mad-House* was issued as *Diez Días en un Manicomio, Narrativa Norteamericana 2* by Buck Press in Barcelona, and in 2011 a German edition was issued as *Zehn Tage im Irrenhaus: Undercover in Der Psychiatrie* by Aviva in Berlin.

6. See, for instance, www.nellieblyonline.com.

7. *The Journalist,* November 10, 1888.

8. She also added an "e" to "Cochran," presumably because it sounded more sophisticated, and she used Cochrane as her legal name until she married in 1895.

9. *Pittsburg Dispatch,* August 21, 1887.

10. In 1888, Bly published her first and only novel, *The Mystery of Central Park,* based loosely on a story she had written about a carriage driver in Central Park who picked up young women new to the city and sought to lure them into prostitution.

11. For more details on Bly's trip, see headnote for *Around the World in Seventy-Two Days.*

12. Thanks to a newly digitized issue of the *New York Family Story Paper,* we do know that before she signed the contract with Munro, Bly had already been listed as the author of at least one piece of serialized fiction, titled "Eva, the Adventuress: A Romance of a Blighted Life," and attributed to "Nellie Bly, who is now attempting to make the circuit of the world in seventy-five days" (6). The *Story Paper*—dated January 25, 1890, the same day thousands of people turned out to witness Bly's triumphant return to New York—was obviously seeking, like everyone else, to capitalize on Bly's name recognition. In the "Eva, the Adventuress" installment published the day Bly finished her race around the world, the vengeful heroine seduces a man who had wronged her (he apparently ruined her reputation, among other things), gets him to agree to rob a bank for her, and exults in the progress of her plan to ruin his life by branding him a thief. If Bly did actually write "Eva, the Adventuress," she would have had to complete it before she embarked on her trip around the world. Told from the perspective of a beautiful, sexually manipulative woman, the story of "Eva, the Adventuress" centers on intimate betrayal and acts of passion. The narrative's fevered tone and its tendency to linger on the sensual details of seduction scenes distinguish it from Bly's relatively brisk journalistic narratives. On the same day that Eva was catching her lover's head between her hands, kissing him full on the lips, and setting his "blood on fire," Nellie Bly the circumnavigator was observing in print: "What a magnificent ride it was across the continent! Allowing for the difference between Pacific and Central time we sped over two thousand five hundred and sixty-six miles in sixty-nine hours and five minutes" ("On the Homestretch," January 20, 1890).

13. Quoted in Kroeger, *Nellie Bly,* 309; image of business card from Kroeger's personal collection, p. 320.

14. *Brooklyn Daily Eagle*, March 4, 1919. See Kroeger, *Nellie Bly*, 449.
15. Arthur Brisbane, "The Death of Nellie Bly," *New York Evening Journal*, January 28, 1922.

I. GATHER UP THE REAL SMART GIRLS

THE GIRL PUZZLE

1. "Anxious Father," *Pittsburg Dispatch*, January 14, 1885.
2. *Madame Neilsons*: Likely a reference to Swedish opera star Christina Nilsson (1843–1921), known as Madame Nilsson, who later became the Countess de Casa Miranda.
3. *Mary Andersons*: popular American stage actress Mary Anderson (1859–1940).
4. *Bessie Brambles*: "Bessie Bramble" was the pseudonym of Pittsburgh newspaper columnist Elizabeth Wilkinson Wade (1838–1889).
5. *Maggie Mitchells*: popular American stage actress Margaret Julia "Maggie" Mitchell (1832–1918).
6. Jane Grey Swisshelm (1815–1884) was a well-known journalist, abolitionist, and advocate for women's rights.
7. *Mr. Quiet Observations*: journalist Erasmus Wilson and his regular column, titled "Quiet Observations." Bly quotes the most inflammatory remark from Wilson's column; see headnote for details. Their disagreement over women's roles notwithstanding, Wilson became a trusted mentor and friend to Bly.
8. The Pullman Palace car was a railroad sleeping car manufactured by the Pullman company, which hired so many African Americans to serve as "Pullman porters" that it became the largest single employer of African Americans after the Civil War. Pullman porters were known for providing first-rate service to rail passengers, but Bly was wrong about it being a good-paying business; the porters relied on tips to supplement their low wages.
9. Omitted sentence fragment: "In the banks, where so many young men are employed."
10. Industrialist and inventor George M. Pullman (1831–1897) designed and manufactured the Pullman sleeping car for trains. In a paternalistic social experiment that attracted widespread attention, he also built a company town for his factory workers near Chicago. Later in her career, Bly would visit Pullman's town and write about the famous Pullman strike, which was organized to protest wage cuts. Moved by the plight of the workers

and their families, she wrote three features on the strike based on their viewpoint. See "Nellie Bly at Pullman," *The New York World*, July 11, 13, and 15, 1894.

NELLIE IN MEXICO

1. Nellie Bly, *Six Months in Mexico* (New York: J. W. Lovell, 1888). The article reprinted here appeared in the book, slightly revised, as Ch. V: "In the Streets of Mexico."
2. *rebozo*: Spanish for shawl.
3. *serape*: Spanish for narrow blanket, worn by men.
4. *Rogers*: John Rogers (1829–1904), a popular sculptor whose statuettes were mass-produced in cast plaster. His relatively affordable figurines, called Rogers Groups, featured ordinary domestic scenes.

II. INTO THE MADHOUSE

BEHIND ASYLUM BARS

1. Blackwell's Island is now called Roosevelt Island.
2. "The Nellie Brown Mystery," *New York World*, October 9, 1887.
3. For more details about the city's response to Bly's report, see Kroeger, *Nellie Bly,* pp. 96–99.
4. *Temporary Home for Females*: A boardinghouse for working-class women, which provided residents with a room, housekeeping service, and meals served at a common table. Bly chose an establishment with an assistant matron named Irene Stenard, in a neighborhood now known as the East Village. Bly refers to Stenard as "Mrs. Stanard" throughout her article.
5. According to legend, Robert the Bruce, who declared himself King of Scotland but was turned into an outlaw by the English king Edward I, was inspired in a moment of despair by watching a determined spider try six times to swing itself from one ceiling beam to another. When the spider finally succeeded on its seventh try, Bruce resolved to continue fighting for Scotland. Years later, Bruce prevailed and drove the English from Scotland. The spider story may have originated with Sir Walter Scott's popular *Tales of a Grandfather, Being Stories Taken from Scottish History* (1828), written with Scott's six-year-old grandson in mind.
6. *Judge Duffy*: Judge Patrick G. Duffy of the Essex Market police court.

7. *private of dragoons*: Company of military cavalrymen.
8. *Moreno*: Spanish for brown.
9. *Warden O'Rourke*: James F. O'Rourke, warden of Bellevue Hospital from 1875 to 1889.
10. *Dr. Field*: Dr. Matthew Dickenson Field, appointed an "examiner in lunacy" in 1882 for New York City's Department of Public Charities and Corrections; worked for many years at the reception pavilion for the insane at Bellevue.

INSIDE THE MADHOUSE

1. As usual, Bly was lying about her age. She had turned twenty-three, not nineteen, in May 1887.
2. *Fritz Emmet*: composer and singer Joseph K. Emmet (1841–1891), who played the character Fritz in popular comedy-melodramas of the late nineteenth century.
3. *Dr. Ingram*: Dr. Frank H. Ingram, assistant superintendent of the Blackwell's Island women's asylum, who later became good friends with Bly. In 1890, at the end of her globe-circling tour, Bly's name was linked even more closely with Ingram's. When Bly's train stopped briefly in Ingram's hometown of Logansport, Indiana, on her triumphant train ride from California to New Jersey, reporters speculated that the two were engaged. When questioned about Ingram, Bly said only that she knew him "intimately" (*Logansport Daily Journal*, January 25, 1890). They apparently remained friends until Ingram died in 1893 at the age of thirty-three.
4. *Supt. Dent*: Dr. E. C. Dent, superintendent of the women's asylum at Blackwell's Island.
5. Bly included the question mark in the original text; presumably she wanted to suggest her skepticism about the nurses' intentions.
6. *the Retreat*: ward where violent patients were housed. Another such ward was the Lodge, where the most violent patients were kept.

III. UNDERCOVER AGAIN

THE GIRLS WHO MAKE BOXES

1. *The New York World*, October 30, 1887, and November 6, 1887.
2. For more details on working women, see Susan Estabrook Kennedy, *If All We Did Was to Weep at Home: A History of White*

Working-Class Women in America (Bloomington: Indiana University Press, 1979), p. 70, and Carol Hymowitz and Michaele Weissman, *A History of Women in America* (New York: Bantam Books, 1978), pp. 235–39.

3. *passementerie*: the art of making elaborate trimmings of braid, cord, silk, or beads; the trimmings are used as ornaments for furnishings and clothing.

4. *Cooper Institute*: Established in 1859, The Cooper Union for the Advancement of Science and Art in New York City's East Village offered a tuition-free education to the working classes, and its doors were open to all regardless of gender, race, or ethnicity. The prestigious school remained tuition-free until 2013, when, under severe financial strain, trustees announced that the entering class of 2014 would be charged on a sliding scale based on their ability to pay.

5. *The Knights of Labor*: National labor organization that advocated equal pay for equal work. Founded in 1869, its original constitution made no provision for women, but in the 1880s the group began actively recruiting women; within a few years, it had chartered more than one hundred women's assemblies and claimed a female membership of more than fifty thousand.

THE KING OF THE LOBBY

1. See note 7. Phelps's profession was listed as "broker" in the 1880 federal census; in the 1900 federal census his job title had generalized to "capitalist."

2. "The Lobby King's Bluff," *The New York World*, April 2, 1888.

3. See pp. 5–6 in No. 90, "Report of the Judiciary Committee, on the Investigation Ordered by the Assembly, in Reference to the Charges Made in the *New York World*, of April 1, 1888, Touching the Legislative Integrity of Certain Members of the Assembly." In *Documents of the Assembly of the State of New York*, One Hundred and Eleventh Session, 1888, vol. X, nos. 75 to 92 inclusive (New York: The Troy Press Co., 1888), pp. 1–98.

4. *J. W. Chesbrough*: Phelps's longtime business partner Julius F. (not W.) Chesbrough, referred to later in the article as J. F. Chesbrough.

5. *boodler*: person involved in political bribery or corruption.

6. *Conkling-Platt Senatorial fight*: Standoff over federal appointments between President James Garfield and two U.S. senators from New York, Roscoe Conkling (1829–1888) and Thomas Platt

(1833–1910). Conkling oversaw a patronage system that depended on his ability to influence federal appointments. He served in the U.S. Senate from 1867 to 1881, when he abruptly ended his own senatorial career, without really intending to do so. Conkling persuaded his newly elected colleague Thomas Platt to resign with him in protest over President Garfield's refusal to nominate Conkling's candidate for a prized federal appointment. The plan backfired; the two expected to demonstrate their power to Garfield and to be reappointed easily (senators were still chosen by state legislatures at this point), but public sentiment turned against them. The legislature voted to appoint new senators instead.

7. Phelps had been implicated in a previous bribery scandal, one that erupted in 1881 when New York state senator Loren B. "Lo" Sessions was accused of trying to rig the vote to replace state senators Conkling and Platt (see note 6). Sessions allegedly offered a New York assemblyman $2,000 to vote for Sessions's candidate of choice. The assemblyman took the money, promptly turned it over to the speaker of the Assembly, and informed the speaker about the attempted bribe (*Geneva Gazette,* June 17, 1881). Sessions was indicted and charged with attempted bribery, as was Phelps, who worked with him. Both denied any wrongdoing. After Sessions was acquitted in 1883 by an Albany County jury, charges against Phelps were dropped. Sessions never claimed the $2,000, which remained in the county treasury until 1890, when a judge awarded the funds to the Albany Hospital (*New York Herald,* March 7, 1890; *New York Times,* December 11, 1883).

8. *Pierce of Buffalo*: probably Buffalo businessman, doctor, and one-term U.S. congressman Ray Vaughn Pierce, who made a fortune selling patent medicines such as Pierce's Golden Medical Discovery and Dr. Pierce's Pleasant Purgative Pellets.

9. *Mr. Crosby, of New York*: Republican assemblyman Ernest H. Crosby from New York County.

10. *Gallagher, of Erie; Tallmadge, of Kings; Prime, of Essex; De Witt, of Ulster; Hagan, of New York, and McLaughlin, of Kings*: New York state assemblymen Edward Gallagher (Republican from Erie County), Daniel W. Tallmadage (Republican from Kings County), Spencer G. Prime (Republican from Essex County), Christopher N. DeWitt (Republican from Ulster County), Edward P. Hagan (Democrat from New York County), and William H. McLaughlin (Democrat from Kings County).

11. *J. W. Smith*: Democrat J. Wesley Smith of New York County.

12. The original text included a facsimile of the list with legislators' names crossed out, some more lightly than others.

13. Phelps's thirty-year-old son, John E. Phelps.
14. Part of this sentence was missing in the original; the illegible phrase was confirmed by consulting a reprint of Bly's story in the *Documents of the Assembly of the State of New York*, One Hundred and Eleventh Session, 1888, vol. 10 (New York: The Troy Press Company), p. 87.
15. According to a report the *World* published along with Bly's article, Phelps and his son lurked outside the St. James Hotel for more than an hour at the designated time, repeatedly checking the ladies' parlor in the hope of seeing Bly and relieving her of the $1,250 check she had promised to bring ("Mr. Phelps's Vain Waiting," *The New York World*, April 1, 1888).

IV. THE WOMAN QUESTION

WOMAN'S PART IN POLITICS

1. *The New York World*, January 20, 1895; May 26, 1889; and February 17, 1889.
2. *Mrs. Cleveland*: Frances Folsom Cleveland Preston (1864–1947), who married President Grover Cleveland during his first term in office, was the youngest presidential wife to become first lady and the only first lady to be married in the White House. Reporters frequently commented on her youth, beauty, and style.
3. *the old adage about certain folks falling out*: English proverb "Thieves falling out, true men coming to their goods," dating back to sixteenth century. Referenced by William Johnston in his 1859 novel *Freshfield*: "There is a not very uncommon proverb about certain people falling out, and certain other people getting their due consequence" (p. 242).
4. *Mrs. Leonard*: suffragist Cynthia Leonard (1828–1908) supported Lockwood's candidacy; she hosted her and organized a political meeting for her supporters.
5. *Lillian Russell*: stage name of actress and singer Helen Louise Leonard (1860–1922), the most famous of Cynthia Leonard's eight children. Lillian Russell was celebrated for her beauty, style, and presence.
6. *Candidate Harrison*: Benjamin Harrison (1833–1901), the Republican nominee for president and the eventual winner of the 1888 election. He defeated incumbent Grover Cleveland (1837–1908).
7. *Panama Canal*: In 1888, after seven years of problems, France's progress on the extraordinarily challenging project of building a

fifty-mile canal across the isthmus of Panama had ground to a halt. The canal, when finished, would change global trade patterns by allowing ships to pass from the Atlantic Ocean to the Pacific Ocean more safely and in half the time. The United States—which stood to benefit significantly from the project's completion—would eventually take over construction, but not until 1904. The Panama Canal opened to ships in 1914.

8. Lura McNall Ormes, Lockwood's daughter, managed correspondence and kept accounts. Clara Bennett Harrison, Lockwood's niece, began living with Lockwood after Clara's mother died in 1877. She worked as a legal assistant and office manager, helping Lura to run the law office when Lockwood was away.

9. *telautograph*: a telegraph used to transmit handwriting and sketches via electrical signals; precursor to the modern fax machine.

10. *Linda Gilbert*: Linda Gilbert (1847–1895) was a well-known advocate for prison reform; she pioneered the establishment of prison libraries. She lost the lieutenant governor race to Democrat Edward F. Jones.

11. *a reduced tariff*: Tariffs (taxes on imports and exports) were a key issue in the election. Harrison and the Republicans wanted to maintain high tariffs to protect American industries while Cleveland and the Democrats advocated lower tariffs to protect consumers. Lockwood tries to strike a middle ground here, although her position is closer to that of the Democratic platform.

12. *What of the Chinese?*: Although Chinese workers provided essential labor in the building of the nation's first transcontinental railroad in the 1860s, U.S. immigration policy reflected widespread American prejudice against the Chinese, who were viewed as racially inferior and as a threat to native-born workers. The Chinese Exclusion Act (1882) halted Chinese immigration and prohibited the Chinese from becoming citizens. It was not repealed until 1943, and restrictions on Chinese immigration persisted until 1965. In Bly's article, Lockwood advocates broadening immigration restrictions and points out the inconsistency of a policy that singled out members of a specific ethnic group.

13. When Lockwood named Frances Cleveland as the woman with the best chance for the presidency (other than herself), she acknowledged that the most prominent woman in the presidential campaign was not an actual candidate, but rather the wife of one of her rivals.

SHOULD WOMEN PROPOSE?

1. According to folk tradition in some countries, including Ireland and Britain, women were allowed to propose only in leap years.

2. *Love is life's end; an end, but never ending*: canto ii, stanza 8, of the erotic poem "Brittain's Ida," by the English poet Phineas Fletcher (1582–1650). Often misattributed to Edmund Spenser, whose name was on the title page of the original edition. The line is punctuated slightly differently in the original: "Love is life's end, (an end, but never ending)."

3. From Shakespeare's *Romeo and Juliet*, act II, scene ii. Juliet is speaking to Romeo: "If thou dost love, pronounce it faithfully:/ Or if thou think'st I am too quickly won,/ I'll frown and be perverse and say thee nay,/So thou wilt woo; but else, not for the world."

4. Matthew 7:7 and Luke 11:9.

5. Railroad lawyer and politician Chauncey M. Depew (1834–1928) was a celebrated orator, known for his wit and storytelling skills. A Republican candidate for president in 1888 (the year Bly's article appeared), Depew withdrew in favor of Benjamin Harrison, who went on to win the election. Depew later served two terms as a U.S. senator from New York.

6. *the election*: The presidential election of 1888, held November 6, 1888, five days before this article was published.

7. *Gen. Harrison*: Benjamin Harrison, who fought in the Civil War as a brigadier general in the Union Army, had just been elected twenty-third president of the United States, in a narrow win over incumbent Grover Cleveland.

8. Publisher and author Mrs. Frank Leslie (1836–1914), born Miriam Florence Folline, was the widow of famous publisher and illustrator Frank Leslie. She took over Leslie's debt-saddled business enterprise after his death in 1880, made it profitable, and legally changed her name to Frank Leslie. She was married four times— twice before she married Leslie, and once after; her other three marriages ended in divorce. When she died, she willed the bulk of her $2 million estate to suffragist Carrie Chapman Catt.

9. *Brigham Young* (1801–1877): famous polygamist and founding figure of the Mormon movement. Leslie interviewed Young and debated polygamy with him during her trip across the country, and at one point he told her that "A woman feeling herself drawn in affinity to a man, and feeling inclined to seal herself to him, should make her idea known to him without scruple. It is her duty, and there can be no indelicacy in obeying the voice of duty"

(Mrs. Frank Leslie, *California: A Pleasure Trip from Gotham to the Golden Gate*, New York: G. W. Carleton & Co., 1877, p. 102).

10. Hugh J. Grant (1858–1910), who had just been elected mayor of New York, would go on to serve two terms as mayor. He remained unmarried until 1895, three years after he left office.

11. William Hooker Gillette (1853–1937) was an American actor, playwright, and stage manager.

12. Quotation from Scottish poet Thomas Campbell's "The Maid's Remonstrance," a poem in three stanzas, c. 1821. Bly misquotes slightly; in the original, "wrong" is plural when the speaker pleads, "Read you not the wrongs you're doing," and the fifth line ends with a comma, not a semicolon.

SUSAN B. ANTHONY

1. The suffragists, like many other Americans, were intensely interested in Cuba's ongoing war to win independence from Spain. In 1898 the United States would intervene to support the Cubans in a ten-week conflict that became known as the Spanish American War. Accounts of Spanish atrocities against the Cubans were especially sensationalized by Joseph Pulitzer's *New York World* and William Randolph Hearst's *New York Journal*; the two newspapers were engaged in an epic circulation battle of their own.

2. Bly had commented extensively about the fashion choices of the suffragists in her recently published reports, "Nellie Bly with the Female Suffragists," *The New York World*, January 26, 1896, and "Woman in the Pulpit," *The New York World*, January 27, 1896.

3. *Horace Greeley* (1811–1872): American newspaper editor, politician, and outspoken opponent of slavery.

4. *Mrs. Stanton and Mrs. Mott had just been in Rochester*: Women's rights advocates Elizabeth Cady Stanton (1815–1902) and Lucretia Mott (1793–1880) had just spoken at the Rochester Woman's Rights Convention in August 1848. Anthony's father, mother, and sister attended the Rochester convention, which was a follow-up to the convention held in Seneca Falls, New York, two weeks earlier, at which Stanton, Mott, and others had launched the organized women's movement in the United States. Both Stanton and Mott came to be close friends with Anthony, especially Stanton. They were the three most influential figures in the women's rights movement of the nineteenth century.

5. Abby Kelley Foster (1811–1887), abolitionist and social activist who encouraged Anthony to become a reformer.

6. *Daughters of Temperance society*: A group that campaigned for more restrictive liquor laws and drew attention to the effects of excessive drinking on families. The "Sons of Temperance" was a men's group with the same goals. Anthony met Elizabeth Cady Stanton at a temperance society meeting in 1851.

7. Abolitionist Lydia Mott (1807–1875), a distant relative of Lucretia Mott's husband James.

8. *Thurlow Weed* (1797–1882): New York politician and newspaper publisher.

9. *David Wright*: Attorney and husband of Martha Coffin Wright, one of the organizers of the 1848 Seneca Falls Women's Rights Convention and a close friend of Anthony's.

10. *Rev. Samuel J. May, father of Rev. Joseph May*: Unitarian minister and social reformer Samuel Joseph May (1797–1871). His son Joseph was also a Unitarian minister.

11. *Henry Ward Beecher* (1813–1887): abolitionist, social reformer, Congregationalist minister, and public speaker who weathered a scandal in the 1870s when Theodore Tilton sued him for damages, alleging that Beecher had had an affair with Tilton's wife, Elizabeth.

12. When Anthony presented the petition to the New York State Legislature, it was the first time a delegation of women had carried their demands before a legislative body in the United States.

V. GLOBETROTTER

FROM *AROUND THE WORLD IN SEVENTY-TWO DAYS*

1. According to the detailed coverage of the contest, it took 33 men 107 hours working "without one minute's intermission" to sort all the coupons.

2. "The Winner," *The New York World*, February 2, 1890. In the same issue, the *World* also published a list of more than one hundred contestants who came within fifteen seconds of winning. Although most were New Yorkers, the list included guessers from Michigan, Kansas, Nebraska, and Wyoming.

3. *Phileas Fogg*: fictional British hero of Jules Verne's 1873 bestselling novel *Around the World in Eighty Days*. The narrative was originally serialized in a Paris newspaper in 1872.

4. *a special passport*: Because Bly had no passport, the *World* sent an editorial writer to Washington, D.C., to make a personal appeal to Secretary of State James G. Blaine, who agreed to arrange a special passport for Bly. The *World* staffer returned to New York with the passport just a few hours before Bly's scheduled departure.

5. *Brindisi*: port town in southern Italy off the coast of the Adriatic Sea.

6. Bly appears to be confusing two separate incidents here. Although she had visited a steamship office much earlier, when she first thought of going around the world, it does not seem likely that she actually accompanied the *World* staffer who was sent to an international travel agency (not a steamship office) to plan her itinerary in November 1889. The travel agency, Thomas Cook & Son, is mentioned in the *World*'s announcement of Bly's trip on November 14, 1889.

7. *Aden*: port town in modern Yemen, on the southern tip of the Arabian Peninsula; a British colony from 1839 to 1967.

8. Although she wouldn't know it until long into her journey, Bly had a competitor. After John Brisben Walker, publisher of the monthly magazine *Cosmopolitan*, read about Bly's trip on the front page of the *World*, he was inspired to send a female journalist around the world in the opposite direction. *Cosmopolitan*'s literary editor, Elizabeth Bisland, started off on a train bound for Chicago a little more than eight hours after Bly sailed on the *Augusta Victoria*.

9. *Commander Albers*: Adolph Albers (1843–1902), genial transatlantic steamship captain, popular among passengers and known for record-breaking crossings of the Atlantic Ocean.

10. *Lunnen*: slang for London.

11. *Yokohama*: major port city in Japan, on the western coast of Tokyo Bay.

12. *Dorothy Maddox*: women's page columnist for *The Philadelphia Inquirer*.

13. *enjoying (?)*: The question mark is in the original text; Bly uses the punctuation to indicate her ironic tone. She doubts that the passengers who spent the voyage below decks enjoyed their trip.

14. Evidence suggests that Bly's account of this incident is inaccurate. Tracey Greaves, the *World* correspondent who escorted Bly through British customs, told a different version in an account published in the December 8, 1888, *World*. According to Greaves, Bly was careful to keep her age a secret during the interview; he said she lured the British official into a corner before she would specify her age, thus inspiring him to discuss how sensitive woman travelers often were about revealing their ages. Neither account reports Bly's actual age, although the passport application does. It

wrongly lists 1867 (not the correct 1864) as her birth year. Bly continued to subtract three years from her age throughout her life. (For details, see Kroeger, *Nellie Bly*, pp. 144–45.)

15. *Peninsular and Oriental Steamship Company*: Major British shipping company established in the early nineteenth century; officially the Peninsular and Oriental Steam Navigation Company, but more often referred to as the P&O.

16. *Charing Cross station*: railway station in central London.

17. *Boulogne, France*: port city on the coast of northern France.

18. Robert H. Sherard, the *World*'s Paris correspondent, who set up the meeting with Verne.

19. *Because I am more anxious to save time than a young widow*: Reference to the romantic life of Phileas Fogg, the circumnavigator of Jules Verne's 1873 novel, who departs on his trip a single man but returns with a wife, a young Indian widow he rescues from a suttee, a now-banned Hindu practice in which a widow burned herself to death on her husband's funeral pyre.

20. The author is Tracey Greaves, the correspondent who met Bly's ship when it arrived in England and accompanied her to Amiens to visit Jules Verne.

21. *The Lizard*: the southernmost point in mainland England, the Lizard is a peninsula in south Cornwall, and the first place from which Bly's ship, the *Augusta Victoria*, would have been spotted on its way to Southampton.

22. *Hurst Castle*: a fortress at the narrow entrance to the Solent, a strait and a major shipping route through which the *Augusta Victoria* would pass as it came into the port of Southampton.

23. *Catherine Elsmere*: fictional character in *Richard Elsmere*, a bestselling 1888 novel by Mary Augusta Ward. Catherine is the exceptionally pious wife of the title character, a brilliant and intellectually curious clergyman.

24. *quoits*: traditional game in which players toss flat rings at a stake.

25. *Port Said*: town in northeast Egypt, near the Suez Canal's northern entrance.

26. *Gladstone*: British Prime Minister William E. Gladstone (1809–1898).

27. *Mrs. Maybricks, Mary Andersons, Lillie Langtrys*: Women with various claims to fame. American Florence Maybrick (1862–1941) became a household name in 1889 when she was convicted in England of murdering her much-older British husband; Mary Anderson (1859–1940) was an American actress; Lillie Langtry (1853–1929) was a British actress who became an American citizen in 1887.

28. *pugaree*: scarf wrapped around the crown of a sun hat.

29. *Suez Canal*: a 101-mile canal that flows through Egypt, linking the Mediterranean and the Red seas. The canal, which separates the African continent from Asia, dramatically reduced transit times for global trade when it opened in 1869.

30. The Egyptian government conscripted peasants to complete much of the work on the canal. By the mid-1860s, with public condemnation of slavery growing, the canal builders were forced to pay free laborers and improve working conditions.

31. *Ismailia*: Egyptian city near the midpoint of the Suez Canal.

32. *bahkshish*: variant of baksheesh, a term of Persian origin that describes tips, gifts, or small bribes. Used to solicit charity in the Middle East and South Asia.

33. *minstrel show*: American theatrical form, founded on the comic performance of racial stereotypes and popular in the nineteenth and early twentieth century. Since Bly goes on to mention the actors' blackened faces, we know that it was a blackface minstrel show, in which white male performers painted their faces black and mimicked the songs and dances of African slaves. The irony of steamship passengers staging a minstrel show to pass the time while sailing through Africa was apparently lost on Bly.

34. tableaux vivants: French for living pictures; scenes presented on stage by costumed actors who remain silent and motionless.

35. *Colombo*: port city on the west coast of Ceylon (now Sri Lanka), a tropical island in the northern Indian Ocean celebrated for its spectacular natural beauty. Ceylon was a British colony from 1796 to 1948.

36. *Adam's Peak*: tallest mountain on the island.

37. *punkas*: large swinging fans made of cloth or canvas stretched on a rectangular frame suspended from a roof and worked manually with a cord.

38. *tiffin*: light meal.

39. Mount Lavinia (not Lavania), just south of Colombo's city center, known for its beaches.

40. *jinrickshas:* single-passenger two-wheeled vehicles drawn by men; eventually Anglicized into rickshaws.

41. *sulky*: light two-wheeled carriage with seating for one person.

42. *Kandy*: ancient highland city not far from Colombo, renowned for its palaces, Hindu and Buddhist temples, and lush gardens.

43. *Penang, or Prince of Wales Island, one of the Straits Settlements*: northernmost seaport on the Malaysian peninsula and a British colony from 1786 to 1946, called Prince of Wales Island by the British. Along with Singapore and Malacca, Penang was part of a collection of British colonies in the Strait of Malacca

known as the Straits Settlements (a fourth colony, Labuan, was added in the early twentieth century).

44. *sampan*: small flat-bottomed Chinese wooden boat, eleven to fourteen feet long.

45. *Hindoo*: archaic spelling of Hindu; lends itself to derogatory use.

46. *joss-house*: Chinese temple or building for idol worship.

47. *josses*: Chinese figures of deities; idols.

48. *joss-sticks*: thin cylinders or sticks of fragrant tinder mixed with clay and used by the Chinese as incense.

49. *coolies*: racial slur for unskilled Asian workers.

50. *Portugese lorchas*: fast sailing vessels built in China with the hull after a European model but rigged in Chinese fashion, usually carrying guns.

51. *Chinese junks*: common type of native sailing vessel in the Chinese seas, flat-bottomed with a square prow.

52. *Ali Baba and the Forty Thieves*: adventure story based on an Arabic folk tale, added by European translators to the popular Middle Eastern story collection *One Thousand and One Nights*. Ali Baba is a poor woodcutter who discovers that the words "open sesame" will open the door to the cave where the forty thieves have hidden their treasure.

53. *Captain Smith, of the Oceanic*: Canadian William M. Smith (1849–1932), known in the China seas as Typhoon Bill because of his skillful and daring seamanship.

54. On the Chinese Exclusion Act, see note 12 in "Woman's Part in Politics."

55. Canton, southern China's largest city, is about eighty miles northwest of Hong Kong.

56. The mass executions occurred during the Taiping Rebellion (1850–1864), a devastating civil war that took an estimated twenty million lives.

57. *fan tan*: Chinese gambling game.

58. British writer Sir Edwin Arnold (1832–1904), best known for the epic poem *The Light of Asia* (1879). He lived in Japan late in his life and his third wife was Japanese.

59. *geisha girls*: professional female companions for men in Japan, trained in the art of conversation, music, and dancing.

60. *samisens*: guitarlike Japanese instrument with a long neck and three strings.

61. *foolscap*: writing paper, varying in size.

62. *Diabutsu*: reference to Kamakura's Daibatsu, a massive bronze statue of Buddha completed in 1252. Japan's second-largest Buddha image, it is Kamakura's most famous sight.

63. *the Mikado*: The emperor of Japan.
64. *snow blockade*: The week before Bly was scheduled to land in San Francisco, the *World* sent a "Nellie Bly escort corps" from New York to welcome her and published reports about the group's progress across the country. But record-breaking snow-falls stopped trains and trapped the correspondents in the Sierra Nevada mountains. To avoid the snow blockade, the *World* chartered a special train to take Bly on a more southerly, less direct route to Chicago. Her celebrated dash across the United States was by far the most expensive leg of her trip; the Santa Fe railroad charged the newspaper $2,190—a dollar a mile—to make the special accommodations.
65. *stringers*: beams running lengthwise to support the portion of a bridge that carries vehicles (in this case, trains).
66. Bly was exaggerating, as is apparent from the report published in the January 23, 1890, *New York World* and excerpted just above this passage. Although the railroad workers feared the bridge would fall, it did not.

VI. ON THE FIRING LINE

NELLIE BLY ON THE BATTLEFIELD

1. The *Journal* published twenty-one of Bly's war dispatches between December 1914 and February 1915.
2. "Taken Prisoner," *The New York Evening Journal*, January 16, 1915.
3. Throughout her war correspondence, Bly refers to her army guide only as "Colonel John, our commander" ("Nellie Bly on the Firing Line," *The New York Evening Journal*, December 4, 1914).
4. Noted Hungarian painter Baron Laszlo Mednyanszky (1852–1919) was born into an aristocratic family but gave much of his income to the poor. In his early sixties, he spent two years making sketches on the front lines of World War I.
5. Bly appears to have garbled somewhat the name and position of Royal Italian Navy lieutenant Cesare Santorre, technical correspondent of the Italian military magazine *Aero Marittima*, who was one of the four foreign correspondents granted press credentials by the Austrian authorities to cover the war. Bly was another one of the four; she was the only woman in the group (Kroeger, *Nellie Bly*, p. 588).

6. Bly describes Exax as "a young photographer from Vienna" ("Nellie Bly Sees Maimed," *The New York Evening Journal*, December 5, 1914).

7. When Bly's ankle-length fur coat proved too unwieldy for the long, muddy trek to the front, she asked one of her companions, the six-foot, 250-pound artist Carl Leopold Hollitzer, if she could wear his cape, which he had taken off because it was too heavy. He agreed, and for the rest of the trek, she wore Hollitzer's folded cape on her shoulders like a shawl ("Nellie Bly Sees Maimed," *The New York Evening Journal*, December 5, 1914).

8. *like the famous lady who turned to salt, I turned to look!*: Lot's wife in the biblical account of Sodom and Gomorrah (Genesis 19:26).

NELLIE BLY DESCRIBES WAR HORRORS

1. *kino*: film.

2. *Galiscze*: historical region made up of parts of Poland and Ukraine, extending northward from the Carpathian Mountains into the Vistula Valley to the San River.

AT SCENE OF SLAUGHTER

1. *the Prince*: identified in an earlier report as Prince Schonburg, commander of the Austrian brigade. Likely Alois Furst Schonburg-Hartenstein (1858–1944), a military officer in the Austro-Hungarian army and a member of the Austrian nobility who commanded several units in World War I.

2. *Soldiers of Francis Joseph and the Czar*: soldiers from opposing sides. Those loyal to Austrian emperor Franz Joseph were fighting those loyal to Nicholas II, the Russian czar.

NELLIE BLY AT FRONT

1. *kino shows*: film screenings.

2. *Dr. MacDonald*: Dr. Charles MacDonald of the American Red Cross.

3. *Mr. Schriner*: Associated Press correspondent George M. Schreiner, an American she met in Budapest.

4. *Von Leidenfrost*: Adolf von Leidenfrost, a Hungarian-American relief worker affiliated with the Red Cross. She met him in Budapest.

VII. DEAR NELLIE

NELLIE BLY FINDS A HOME AND FATHER FOR LITTLE WAIF

1. *The New York Evening Journal*, December 10, 1919.
2. The "love of Mike" baby's history turned out to be complicated; for details, see Kroeger, *Nellie Bly*, pp. 468–70.
3. Bly was living in the Hotel McAlpin, at the corner of Broadway and Thirty-fourth Street in Manhattan.
4. In the next two installments of the series on "little waif" Richard, Bly reported that when "Mr. O." met Richard's foster mother, he insisted that she travel with him and the child back to his home in the West, and that she live as part of his family. Then, while the foster mother packed her trunk for the trip, Mr. O. took Richard and Bly out to a fancy lunch, a matinee, and a shopping spree. A *New York World* photographer showed up to take the boy's photograph in one of his new outfits (*The New York Evening World*, December 1 and December 2, 1919).